More Praise for *The Chalice and the Blade:*

"I have never before praised a book so highly. . . . Everyone . . . should have the opportunity to read it."—Ashley Montagu

"Eisler gives us a revealing study of history and an offer of hope. She demonstrates that to be human can be to affirm life, not death, in one of the most compelling books of the year."—*Minneapolis Star Tribune*

"A notable application of science to the growth and survival of human understanding."—Marija Gimbutas, author of *Goddesses and Gods of Old Europe*

"Excellent from every point of view. . . . A very important picture of human evolution."—Nicolas Platon, author of *Crete* and former director of the Acropolis Museum

"A daring journey from pole to pole of human existence."—Charles Tilly, professor of history, New School for Social Research

"Casts a new light on all of the major problems confronting us today . . . brings new clarity to the entire man-woman question. . . . A major contribution."—Jean Baker Miller, author of *Toward a New Psychology of Women*

"Shows how our political and economic system may attain a new balance."—Hazel Henderson, author of *Creating Alternative Futures*

"A major breakthrough."—Barbara Walker, author of *The Woman's Encyclopedia of Myths and Secrets*

"It opens a window to a new vista, a new perspective with which to see and understand the human condition. . . . So empowering that things that did not seem possible before now come within reach."—*Sojourner*

"An *extremely* important book."—Merlin Stone, author of *When God Was A Woman* and *Ancient Mirrors of Womanhood*

"A seminal work, destined to be debated and discussed for years to come. . . . Required reading for anyone concerned about our destiny on earth."—Ervin Laszlo, author of *Evolution: The Grand Synthesis*

"As important, perhaps more important, than the unearthing of Troy or the deciphering of cuneiform."—Bruce Wilshire, professor of philosophy, Rutgers, The State University of New Jersey

"Immeasurably valuable . . . really extraordinary in its vastness and vision."—Gloria Orenstein, professor, Program for the Study of Women and Men in Society, University of Southern California

"A very important book . . . opens up the entire question of the value, purpose, and cosmic fulfillment of the individual."—Robert Muller, chancellor, United Nations University for Peace

"To read Eisler is to glimpse new vistas of human possibility, fueled by the nurturing and regenerating powers associated with women."
—*New Woman*

"The most significant work published in our lifetimes . . . might make the future possible."—*Los Angeles Weekly*

"Eisler's highly readable synthesis . . . is an important contribution to social history."—*Publisher's Weekly*

"An imaginative and persuasive work."—*Library Journal*

"This clear and uncluttered study makes fascinating reading."—*Booklist*

"Clears up many historical mysteries . . . provides foundations upon which to build a more humanistic world."—*The Humanist*

"Fascinating. . . . Sweeping. . . . Examines the past, the present, and even the future to answer some of the central questions of our time."
—*San Diego Weekly*

"Rejuvenates my hope that things can change, that it is possible for all of us to create and live in the kind of world we have dreamt of."
—*Woman of Power*

To David Loye,
my partner in life and work

Contents

Figures

Acknowledgments

In many ways this book has been a cooperative effort, drawing on the work and vision of countless women and men, many of whom have been acknowledged in the notes. Beyond this, there have been many others whose critiques, suggestions, help with editing and manuscript preparation, and above all, support and encouragement over the past ten years have been invaluable.

The contribution of David Loye, to whom this book is dedicated, has been so enormous that there is no way I can adequately express my gratitude. It is no exaggeration to say that this book would not have been possible without the full and active partnership over many years of this remarkable man, who often put aside his own important work as a pioneering social scientist to generously give of his scholarship, thinking, editing skills, and understanding with a selfless dedication and patience that truly transcended human limits.

Of the many women who have given generously to this book, I am particularly indebted to my friend and colleague Annette Ehrlich, who out of a busy life as a professor of psychology and scientific editorial consultant made the time to several times read the much longer manuscripts out of which *The Chalice and the Blade* finally evolved. Her no-holds-barred editorial critiques as well as her steadfast support for my sometimes flagging spirits and energy were of enormous help. I am also very grateful to Carole Anderson, Fran Hosken, Mara Keller, Rebecca McCann, Isolina Ricci, and the late Wilma Scott Heide. Each read all or most of the manuscript at various stages, made important suggestions, and gave generously of their support and love. *The Chalice and the Blade* and I also owe an enormous debt of gratitude to Ashley Montagu, who put aside completion of two of his own books to go over this book line by line and note by note. This, and other expressions of belief in my work by a man who has devoted most of his long and extraordinarily productive life to human betterment, have been of great help and encouragement to me.

It would take another book to adequately thank everyone who has contributed in important ways to this book: my daughters Andrea and Loren Eisler, my agent Ellen Levine, my editor Jan Johnson, as well as the many others at Harper & Row, including Clayton Carlson, Tom Dorsaneo, Mike Kehoe, Yvonne Keller, Dorian Gossy, and Virginia Rich, and all the others who have taken such good care of the book in its final production stages.

Some of those who from the perspective of their various disciplines read portions of *The Chalice and the Blade* as a work in process and made important contributions include archaeologists Marija Gimbutas and Nicolas Platon, sociologists Jessie Bernard and Joan Rockwell, psychiatrist Jean Baker Miller, cultural and art historians Elinor Gadon and Merlin Stone, literary comparatist Gloria Orenstein, biologist Vilmos Csanyi, "chaos" and "self-organizing systems" theorists Ervin Laszlo and Ralph Abraham, physicist Fritjof Capra, futurists Hazel Henderson and Robert Jungk, and theologian Carol Christ. Others who read portions of the manuscript or provided important suggestions, information, encouragement, and support include, in alphabetical order: Andra Akers, Lettie Bennett, Anna Binicus, June Brindel, Marie Cantlon, Olga Eleftheriades, Julia Eisler, Maier Greif, Mary Hardy, Helen Helmer, Allie Hixson, Elizabeth Holm, Barbara Honegger, Al Ikof, Ed Jarvis, Abida Khanum, Samson Knoll, Pat Lala, Susan Mehra, Mary and Lloyd Morain, Hilkka Pietila, and Cosette Thomson. The list goes on, but limitations of space make it impossible to mention everyone, and for this, and for any lapses of memory, I apologize, as I would have liked to thank by name all who, through many years of research and writing, gave me both intellectual stimulation and emotional support.

I do want to give special thanks to those who participated in the seemingly endless process of manuscript preparation, particularly to Jeannie Adams, Ryan Bounds, Kedron Bryson, Kathy Campbell, Sylvia Edgren, Elizabeth Dolmat, DiAna, Elizabeth Harrington, Cherie Long, Jeannie McGregor, Mike Rosenberg, Cindy Sprague, Susanne Shavione, Elizabeth Wahbe, and Jo Warley.

Introduction: The Chalice and the Blade

This book opens a door. The key to unlock it was fashioned by many people and many books, and it will take many more to fully explore the vast vistas that lie behind it. But even opening this door a crack reveals fascinating new knowledge about our past—and a new view of our potential future.

For me, the search for this door has been a life-long quest. Very early in my life I saw that what people in different cultures consider given—just the way things are—is not the same everywhere. I also very early developed a passionate concern about the human situation. When I was very small, the seemingly secure world I had known was shattered by the Nazi takeover of Austria. I watched as my father was dragged away, and after my mother miraculously obtained his release from the Gestapo, my parents and I fled for our lives. Through that flight, first to Cuba and finally to the United States, I experienced three different cultures, each with its own verities. I also began to ask many questions, questions that to me are not, and never have been, abstract.

Why do we hunt and persecute each other? Why is our world so full of man's infamous inhumanity to man—and to woman? How can human beings be so brutal to their own kind? What is it that chronically tilts us toward cruelty rather than kindness, toward war rather than peace, toward destruction rather than actualization?

Of all life-forms on this planet, only we can plant and harvest fields, compose poetry and music, seek truth and justice, teach a child to read and write—or even laugh and cry. Because of our unique ability to imagine new realities and realize these through ever more advanced technologies, we are quite literally partners in our own evolution. And yet, this same wondrous species of ours now seems bent on putting an end not only to its own evolution but to that of most life on our globe, threatening our planet with ecological catastrophe or nuclear annihilation.

As time went on, as I pursued my professional studies, had children, and increasingly focused my research and writing on the future, my concerns broadened and deepened. Like many people, I became convinced that we are rapidly approaching an evolutionary crossroads—that never before has the course we choose been so critical. But what course should we take?

Socialists and communists assert that the root of our problems is capitalism; capitalists insist socialism and communism are leading us to ruin. Some argue our troubles are due to our "industrial paradigm," that our "scientific worldview" is to blame. Still others blame humanism, feminism, and even secularism, pressing for a return to the "good old days" of a smaller, simpler, more religious age.

Yet, if we look at ourselves—as we are forced to by television or the grim daily ritual of the newspaper at breakfast—we see how capitalist, socialist, and communist nations alike are enmeshed in the arms race and all the other irrationalities that threaten both us and our environment. And if we look at our past—at the routine massacres by Huns, Romans, Vikings, and Assyrians or the cruel slaughters of the Christian Crusades and Inquisition—we see there was even more violence and injustice in the smaller, prescientific, preindustrial societies that came before us.

Since going backward is not the answer, how do we move forward? A great deal is being written about a New Age, a major and unprecedented cultural transformation.[1] But in practical terms, what does this mean? A transformation from what to what? In terms of both our everyday lives and our cultural evolution, what precisely would be different, or even possible, in the future? Is a shift from a system leading to chronic wars, social injustice, and ecologial imbalance to one of peace, social justice, and ecological balance a realistic possibility? Most important, what changes in social structure would make such a transformation possible?

The search for answers to these questions led me to the re-examination of our past, present, and future on which this book is based. *The Chalice and the Blade* reports part of this new study of human society, which differs from most prior studies in that it takes into account the *whole* of human history (including our prehistory) as well as the *whole* of humanity (both its female and male halves).

Weaving together evidence from art, archaeology, religion, social science, history, and many other fields of inquiry into new patterns that more accurately fit the best available data, *The Chalice and the Blade* tells a new story of our cultural origins. It shows that war and the "war of the sexes" are neither divinely nor biologically ordained. And it provides verification that a better future *is* possible—and is in fact firmly rooted in the haunting drama of what actually happened in our past.

Human Possibilities: Two Alternatives

We are all familiar with legends about an earlier, more harmonious and peaceful age. The Bible tells of a garden where woman and man lived in harmony with each other and nature—before a male god decreed that woman henceforth be subservient to man. The Chinese *Tao Te Ching* describes a time when the yin, or feminine principle, was not yet ruled by the male principle, or yang, a time when the wisdom of the mother was still honored and followed above all. The ancient Greek poet Hesiod wrote of a "golden race" who tilled the soil in "peaceful ease" before a "lesser race" brought in their god of war. But though scholars agree that in many respects these works are based on prehistoric events, references to a time when women and men lived in partnership have traditionally been viewed as no more than fantasy.

When archaeology was still in its infancy, the excavations of Heinrich and Sophia Schliemann helped establish the reality of Homer's Troy. Today new archaeological excavations, coupled with reinterpretations of older digs using more scientific methods, reveal that stories such as our expulsion from the Garden of Eden also derive from earlier realities: from folk memories of the first agrarian (or Neolithic) societies, which planted the first gardens on this earth. Similarly (as the Greek archaeologist Spyridon Marinatos already suggested almost fifty years ago), the legend of how the glorious civilization of Atlantis sank into the sea may well be a garbled recollection of Minoan civilization—now believed to have ended when Crete and surrounding islands were massively damaged by earthquakes and enormous tidal waves.[2]

Just as in Columbus's time the discovery that the earth is not flat made it possible to find an amazing new world that had been there all the time, these archaeological discoveries—deriving from what the British archaeologist James Mellaart calls a veritable archaeological revolution—open up the amazing world of our hidden past.³ They reveal a long period of peace and prosperity when our social, technological, and cultural evolution moved upward: many thousands of years when all the basic technologies on which civilization is built were developed in societies that were not male dominant, violent, and hierarchic.

Further verifying that there were ancient societies organized very differently from ours are the many otherwise inexplicable images of the Deity as female in ancient art, myth, and even historical writings. Indeed, the idea of the universe as an all-giving Mother has survived (albeit in modified form) into our time. In China, the female deities Ma Tsu and Kuan Yin are still widely worshiped as beneficent and compassionate goddesses. In fact, the anthropologist P. S. Sangren notes that "Kuan Yin is clearly the most popular of Chinese deities."⁴ Similarly, the worship of Mary, the Mother of God, is widespread. Although in Catholic theology she is demoted to nondivine status, her divinity is implicitly recognized by her appellation Mother of God as well as by the prayers of millions who daily seek her compassionate protection and solace. Moreover, the story of Jesus' birth, death, and resurrection bears a striking resemblance to those of earlier "mystery cults" revolving around a divine Mother and her son or, as in the worship of Demeter and Kore, her daughter.

It of course makes eminent sense that the earliest depiction of divine power in human form should have been female rather than male. When our ancestors began to ask the eternal questions (Where do we come from before we are born? Where do we go after we die?), they must have noted that life emerges from the body of a woman. It would have been natural for them to image the universe as an all-giving Mother from whose womb all life emerges and to which, like the cycles of vegetation, it returns after death to be again reborn. It also makes sense that societies with this image of the powers that govern the universe would have a very different social structure from societies that worship a divine Father who wields a thunderbolt and/or sword. It further seems logical that women would not be seen as subservient in societies that conceptualized the powers governing the universe in female form—and that "effeminate" qualities such as caring, compassion, and nonviolence would be highly valued in these societies. What does *not* make sense is to conclude that societies in which men did not dominate women were societies in which women dominated men.

Nonetheless, when the first evidence of such societies was unearthed in the nineteenth century, it was concluded that they must have been "matriarchal." Then, when the evidence did not seem to support this conclusion, it again became customary to argue that human society always was—and always will be—dominated by men. But if we free ourselves from the prevailing models of reality, it is evident that there is another logical alternative: that there can be societies in which difference is not necessarily equated with inferiority or superiority.

One result of re-examining human society from a gender-holistic perspective has been a new theory of cultural evolution. This theory, which I have called Cultural Transformation theory, proposes that underlying the great surface diversity of human culture are two basic models of society.

The first, which I call the *dominator* model, is what is popularly termed either patriarchy or matriarchy—the *ranking* of one half of humanity over the other. The second, in which social relations are primarily based on the principle of *linking* rather than ranking, may best be described as the *partnership* model. In this model—beginning with the most fundamental difference in our species, between male and female—diversity is not equated with either inferiority or superiority.[5]

Cultural Transformation theory further proposes that the original direction in the mainstream of our cultural evolution was toward partnership but that, following a period of chaos and almost total cultural disruption, there occurred a fundamental social shift. The greater availability of data on Western societies (due to the ethnocentric focus of Western social science) makes it possible to document this shift in more detail through the analysis of Western cultural evolution. However, there are also indications that this change in direction from a partnership to a dominator model was roughly paralleled in other parts of the world.[6]

The title *The Chalice and the Blade* derives from this cataclysmic turning point during the prehistory of Western civilization, when the direction of our cultural evolution was quite literally turned around. At this pivotal branching, the cultural evolution of societies that worshiped the life-generating and nurturing powers of the universe—in our time still symbolized by the ancient chalice or grail—was interrupted. There now appeared on the prehistoric horizon invaders from the peripheral areas of our globe who ushered in a very different form of social organization. As the University of California archaeologist Marija Gimbutas writes, these were people who worshiped "the lethal power of the blade"[7]—the power to take rather than give life that is the ultimate power to establish and enforce domination.

The Evolutionary Crossroads

Today we stand at another potentially decisive branching point. At a time when the lethal power of the Blade—amplified a millionfold by megatons of nuclear warheads—threatens to put an end to all human culture, the new findings about both ancient and modern history reported in *The Chalice and the Blade* do not merely provide a new chapter in the story of our past. Of greatest importance is what this new knowledge tells us about our present and potential future.

For millennia men have fought wars and the Blade has been a male symbol. But this does not mean men are inevitably violent and warlike.[8] Throughout recorded history there have been peaceful and nonviolent men. Moreover, obviously there were both men and women in the prehistoric societies where the power to give and nurture, which the Chalice symbolizes, was supreme. The underlying problem is not men as a sex. The root of the problem lies in a social system in which the power of the Blade is idealized—in which both men and women are taught to equate true masculinity with violence and dominance and to see men who do not conform to this ideal as "too soft" or "effeminate."

For many people it is difficult to believe that any other way of structuring human society is possible—much less that our future may hinge on anything connected with women or femininity. One reason for these beliefs is that in male-dominant societies anything associated with women or femininity is automatically viewed as a secondary, or women's, issue—to be addressed, if at all, only after the "more important" problems have been resolved. Another reason is that we have not had the necessary information. Even though humanity obviously consists of two halves (women and men), in most studies of human society the main protagonist, indeed often the sole actor, has been male.

As a result of what has been quite literally "the study of man," most social scientists have had to work with such an incomplete and distorted data base that in any other context it would immediately have been recognized as deeply flawed. Even now, information about women is primarily relegated to the intellectual ghetto of women's studies. Moreover, and quite understandably because of its immediate (though long neglected) importance for the lives of women, most research by feminists has focused on the implications of the study of women for women.

This book is different in that it focuses on the implications of how we organize the relations between the two halves of humanity for the *totality* of a social system. Clearly, how these relations are structured has decisive implications for the personal lives of both men and women, for our day-to-day roles and life options. But equally important, although still generally ignored, is something that once articulated seems obvious. This is that the way we structure the most fundamental of all human relations (without which our species could not go on) has a profound effect on every one of our institutions, on our values, and— as the pages that follow show—on the direction of our cultural evolution, particularly whether it will be peaceful or warlike.

If we stop and think about it, there are only two basic ways of structuring the relations between the female and male halves of humanity. All societies are patterned on either a dominator model—in which human hierarchies are ultimately backed up by force or the threat of force—or a partnership model, with variations in between. Moreover, if we reexamine human society from a perspective that takes into account *both* women and men, we can also see that there are patterns, or systems configurations, that characterize dominator, or alternatively, partnership, social organization.

For example, from a conventional perspective, Hitler's Germany, Khomeini's Iran, the Japan of the Samurai, and the Aztecs of Meso-America are radically different societies of different races, ethnic origins, technological development, and geographic location. But from the new perspective of cultural transformation theory, which identifies the social configuration characteristic of rigidly male-dominated societies, we see striking commonalities. All these otherwise widely divergent societies are not only rigidly male dominant but also have a generally hierarchic and authoritarian social structure and a high degree of social violence, particularly warfare.[9]

Conversely, we can also see arresting similarities between otherwise extremely diverse societies that are more sexually equalitarian. Characteristically, such "partnership model" societies tend to be not only much more peaceful but also much less hierarchic and authoritarian. This is evidenced by anthropological data (i.e., the BaMbuti and the !Kung), by contemporary studies of trends in more sexually equalitarian modern societies (i.e., Scandinavian nations such as Sweden), and by the prehistoric and historic data that will be detailed in the pages that follow.[10]

Through the use of the dominator and partnership models of social organization for the analysis of both our present and our potential future, we can also begin to transcend the conventional polarities between right and left, capitalism and communism, religion and secularism, and even masculinism and feminism. The larger picture that emerges indicates that all the modern, post-Enlightenment movements for social justice, be they religious or secular, as well as the more recent feminist, peace, and ecology movements, are part of an underlying thrust for the transformation of a dominator to a partnership system. Beyond this, in our time of unprecedentedly powerful technologies, these movements may be seen as part of our species' evolutionary thrust for survival.

If we look at the whole span of our cultural evolution from the perspective of cultural transformation theory, we see that the roots of our present global crises go back to the fundamental shift in our pre-history that brought enormous changes not only in social structure but also in technology. This was the shift in emphasis from technologies that sustain and enhance life to the technologies symbolized by the Blade: technologies designed to destroy and dominate. This has been the technological emphasis through most of recorded history. And it is this technological emphasis, rather than technology per se, that today threatens all life on our globe.[11]

There will undoubtedly be those who will argue that because in prehistory there was a shift from a partnership to a dominator model of society it must have been adaptive. However, the argument that because something happened in evolution it was adaptive does not hold up—as the extinction of the dinosaurs so amply evidences. In any event, in evolutionary terms the span of human cultural evolution is far too short to make any such judgment. The real point would seem to be that, given our present high level of technological development, a dominator model of social organization is maladaptive.

Because this dominator model now seems to be reaching its logical limits, many men and women are today rejecting long-standing principles of social organization, including their stereotypical sexual roles. For many others these changes are only signs of systems breakdown, chaotic disruptions that at all costs must be quelled. But it is precisely because the world we have known is changing so rapidly that more and more people over ever larger parts of this world are able to see that there are other alternatives.

The Chalice and the Blade explores these alternatives. But while the material that follows shows that a better future is possible, it by no means follows (as some would have us believe) that we will inevitably move beyond the threat of nuclear or ecological holocaust into a new and better age. In the last analysis, that choice is up to us.

Chaos or Transformation

The study on which *The Chalice and the Blade* is based is what social scientists call action research.[12] It is not merely a study of what was, or is, or even of what can be, but also an exploration of how we may more effectively intervene in our own cultural evolution. The rest of this introduction is intended primarily for the reader interested in learning more about this study. Other readers may want to go straight to chapter 1, perhaps returning to this section later.

Until now, most studies of cultural evolution have primarily focused on the progression from simpler to more complex levels of technological and social development.[13] Particular attention has been paid to major technological shifts, such as the invention of agriculture, the industrial revolution, and, more recently, the move into our postindustrial or nuclear/electronic age.[14] This type of movement obviously has extremely important social and economic implications. But it only gives us part of the human story.

The other part of the story relates to a different type of movement: the social shifts toward either a partnership or a dominator model of social organization. As already noted, the central thesis of Cultural Transformation theory is that the direction of the cultural evolution for dominator and partnership societies is very different.

This theory in part derives from an important distinction that is not generally made. This is that the term *evolution* has a double meaning. In scientific parlance, it describes the biological and, by extension, cultural history of living species. But evolution is also a normative term. Indeed, it is often used as a synonym for progress: for the movement from lower to higher levels.

In actual fact, not even our technological evolution has been a linear movement from lower to higher levels, but rather a process punctuated by massive regressions, such as the Greek Dark Age and the Middle Ages.[15] Nonetheless, there seems to be an underlying thrust toward greater technological and social complexity. Similarly, there seems to be a human thrust toward higher goals: toward truth, beauty, and justice. But as the brutality, oppression, and warfare that characterize recorded history all too vividly demonstrate, the movement toward these goals has hardly been linear. Indeed, as the data we will examine documents, here too there has been massive regression.

In gathering the data to chart, and test, the social dynamics I have been studying, I have brought together findings and theories from many fields in both the social and natural sciences. Two sources have been particularly useful: the new feminist scholarship and new scientific findings about the dynamics of change.

A reassessment of how systems are formed, maintain themselves, and change is rapidly spreading across many areas of science, through works such as those of Nobel Prize winner Ilya Prigogine and Isabel Stengers in chemistry and general systems, Robert Shaw and Marshall Feigenbaum in physics, and Humberto Maturana and Francisco Varela in biology.[16] This emerging body of theory and data is sometimes identified with the "new physics" popularized by books such as Fritjof Capra's *Tao of Physics* and *The Turning Point*.[17] It is sometimes also called "chaos" theory because, for the first time in the history of science, it focuses on sudden and fundamental change—the kind of change that our world is increasingly experiencing.

Of particular interest are the new works investigating evolutionary change by biologists and paleontologists such as Vilmos Csanyi, Niles Eldredge, and Stephen Jay Gould, as well as by scholars such as Erich Jantsch, Ervin Laszlo, and David Loye on the implications of "chaos" theory for cultural evolution and social science.[18] This is by no means to suggest that human cultural evolution is the same as biological evolution. But although there are important differences between the natural and social sciences, and the study of social systems must avoid mechanistic reductionism, there are also important similarities regarding both systems change and systems self-organization.

All systems are maintained through the mutually reinforcing interaction of critical systems parts. Accordingly, in some striking respects the Cultural Transformation theory presented in this book and the "chaos" theory being developed by natural and systems scientists are similar in what they tell us of what happened—and may now again happen—at critical systems branching or bifurcation points, when rapid transformation of a whole system may occur.[19]

For example, Eldredge and Gould propose that rather than always proceeding in gradual upward stages, evolution consists of long stretches of equilibrium, or lack of major change, punctuated by evolutionary branching or bifurcation points when new species spring up on the periphery or fringe of a parental species' habitat.[20] And even though there are obvious differences between the branching off of new species and shifts from one type of society to another, as we shall see, there are startling similarities to Gould and Eldredge's model of "peripheral isolates" and the concepts of other evolutionary and "chaos" theorists in what has happened and may now again be happening in our cultural evolution.

The contribution of feminist scholarship to a holistic study of cultural evolution—encompassing the whole span of human history and *both* halves of humanity—is more obvious: it provides the missing data not found in conventional sources. In fact, the reevaluation of our past, present, and future presented in this book would not have been possible without the work of scholars such as Simone de Beauvoir, Jessie Bernard, Ester Boserup, Gita Sen, Mary Daly, Dale Spender, Florence Howe, Nancy Chodorow, Adrienne Rich, Kate Millett, Barbara Gelpi, Alice Schlegel, Annette Kuhn, Charlotte Bunch, Carol Christ, Judith Plaskow, Catharine Stimpson, Rosemary Radford Ruether, Hazel Henderson, Catharine MacKinnon, Wilma Scott Heide, Jean Baker Miller, and Carol Gilligan, to name but a few.[21] Dating from the time of Aphra Behn in the seventeenth century and even earlier,[22] but only coming into its own during the past two decades, the emerging body of data and insight provided by feminist scholars is, like "chaos" theory, opening new frontiers for science.

Though poles apart in origin—one from the traditional male, the other from a radically different female experience and worldview—feminist and "chaos" theories in fact have a good deal in common. Within mainstream science both are still often viewed as mysterious activities at or beyond the fringe of the sanctified endeavors. And in their focus on *transformation*, these two bodies of thought share the growing awareness that the present system is breaking down, that we must find ways to break through to a different kind of future.

The chapters that follow explore the roots of—and paths to—that future. They tell a story that begins thousands of years before our recorded (or written) history: the story of how the original partnership direction of Western culture veered off into a bloody five-thousand-year dominator detour. They show that our mounting global problems are in large part the logical consequences of a dominator model of social organization at our level of technological development—hence can *not* be solved within it. And they also show that there is another course which, as co-creators of our own evolution, is still ours to choose. This is the alternative of break*through* rather than breakdown: how through new ways of structuring politics, economics, science, and spirituality we can move into the new era of a partnership world.

CHAPTER 1

Journey into a Lost World: The Beginnings of Civilization

Preserved in a cave sanctuary for over twenty thousand years, a female figure speaks to us about the minds of our early Western ancestors. She is small and carved out of stone: one of the so-called Venus figurines found all over prehistoric Europe.

Unearthed in excavations over a wide geographical area—from the Balkans in eastern Europe to Lake Baikal in Siberia, all the way west to Willendorf near Vienna and the Grotte du Pappe in France—these figurines have been described by some scholars as expressions of male eroticism: that is, an ancient analogue for today's *Playboy* magazine. To other scholars they are only something used in primitive, and presumably obscene, fertility rites.

But what is the actual significance of these ancient sculptures? Can they really be dismissed as the "products of unregenerated male imagination"?[1] Is the term *Venus* even appropriate to describe these broad-hipped, sometimes pregnant, highly stylized, and often faceless figures? Or do these prehistoric sculptures tell us something important about ourselves, about how both women and men once venerated the *life*-giving powers of the universe?

The Paleolithic

Along with their wall paintings, cave sanctuaries, and burial sites, the female figurines of the peoples of the Paleolithic are important psychic records. They attest to our forebears' awe at both the mystery of life and the mystery of death. They indicate that very early in human history the human will to live found expression and reassurance through a variety of rituals and myths that seem to have been associated with the still widely held belief that the dead can return to life through rebirth.

"In a great cavern sanctuary like Les Trois Frères, Niaux, Font de Gaume or Lascaux," writes the religious historian E. O. James, "the ceremonies must have involved an organized attempt on the part of the community . . . to control natural forces and processes by supernatural means directed to the common good. The sacred tradition, be it in relation to the food supply, the mystery of birth and propagation, or of death, arose and functioned, it would appear, in response to the will to live here and hereafter."[2]

This sacred tradition found expression in the remarkable art of the Paleolithic. And an integral component of this sacred tradition was the association of the powers that govern life and death with woman.

We can see this association of the feminine with the power to give life in Paleolithic burials. For example, in the rock shelter known as Cro-Magnon in Les Eyzies, France (where in 1868 the first skeletal remains of our Upper Paleolithic ancestors were found), around and on the corpses were carefully arranged cowrie shells. These shells, shaped in the form of what James discreetly calls "the portal through which a child enters the world," seem to have been associated with some kind of early worship of a female deity. As he writes, the cowrie was a life-giving agent. So also was red ocher, still in later traditions the surrogate of the life-giving or menstrual blood of woman.[3]

The main emphasis seems to have been on the association of woman with the giving and sustaining of life. But at the same time, death—or, more specifically, resurrection—also appears to have been a central religious theme. Both the ritualized placement of the vagina-shaped cowrie shells around and on the dead and the practice of coating these shells and/or the dead with red ocher pigment (symbolizing the vitalizing power of blood) appear to have been part of funerary rites intended to bring the deceased back through rebirth. Even more specifically, as James notes, they "point to mortuary rituals in the nature of a life-giving ritual closely connected with the female figurines and other symbols of the Goddess cult."[4]

In addition to this archaeological evidence of Paleolithic funerary rites, there is also evidence of rites seemingly designed to encourage the fecundity of the wild animals and plants that provided our forebears with life support. For example, in the gallery of the inaccessible cavern of Tuc d'Audoubert in Ariège, on the soft clay floor underneath the wall painting of two bisons (a female followed by a male), we find impressions of human feet believed by scholars to have been made in ritual dances. Similarly, in the Cogul rock shelter in Catalonia, we find a scene of women, possibly priestesses, dancing around a smaller naked male figure in what seems to be a religious ceremony.

These cave sanctuaries, figurines, burials, and rites all seem to have been related to a belief that the same source from which human life springs is also the source of all vegetable and animal life—the great Mother Goddess or Giver of All we still find in later periods of Western civilization. They also suggest that our early ancestors recognized that we and our natural environment are integrally linked parts of the great mystery of life and death and that all nature must therefore be treated with respect. This consciousness—later emphasized in Goddess figurines either surrounded by natural symbols such as animals, water, and trees or themselves partly animal—evidently was central to our lost psychic heritage. Also central to that lost heritage is the apparent awe and wonder at the great miracle of our human condition: the miracle of birth incarnated in woman's body. Judging from these early psychic records, this was a central theme of prehistoric Western systems of belief.

Now what we have been developing to this point is still not the view of many scholars. Nor is it the view still taught in most survey classes about the origins of civilization. For here, as in most popularized writings on the subject, there still prevail the preconceptions of earlier scholars who saw Paleolithic art in terms of the conventional stereotype of "primitive man": bloodthirsty, warlike hunters, in fact very unlike some of the most primitive gathering-hunting societies discovered in modern times.[5] Based on this interpretation of the very fragmentary materials available from Paleolithic times, male-centered theories of proto- and prehistoric social organization were constructed. And even when new discoveries were made, these too were usually interpreted by scholars so as to fit into the old theoretical molds.

One of the assumptions of these scholars was—as it still generally is—that only prehistoric *man* was responsible for Paleolithic art. This too was not based on any factual evidence. Rather, it was the result of scholarly preconceptions, which actually fly in the face of findings that, for example, among the contemporary Vedda in Sri Lanka (Ceylon) it is in fact the women, not the men, who do the rock painting.[6]

Basic to these preconceptions was the idea, as John Pfeiffer put it in *The Emergence of Man*, that "hunting dominated the attention and imagination of prehistoric man" and that "if he was anything like modern man, he used ritual on numerous occasions to help replenish and increase his power."[7] In keeping with this bias, Paleolithic wall paintings were interpreted as relating to hunting even when they showed women dancing. Similarly, as already noted, the evidence of a female-centered anthropomorphic form of worship—such as finds of broad-hipped and pregnant female representations—had to either be ignored or classified as merely male sex objects: obese erotic "Venuses" or "barbaric images of beauty."[8]

Although there have been exceptions, the evolutionary model of man the hunter-warrior has colored most interpretations of Paleolithic art. Only in later twentieth-century excavations in eastern and western Europe and Siberia has the interpretation of both new and old finds gradually begun to change. Some of the new researchers were women, who noted the female genital imagery and also leaned toward more complex religious rather than the "hunting magic" explanations of Paleolithic art.[9] And as more scholars were secular scientists rather than monks like Abbé Breuil (whose "moral" interpretations of religious practices colored so much of the nineteenth- and early twentieth-century Paleolithic research), some of the men who reexamined the cave paintings, figurines, and other Paleolithic finds now also began to question tenets once accepted by the scholarly establishment.

An interesting example of this questioning relates to the stick and line forms painted on the walls of Paleolithic caves and engraved in bone or stone objects. To many scholars, it seemed obvious that they depict weapons: arrows, barbs, spears, harpoons. But as Alexander Marshack writes in *The Roots of Civilization*, one of the first works to frontally challenge this standard interpretation, these line paintings and engravings could just as easily be plants, trees, branches, reeds, and leaves.[10] Moreover, this new interpretation would account for what would otherwise be a remarkable absence of pictures of such vegetation among a people who, like contemporary gatherer-hunter peoples, must have relied heavily on vegetation for food.

In *Paleolithic Cave Art*, Peter Ucko and Andrée Rosenfeld had also wondered about the peculiar absence of vegetation in Paleolithic art. They further noted another curious incongruity. All other evidence showed that a particular kind of harpoon called biserial didn't appear until the late Paleolithic or Magdalenian age—even though scholars kept "finding" them in "sticks" thousands of years earlier in the wall paintings of prehistoric caves. Moreover, why would Paleolithic artists want to depict so many hunting *failures?* For if the sticks and lines were in fact weapons, the pictures had them chronically *missing* their targets.[11]

To probe such mysteries, Marshack, who was not an archaeologist, hence not bound by earlier archeological conventions, thoroughly examined the engravings on a bone object that had been described as pictures of harpoons. Under a microscope he discovered that not only were the barbs of this supposed harpoon turned the wrong way but the points of the long shaft were also at the wrong end. But what did these engravings represent if they were not "wrong way" weapons? As it turned out, the lines easily conformed to the proper angle of branches growing at the top of a long stem. In other words, these and other engravings conventionally described as "barbed signs" or "masculine objects" were probably nothing more than stylized representations of trees, branches, and plants.[12]

So time and time again, under closer scrutiny, the traditional view of Paleolithic art as primarily primitive hunting magic can be seen as projection of stereotypes rather than logical interpretation of what is seen. And so also can the explanation of Paleolithic female figurines as either obscene male sex objects or expressions of a primitive fertility cult.

Because of the scarceness of their remains and the long time span between us and them, we probably never will be entirely certain of the specific meaning their paintings, figurines, and symbols had for our Paleolithic forebears. But, following the impact of the first publication of Paleolithic cave paintings in magnificent color plates, the evocative power of this art has become legendary. Some of the renditions of animals are as fine as the work of the best of modern artists and offer a fresh vision few moderns can recapture. Therefore there is one thing we can be certain of: Paleolithic art is far more than the crude scratching of undeveloped primitives. Rather, it bespeaks psychic traditions we must understand if we are to know not only what humans were and are but also what they can become.

As André Leroi-Gourhan, director of the Sorbonne's Center for Prehistoric and Protohistoric Studies, wrote in one of the most important recent studies of Paleolithic art, it is "unsatisfactory and ridiculous" to dismiss the belief system of the period as a "primitive fertility cult." We can, "without forcing the materials, take the whole of the figurative Paleolithic art as an expression of concepts about the natural and supernatural organization of the living world," he observed, adding that the people of the Paleolithic "undoubtedly knew of the division of the animal and human world into confronted halves and conceived that the union of these two halves ruled the economy of living beings."[13]

Leroi-Gourhan's conclusion that Paleolithic art reflects the importance our early forebears attached to their observation that there are two sexes was based on analysis of thousands of paintings and objects in some sixty excavated Paleolithic caves. Even though he speaks in terms of sadomasochistic male-female stereotypes and in other respects follows earlier archaeological conventions, he verifies that Paleolithic art expressed some form of early religion in which feminine representations and symbols played a central part. In this connection, he makes two fascinating observations. Characteristically, the female figures and the symbols he interpreted as feminine were located in a central position in the excavated chambers. In contrast, the masculine symbols typically either occupied peripheral positions or were arranged around the female figures and symbols.[14]

Leroi-Gourhan's findings are in line with the view I proposed earlier: that the vagina-shaped cowrie shells, the red ocher in burials, the so-called Venus figurines, and the hybrid woman-animal figurines earlier writers dismissed as "monstrosities" all relate to an early form of worship in which the life-giving powers of woman played a major part. They were all expressions of our forebears' attempts to understand their world, attempts to answer such universal human questions as where we come from when we are born and where we go after we die. And they confirm what we would logically assume: along with the first awareness of self in relation to other humans, animals, and the rest of nature must have come awareness of the awesome mystery— and practical importance—of the fact that life emerges from the body of woman.

It would seem only logical that the visible dimorphism, or difference in form, between the two halves of humanity had a profound effect on Paleolithic systems of belief. And it would seem equally logical that the fact that both human and animal life is generated from the female body and that, like the seasons and the moon, woman's body also goes through cycles led our ancestors to see the life-giving and sustaining powers of the world in female, rather than male, form.

In sum, instead of being random and unconnected materials, the Paleolithic remains of female figurines, red ocher in burials, and vagina-shaped cowrie shells appear to be early manifestations of what was later to develop into a complex religion centering on the worship of a Mother Goddess as the source and regeneratrix of all forms of life.

This Goddess worship, as James and other scholars note, survived well into historic times "in the composite figure of the Magna Mater of the Near East and the Greco-Roman world."[15] We clearly see this religious continuity in such well-known deities as Isis, Nut, and Maat in Egypt; Ishtar, Astarte, and Lilith in the Fertile Crescent; Demeter, Kore, and Hera in Greece; and Atargatis, Ceres, and Cybele in Rome. Even later, in our own Judeo-Christian heritage, we can still see it in the Queen of Heaven, whose groves are burned in the Bible, in the Shekhina of Hebrew kabalistic tradition, and in the Catholic Virgin Mary, the Holy Mother of God.

Again the question arises of why if these connections are so obvious they have for so long been downplayed, or simply ignored, in the conventional archaeological literature. One reason, already noted, is that they do not fit the proto- and prehistoric model of a male-centered and male-dominated form of social organization. But still another reason is that it was not until after World War II that some of the most important new evidence was unearthed of this religious tradition extending over thousands of years into the fascinating period that followed the Paleolithic. This was the long period in our cultural evolution that came between the first crucial developments for human culture during the Paleolithic and the later civilizations of the Bronze Age: the time when our forebears settled down in the first agrarian communities of the Neolithic.

The Neolithic

At about the same time Leroi-Gourhan wrote of his findings, our knowledge of prehistory was immeasurably advanced by the exciting discovery and excavation of two new Neolithic sites: the towns of Catal Huyuk and Hacilar. They were found in what used to be called the plains of Anatolia, now modern Turkey. Of particular interest, according to the man who directed these excavations for the British Institute of Archaeology at Ankara, James Mellaart, was that the knowledge unearthed at these two sites showed a stability and continuity of growth over many thousands of years for progressively more advanced Goddess-worshiping cultures.

"A. Leroi-Gourhan's brilliant reassessment of Upper Paleolithic religion," wrote Mellaart, "has cleared away many misunderstandings. . . . The resulting interpretation of Upper Paleolithic art centered around the theme of complex and female symbolism (in the form of symbols and animals) shows strong similarities to the religious imagery of Catal Huyuk." Moreover, there are also obvious Upper Paleolithic influences "in numerous cult-practices of which the red-ocher burials, red-stained floors, collections of stalactites, fossils, shells, are but a few examples."[16]

Mellaart further observed that as long as it was thought that the highly developed and stylized Upper Paleolithic art was nothing more than "an expression of hunting magic, a view borrowed from backward societies like Australian aborigines," there had been little hope of "establishing any link with the later fertility-cults of the Near East which center around the figure of the Great Goddess and her son, even if the presence of such a goddess in the Upper Paleolithic could hardly be denied, which it is not." But now, he stated, this position has "radically changed in light of the available data."[17]

In other words, the Neolithic culture of Catal Huyuk and Hacilar have provided extensive information about a long-missing piece of the puzzle of our past—the missing link between the Paleolithic Age and the later, more technologically advanced Chalcolithic, Copper, and Bronze Ages. As Mellaart writes, "Catal Huyuk and Hacilar have established a link between these two great schools of art. A continuity in religion can be demonstrated from Catal Huyuk to Hacilar and so on till the great 'Mother-Goddesses' of archaic and classical times."[18]

As in Paleolithic art, female figurines and symbols occupy a central position in the art of Catal Huyuk, where shrines to the Goddess and Goddess figurines are found everywhere. Moreover, Goddess figurines are characteristic of Neolithic art in other areas of the Near and Middle East. For example, in the Middle Eastern Neolithic site of Jericho (now in Israel), where back in 7000 B.C.E. people were already living in plastered brick houses—some with clay ovens with chimneys and even sockets for doorposts—clay Goddess figurines have been found.[19] At Tell-es-Sawwan, a site on the banks of the Tigris distinguished by early irrigation farming and the striking geometrically decorated pottery known as Samarra, a variety of figurines, among them a cache of highly sophisticated painted female sculptures, have been unearthed. In Cayonu, a Neolithic site in northern Syria, where we find the earliest use of hammered native copper and the first use of clay bricks, similar female figurines have been excavated, some of them dating to the site's earliest levels. These small Goddess figurines have later parallels at Jarmo, and even as far west as Aceramic Sesklo, where they were manufactured even before ceramic pottery was introduced.[20]

Although this too is not generally brought out, the numerous Neolithic excavations that have yielded Goddess figurines and symbols span a wide geographical area going far beyond the Near and Middle East. As far east as Harappa and Mohenjo-Daro in India, large numbers of terra-cotta female figurines had earlier been found. These, too, as Sir John Marshall wrote, probably represented a Goddess "with attributes very similar to those of the great Mother Goddess, the Lady of Heaven."[21] Goddess figurines have also been found in European sites as far west as those of the so-called megalithic cultures who built the huge, carefully engineered stone monuments at Stonehenge and Avebury in England. And some of these megalithic cultures went as far south as the Mediterranean island of Malta, where a giant ossuary of seven thousand burial sites was apparently also an important sanctuary for oracular and initiary rites in which, as James writes, "the Mother-goddess probably played an important part."[22]

Gradually a new picture of the origins and development of both civilization and religion is emerging. The Neolithic agrarian economy was the basis for the development of civilization leading over thousands of years into our own time. And almost universally, those places where the first great breakthroughs in material and social technology were made had òne feature in common: the worship of the Goddess.

What are the implications of these findings for our present and future? And why should we believe this new view of our cultural development instead of the old sanctified androcentric lore of so many beautifully illustrated books of bedtime and coffee table archaeology?

One reason is that the finds of female figurines and other archaeological records attesting to a gynocentric (or Goddess-based) religion in Neolithic times are so numerous that just cataloging them would fill several volumes. But the main reason is that this new view of prehistory is the result of a profound change in both methods and emphasis for archaeological investigation.

Digging up the buried treasure of antiquity is as old as the grave robbers who plundered the tombs of the Egyptian pharaohs. But archaeology as a science dates back only to the late 1800s. Even then, the earliest archaeological excavations, though also motivated by intellectual curiosity about our past, primarily served a purpose akin to that of grave robbing: the acquisition of striking antiquities by museums in England, France, and other colonial nations. The idea of archaeological excavation as a way to extract the maximum information from a site—whether or not it contained archaeological treasures—took hold only much later. In fact, it was not until after World War II that archaeology as a systematic inquiry into the life, thought, technology, and social organization of our forebears truly began to come into its own.

New excavations are increasingly conducted not by the lone scholar or explorer of earlier days but by teams of scientists—zoologists, botanists, climatologists, anthropologists, paleontologists, as well as archaeologists. This interdisciplinary approach characterizing more recent digs like Mellaart's at Catal Huyuk is yielding much more accurate understanding of our prehistory.

But perhaps most important is that a number of remarkable technological breakthroughs, such as the Nobel Prize winner Willard Libby's dating by means of radiocarbon, or C–14, and the dendrochronological methods of dating by the girth of trees, have vastly increased archaeology's grasp of the past. Formerly dates were largely a matter of conjecture—of comparisons of objects estimated to be less, equally, or more "advanced" than one another. But as dating became a function of repeatable and verifiable techniques, one could no longer get away with saying that if an artifact was more artistically or technologically developed, it must date to a later and thus presumably more civilized time.

As a consequence, there has been a dramatic reassessment of time sequences, which in turn has radically changed earlier views about prehistory. We now know that agriculture—the domestication of wild plants as well as animals—dates back much earlier than previously believed. In fact, the first signs of what archaeologists call the Neolithic or agricultural revolution begin to appear as far back as 9000 to 8000 B.C.E.—that is, more than ten thousand years ago.

The agricultural revolution was the single most important breakthrough in the material technology of our species. Accordingly, the beginnings of what we call Western civilization are also much earlier than was previously thought.

With a regular, and sometimes even surplus, food supply came an increase in population and the first sizable towns. Here hundreds, sometimes thousands, of people lived and worked, tilling and in many places also irrigating the land. Technological specialization as well as trade accelerated in the Neolithic. And, as agriculture freed human energy and imagination, such crafts as pottery and basket making, textile weaving and leather crafting, jewelry making and wood carving and such arts as painting, clay modeling, and stone carving flourished.

At the same time, the evolution of human spiritual consciousness continued. The first anthropomorphic religion, focusing on the worship of the Goddess, now evolved into a complex system of symbols, rituals, and divine commands and prohibitions, all of which found expression in the rich art of the Neolithic period.

Some of the most vivid evidence of this gynocentric artistic tradition comes to us from Mellaart's excavation of Catal Huyuk. Here, at the largest known Neolithic site in the Near East, there are thirty-two acres of archaeological remains. Only one twentieth of the mound has been excavated, but this digging alone uncovered a period spanning approximately eight hundred years, from about 6500 to about 5700 B.C.E. And what we find here is a remarkably advanced center of art, with wall paintings, plaster reliefs, stone sculptures, and large quantities of Goddess figurines made of clay, all focusing on the worship of a female deity.

"Its numerous sanctuaries," wrote Mellaart about Catal Huyuk in summarizing his first three seasons of work (1961 through 1963), "testify to an advanced religion, complete with symbolism and mythology; its buildings to the birth of architecture and conscious planning; its economy to advanced practices in agriculture and stockbreeding; and its numerous imports to a flourishing trade in raw materials."[23]

But while the excavations carried out at Catal Huyuk, as well as at nearby Hacilar (inhabited from approximately 5700 to 5000 B.C.E.), have yielded some of the richest data about this early civilization, the southern Anatolian plain is only one of several areas where settled agricultural societies worshiping the Goddess have been archaeologically documented. In fact, by circa 6000 B.C.E., not only was the agricultural revolution an established fact, but—to quote Mellaart—"fully agricultural societies began expanding into hitherto marginal territories such as the alluvial plains of Mesopotamia, Transcaucasia and Transcaspia on the one hand, and into southeastern Europe on the other." Moreover, "some of this contact, as in Crete and Cyprus, definitely went by sea," and in each case "the newcomers arrived with a fully fledged Neolithic economy."[24]

In short, though only twenty-five years earlier archaeologists were still talking of Sumer as the "cradle of civilization" (and though this is *still* the prevailing impression among the general public), we now know there was not one cradle of civilization but several, all of them dating back millennia earlier than was previously known—to the Neolithic. As Mellaart wrote in his 1975 work *The Neolithic of the Near East*, "urban civilization, long thought to be a Mesopotamian invention, has predecessors at sites like Jericho or Catal Huyuk, in Palestine and Anatolia, long regarded as backwaters."[25] Moreover, we now also know something else of great significance for the original development of our cultural evolution. This is that in all these places where the first great breakthroughs in our material and social technology were made—to use the phrase Merlin Stone immortalized as a book title—God was a woman.

The new knowledge that civilization is much older and more widespread than was previously believed is understandably producing much new scholarly writings, with massive reassessment of earlier archaeological theories. But the centrally striking fact that in these first civilizations ideology was gynocentric has not, except among feminist scholars, generated much interest. If mentioned by nonfeminist scholars, it is usually in passing. Even those who, like Mellaart, do mention it, generally do so only as a matter of purely artistic and religious significance, without probing its social and cultural implications.

Indeed, the prevailing view is still that male dominance, along with private property and slavery, were all by-products of the agrarian revolution. And this view maintains its hold despite the evidence that, on the contrary, equality between the sexes—and among all people—was the general norm in the Neolithic.

We will pursue this fascinating evidence in the chapters that follow. But first we turn to another important area where old archaeological notions are currently being demolished by new findings.

Old Europe

Some of the most revealing evidence of what life was like during thousands of previously unknown years of human culture has come to us from what was a totally unexpected place. In line with the long-accepted theory that the Fertile Crescent of the Mediterranean was the cradle of civilization, ancient Europe was long considered to be only a cultural backwater that later flowered briefly into the Minoan and Greek civilizations, and then only as a result of influences from the East. But the picture now emerging is very different.

"A new designation, *Civilization of Old Europe,* is introduced here in recognition of the collective identity and achievement of the different cultural groups in Neolithic-Chalcolithic southeastern Europe," writes the University of California archaeologist Marija Gimbutas in *The Goddesses and Gods of Old Europe.* This ground-breaking work catalogs and analyzes hundreds of archaeological finds in an area extending roughly northward from the Aegean and Adriatic (including the islands) all the way up into Czechoslovakia, southern Poland, and the western Ukraine.[26]

The inhabitants of southeastern Europe seven thousand years ago were hardly primitive villagers. "During two millennia of agricultural stability their material welfare had been persistently improved by the increasingly efficient exploitation of the fertile river valleys," reports Gimbutas. "Wheat, barley, vetch, peas, and other legumes were cultivated, and all the domesticated animals present in the Balkans today, except for the horse, were bred. Pottery technology and bone- and stone-working techniques had advanced, and copper metallurgy was introduced into east central Europe by 5500 B.C.E. Trade and communications, which had expanded through the millennia, must have provided a tremendous cross-fertilizing impetus to cultural growth. . . . The use of sailing-boats is attested from the sixth millennia onwards by their incised depictions on ceramics."[27]

Between circa 7000 and 3500 B.C.E. these early Europeans developed a complex social organization involving craft specialization. They created complex religious and governmental institutions. They used metals such as copper and gold for ornaments and tools. They even evolved what appears to be a rudimentary script. In Gimbutas's words, "If one defines civilization as the ability of a given people to adjust to its environment and to develop adequate arts, technology, script, and social relationships it is evident that Old Europe achieved a marked degree of success."[28]

The image of the Old European most of us carry within us today is of those frightfully barbaric tribesmen who kept pushing southward and finally outdid even the Romans in butchery by sacking Rome. For this reason one of the most remarkable and thought-provoking features of Old European society revealed by the archaeological spade is its essentially *peaceful* character. "Old Europeans never tried to live in inconvenient places such as high, steep hills, as did the later Indo-Europeans who built hill forts in inaccessible places and frequently surrounded their hill sites with cyclopean stone walls," reports Gimbutas. "Old European locations were chosen for their beautiful setting, good water and soil, and availability of animal pastures. Vinca, Butmir, Petresti, and Cucuteni settlement areas are remarkable for their excellent views of the environs, but not for their defensive value. The characteristic absence of heavy fortifications and of thrusting weapons speaks for the peaceful character of most of these art-loving peoples."[29]

Moreover, here, as in Catal Huyuk and Hacilar—which show no signs of damage through warfare for a time span of over fifteen

hundred years[30]—the archaeological evidence indicates that male dominance was *not* the norm. "A division of labor between the sexes is
indicated, but not a superiority of either," writes Gimbutas. "In the 53-
grave cemetary of Vinca, hardly any difference in wealth of equipment
was discernible between male and female graves. . . . In respect to the
role of women in the society, the Vinca evidence suggests an equalitarian and clearly non-patriarchal society. The same can be adduced of
the Varna society: I can see there no ranking along a patriarchal mas-
culine-feminine value scale."[31]

In sum, here, as in Catal Huyuk, the evidence indicates a generally
unstratified and basically equalitarian society with no marked distinctions based on either class or sex. But the difference is that in Gimbutas's work this is not simply noted in passing. It is brought to our
attention time and time again by this remarkable archaeological pioneer, who has had the courage to stress what so many others prefer
to ignore: that in these societies we see no signs of the sexual inequality
we have all been taught is only "human nature."

"An equalitarian male-female society is demonstrated by the grave
equipment in practically all the known cemeteries of Old Europe,"
writes Gimbutas. She also notes numerous indicators that this was a
matrilinear society—that is, one in which descent and inheritance is
traced through the mother.[32] Moreover, she points out that the archaeological evidence leaves little doubt that women played key roles
in all aspects of Old European life.

"In the models of house-shrines and temples, and in actual temple
remains," writes Gimbutas, "females are shown supervising the preparation and performance of rituals dedicated to the various aspects and
functions of the Goddess. Enormous energy was expended in the production of cult equipment and votive gifts. Temple models show the
grinding of grain and the baking of sacred bread. . . . In the temple
workshops which usually constitute half the building or occupy the
floor below the temple proper, females made and decorated quantities
of various pots appropriate to different rites. Next to the altar of the
temple stood a vertical loom on which were probably woven the sacred
garments and temple appurtenances. The most sophisticated creations
of Old Europe—the most exquisite vases, sculptures, etc. now extant—
were woman's work."[33]

The artistic heritage left us by these ancient communities—where
the worship of the Goddess was central to all aspects of life—is still
being unearthed by the archaeological spade. By 1974, when Gimbutas
first published a compendium of findings from her own excavations

and from over three thousand other sites, no less than thirty thousand miniature sculptures of clay, marble, bone, copper, and gold had been uncovered, in addition to enormous quantities of ritual vessels, altars, temples, and paintings on both vases and the walls of shrines.[34]

Of these finds, the most eloquent vestiges of this European Neolithic culture are the sculptures. They provide information on facets of life otherwise inaccessible to the archaeologist: fashions of dress and even hairstyles. They give us a firsthand view into the mythical images of the period's religious rites. And what these sculptures show, as was the case in the caves of the Paleolithic and later on in the open plains of Anatolia and other Near Eastern and Middle Eastern Neolithic sites, is that here too feminine figures and symbols occupied the central place.

Even beyond this, they provide arresting evidence pointing to the next step in the aesthetic and social evolution of this lost earlier civilization. For both in style and theme, many of these female figurines and symbols are strikingly similar to those of a place that is still visited by hundreds of thousands of tourists today with practically no knowledge of what they are really looking at: the Bronze Age civilization that later flourished on the fabled island of Crete.

Before we look at Crete—the only known "high" civilization where the worship of the Goddess survived into historical times—let us first more closely examine what we can infer from the archaeological remains of the Neolithic Age about the early direction of Western cultural evolution—and its relevance to our own present and future.

CHAPTER 2

Messages from the Past: The World of the Goddess

What kind of people were our prehistoric ancestors who worshiped the Goddess? What was life like during the millennia of our cultural evolution before recorded or written history? And what can we learn from those times that is relevant to our own?

Because they left us no written accounts, we can only infer, like Sherlock Holmes turned scientist, how the people of the Paleolithic and of the later, more advanced Neolithic thought, felt, and behaved. But almost everything we have been taught about antiquity is based on conjecture. Even the records we have from early historic cultures, such as Sumer, Babylon, and Crete, are at best scanty and fragmentary and largely concerned with inventories of goods and other mercantile matters. And the more detailed later written accounts about both prehistory and early history from classical Greek, Roman, Hebrew, and Christian times are also mainly based on inferences—made without even the aid of modern archaeological methods.

Indeed, most of what we have learned to think of as our cultural evolution has in fact been interpretation. Moreover, as we saw in the preceding chapter, this interpretation has more often than not been the projection of the still prevailing dominator worldview. It has consisted of conclusions drawn from fragmentary data interpreted to conform to the traditional model of our cultural evolution as a linear progression from "primitive man" to so-called "civilized man," who, despite their many differences, shared a common preoccupation with conquering, killing, and dominating.

Through scientific excavations of ancient sites, archaeologists have in recent years obtained a great deal of primary information about prehistory, particularly about the Neolithic, when our ancestors first settled in communities sustained by farming and the breeding of stock. Analyzed from a fresh perspective, these excavations provide the data base for a re-evaluation, and reconstruction, of our past.

One important source of data is excavations of buildings and their contents—including clothing, jewelry, food, furniture, containers, tools, and other objects used in daily life. Another is the excavation of burial sites, which tell us not only about people's attitudes about death but also about their lives. And overlapping both of these data sources is our richest source of information about prehistory: art.

Even when there is a written as well as an oral literary tradition, art is a form of symbolic communication. The extensive art of the Neolithic—be it wall paintings about daily life or about important myths, statuary of religious images, friezes depicting rituals, or simply vase decorations, pictures on seals, or engravings on jewelry—tells us a great deal about how these people lived and died. It also tells us a great deal about how they thought, for in a very real sense Neolithic art is a kind of language or shorthand symbolically expressing how people in that time experienced, and in turn shaped, what we call reality.[1] And if we let this language speak for itself, without projecting on it prevailing models of reality, it tells a fascinating—and in comparison to the stereotype, a far more hopeful—story of our cultural origins.

Neolithic Art

One of the most striking things about Neolithic art is what it does *not* depict. For what a people do not depict in their art can tell us as much about them as what they do.

In sharp contrast to later art, a theme notable for its absence from Neolithic art is imagery idealizing armed might, cruelty, and violence-based power. There are here no images of "noble warriors" or scenes of battles. Nor are there any signs of "heroic conquerors" dragging captives around in chains or other evidences of slavery.

Also in sharp contrast to the remains of even their earliest and most primitive male-dominant invaders, what is notable in these Neolithic Goddess-worshiping societies is the absence of lavish "chieftain" burials. And in marked contrast to later male-dominant civilizations like that of Egypt, there is here no sign of mighty rulers who take with them into the afterlife less powerful humans sacrificed at their death.

Nor do we here find, again in contrast to later dominator societies, large caches of weapons or any other sign of the intensive application of material technology and natural resources to arms. The inference that this was a much more, and indeed characteristically, peaceful era is further reinforced by another absence: military fortifications. Only gradually do these begin to appear, apparently as a response to pressures from the warlike nomadic bands coming from the fringe areas of the globe, which we will examine later.

In Neolithic art, neither the Goddess nor her son-consort carry the emblems we have learned to associate with might—spears, swords, or thunderbolts, the symbols of an earthly sovereign and/or deity who exacts obedience by killing and maiming. Even beyond this, the art of this period is strikingly devoid of the ruler–ruled, master–subject imagery so characteristic of dominator societies.

What we do find everywhere—in shrines and houses, on wall paintings, in the decorative motifs on vases, in sculptures in the round, clay figurines, and bas reliefs—is a rich array of symbols from nature. Associated with the worship of the Goddess, these attest to awe and wonder at the beauty and mystery of life.

There are the life-sustaining elements of sun and water, for instance, the geometric patterns of wavy forms called meanders (which symbolized flowing waters) incised on an Old European altar from about 5000 B.C.E. in Hungary. There are the giant stone heads of bulls with enormous curled horns painted on the walls of Catal Huyuk shrines, terra-cotta hedgehogs from southern Romania, ritual vases in the form of does from Bulgaria, egg-shaped stone sculptures with the faces of fish, and cult vases in the form of birds.[2]

There are serpents and butterflies (symbols of metamorphosis) which are in historic times still identified with the transformative powers of the Goddess, as in the seal impression from Zakro, in eastern Crete, portraying the Goddess with the wings of an eyed butterfly. Even the later Cretan double axe, reminiscent of the hoe axes used to clear farm lands, was a stylization of the butterfly.[3] Like the serpent, which sheds its skin and is "reborn," it was part of the Goddess's epiphany, yet another symbol of her powers of regeneration.[4]

And everywhere—in murals, statues, and votive figurines—we find images of the Goddess. In the various incarnations of Maiden, Ancestress, or Creatrix, she is the Lady of the waters, the birds, and the underworld, or simply the divine Mother cradling her divine child in her arms.[5]

Some images are so realistic that they are almost lifelike, like the slithering snake on a dish found in an early fifth millennium B.C.E.

cemetery in western Slovakia. Others are so stylized that they are more abstract than even our most "modern" art. Among these are the large stylized sacramental vase or chalice in the shape of an enthroned Goddess incised with ideograms from the Tisza culture of southeastern Hungary, the pillar-headed Goddess with folded arms from 5000 B.C.E. Romania, and the marble Goddess figurine from Tell Azmak, central Bulgaria, with schematized arms and an exaggerated pubic triangle, dating from 6000 B.C.E. Still other images are strangely beautiful, such as an 8000-year-old horned terra-cotta stand with female breasts, somehow reminiscent of the classical Greek statue called the Winged Victory, and the painted Cucuteni vases with their graceful shapes and rich geometric snake-spiral designs. And others, such as the crosses incised on the navel or near the breasts of the Goddess, raise interesting questions about the earlier meanings of some of our own most important symbols.[6]

There is a sense of fantasy about many of these images, a dreamlike and sometimes bizarre quality suggestive of arcane rituals and long-forgotten myths. For example, a bird-faced woman on a Vinca sculpture and a bird-faced baby she is holding would seem to be masked protagonists of ancient rites, probably enacting a mythological story about a bird Goddess and her divine child. Similarly, a terra-cotta head of a bull with human eyes from 4000 B.C.E. Macedonia suggests a masked protagonist of some other Neolithic ritual and myth. Some of these masked figures seem to represent cosmic powers, either benevolent or threatening. Others have a humorous effect, such as the masked man with padded knickers and exposed belly from fifth millennium B.C.E. Fafkos, described by Gimbutas as probably a comic actor. There are also what Gimbutas calls cosmic eggs. These too are symbols of the Goddess, whose body is the divine Chalice containing the miracle of birth and the power to transform death into life through the mysterious cyclical regeneration of nature.[7]

Indeed, this theme of the unity of all things in nature, as personified by the Goddess, seems to permeate Neolithic art. For here the supreme power governing the universe is a divine Mother who gives her people life, provides them with material and spiritual nurturance, and who even in death can be counted on to take her children back into her cosmic womb.

For instance, in the shrines of Catal Huyuk we find representations of the Goddess both pregnant and giving birth. Often she is accompanied by powerful animals such as leopards and particularly bulls.[8] As a symbol of the unity of all life in nature, in some of her representations she is herself part human and part animal.[9] Even in her darker aspects, in what scholars call the chthonic, or earthy, she is still portrayed as part of the natural order. Just as all life is born from her, it also returns to her at death to be once again reborn.

It could be said that what scholars term the chthonic aspect of the Goddess—her portrayal in surrealistic and sometimes grotesque form—represented our forebears' attempt to deal with the darker aspects of reality by giving our human fears of the shadowy unknown a name and shape. These chthonic images—masks, wall paintings, and statuettes symbolizing death in fantastic and sometimes also humorous forms—would also be designed to impart to the religious initiate a sense of mystical unity with both the dangerous as well as the benign forces governing the world.

Thus, in the same way that life was celebrated in religious imagery and ritual, the destructive processes of nature were also recognized and respected. At the same time that religious rites and ceremonies were designed to give the individual and the community a sense of participation in and control over the life-giving and preserving processes of nature, other rites and ceremonies attempted to keep the more fearful processes at bay.

But with all of this, the many images of the Goddess in her dual aspect of life and death seem to express a view of the world in which the primary purpose of art, and of life, was not to conquer, pillage, and loot but to cultivate the earth and provide the material and spiritual wherewithal for a satisfying life. And on the whole, Neolithic art, and even more so the more developed Minoan art, seems to express a view in which the primary function of the mysterious powers governing the universe is not to exact obedience, punish, and destroy but rather to give.

We know that art, particularly religious or mythical art, reflects not only peoples' attitudes but also their particular form of culture and social organization. The Goddess-centered art we have been examining, with its striking absence of images of male domination or warfare, seems to have reflected a social order in which women, first as heads of clans and priestesses and later on in other important roles, played a central part, and in which both men and women worked together in equal partnership for the common good. If there was here no glorification of wrathful male deities or rulers carrying thunderbolts or arms, or of great conquerors dragging abject slaves about in chains, it is not unreasonable to infer it was because there were no counterparts for those images in real life.[10] And if the central religious image was a woman giving birth and not, as in our time, a man dying on a cross, it would not be unreasonable to infer that life and the love of life—rather than death and the fear of death—were dominant in society as well as art.

The Worship of the Goddess

One of the most interesting aspects of the prehistoric worship of the Goddess is what the mythologist and religious historian Joseph Campbell calls its "syncretism."[11] Essentially, what this means is that the worship of the Goddess was both polytheistic and monotheistic. It was polytheistic in the sense that she was worshiped under different names and in different forms. But it was also monotheistic—in the sense that we can properly speak of faith in the Goddess in the same way we speak of faith in God as a transcending entity. In other words, there are striking similarities between the symbols and images associated in various places with the worship of the Goddess in her various aspects of mother, ancestress or creatrix, and virgin or maid.

One possible explanation for this remarkable religious unity could be that the Goddess appears to have been originally worshiped in all ancient agricultural societies. We find evidence of the deification of the female—who in her biological character gives birth and nourishment just as the earth does—in the three main centers for the origins of agriculture: Asia Minor and southeastern Europe, Thailand in Southeast Asia, and later on also Middle America.[12]

In many of the earliest known creation stories from very different parts of the world, we find the Goddess-Mother as the source of all being. In the Americas, she is the Lady of the Serpent Skirt—of interest also because, as in Europe, the Middle East, and Asia, the serpent is one of her primary manifestations. In ancient Mesopotamia this same concept of the universe is found in the idea of the world mountain as the body of the Goddess-Mother of the universe, an idea that survived into historic times. And as Nammu, the Sumerian Goddess who gives birth to heaven and earth, her name is expressed in a cuneiform text of circa 2000 B.C.E. (now in the Louvre) by an ideogram signifying sea.[13]

The association of the feminine principle with the primal waters is also a ubiquitous theme. For example, in the decorated pottery of Old Europe, the symbolism of water—often in association with the primal egg—is a frequent motif. Here the Great Goddess, sometimes in the form of the bird or snake Goddess, rules over the life-giving force of water. In both Europe and Anatolia, rain-bearing and milk-giving mo-

tifs are interwoven, and ritual containers and vases are standard equipment in her shrines. Her image is also associated with water containers,
which are sometimes in her anthropomorphic shape. As the Egyptian
Goddess Nut, she is the flowing unity of celestial primordial waters.
Later on, as the Cretan Goddess Ariadne (the Very Holy One), and
the Greek Goddess Aphrodite, she rises from the sea.[14] In fact, this
image was still so powerful in Christian Europe that it inspired Botti-
celli's famous Venus rising from the sea.

Although this too is rarely included in what we are taught about
our cultural evolution, much of what evolved in the millennia of Neolithic history is still with us today. As Mellaart writes, "it formed the
basis on which all later cultures and civilizations have built."[15] Or as
Gimbutas put it, even after the world they represented was destroyed,
the mythic images of our Goddess-worshiping Neolithic forebears "lingered in the substratum which nourished further European cultural
developments," enormously enriching the European psyche.[16]

Indeed, if we look closely at the art of the Neolithic, it is truly
astonishing how much of its Goddess imagery has survived—and that
most standard works on the history of religion fail to bring out this
fascinating fact. Just as the Neolithic pregnant Goddess was a direct
descendant of the full-bellied Paleolithic "Venuses," this same image
survives in the pregnant Mary of medieval Christian iconography. The
Neolithic image of the young Goddess or Maiden is also still worshiped
in the aspect of Mary as the Holy Virgin. And of course the Neolithic
figure of the Mother-Goddess holding her divine child is still everywhere dramatically in evidence as the Christian Madonna and Child.

Images traditionally associated with the Goddess, such as the bull
and the bucranium, or horns of the bull, as symbols of the power of
nature, also survived well into classical, and later Christian, times. The
bull was appropriated as a central symbol of later "pagan" patriarchal
mythology. Still later, the horned bull god was in Christian iconography
converted from a symbol of male power to a symbol of Satan or evil.
But in Neolithic times, the bull horns we now routinely associate with
the devil had a very different meaning. Images of bull horns have been
excavated in both houses and shrines at Catal Huyuk, where horns of
consecration sometimes form rows or altars under representations of
the Goddess.[17] And the bull itself is here also still a manifestation of
the ultimate power of the Goddess. It is a symbol of the male principle,
but it is one that, like all else, issues from an all-giving divine womb—
as graphically depicted in a Catal Huyuk shrine where the Goddess is
shown giving birth to a young bull.

Even the Neolithic imagery of the Goddess in two simultaneous forms—such as the twin Goddesses excavated in Catal Huyuk—survived into historic times, as in the classical Greek images of Demeter and Kore as the two aspects of the Goddess: Mother and Maid as symbols of the cyclical regeneration of nature.[18] Indeed, the children of the Goddess are all integrally connected with the themes of birth, death, and resurrection. Her daughter survived into classical Greek times as Persephone, or Kore. And her son-lover/husband likewise survived well into historic times under such diverse names as Adonis, Tammutz, Attis—and finally, Jesus Christ.[19]

This seemingly remarkable continuity of religious symbolism becomes more understandable if we consider that in both the Neolithic-Chalcolithic of Old Europe and the later Minoan-Mycenaean Bronze Age civilization the religion of the Great Goddess appears to have been the single most prominent and important feature of life. In the Anatolian site of Catal Huyuk the worship of the Goddess appears to permeate all aspects of life. For example, out of 139 rooms excavated between 1961 and 1963, more than 40 appear to have served as shrines.[20]

This same pattern prevails in Neolithic and Chalcolithic Europe. In addition to all the shrines dedicated to various aspects of the Goddess, the houses had sacred corners with ovens, altars (benches), and offering places. And the same holds true for the later civilization of Crete, where, as Gimbutas writes, "shrines of one kind or another are so numerous that there is reason to believe that not only every palace but every private house was put to some such use. . . . To judge by the frequency of shrines, horns of consecration, and the symbol of the double-axe, the whole palace of Knossos must have resembled a sanctuary. Wherever you turn, pillars and symbols remind one of the presence of the Great Goddess."[21]

To say the people who worshiped the Goddess were deeply religious would be to understate, and largely miss, the point. For here there was no separation between the secular and the sacred. As religious historians point out, in prehistoric and, to a large extent, well into historic times, religion was life, and life was religion.

One reason this point is obscured is that scholars have in the past routinely referred to the worship of the Goddess, not as a religion, but as a "fertility cult," and to the Goddess as an "earth mother." But though the fecundity of women and of the earth was, and still is, a requisite for species survival, this characterization is far too simplistic. It would be comparable, for example, to characterizing Christianity as just a death cult because the central image in its art is the Crucifixion.

Neolithic religion—like present-day religious and secular ideologies—expressed the worldview of its time. How different this worldview was from ours is dramatically illustrated if we contrast the Neolithic religious pantheon with the Christian one. In the Neolithic, the head of the holy family was a woman: the Great Mother, the Queen of Heaven, or the Goddess in her various aspects and forms. The male members of this pantheon—her consort, brother, and/or son—were also divine. By contrast, the head of the Christian holy family is an all-powerful Father. The second male in the pantheon—Jesus Christ—is another aspect of the godhead. But though father and son are immortal and divine, Mary, the only woman in this religious facsimile of patriarchal family organization, is merely mortal—clearly, like her earthly counterparts, of an inferior order.

Religions in which the most powerful or only deity is male tend to reflect a social order in which descent is patrilinear (traced through the father) and domicile is patrilocal (the wife goes to live with the family or clan of her husband). Conversely, religions in which the most powerful or sole deity is female tend to reflect a social order in which descent is matrilinear (traced through the mother) and domicile is likewise matrilocal (a husband goes to live with his wife's family or clan).[22] Moreover, a male-dominated and generally hierarchic social structure has historically been reflected and maintained by a male-dominated religious pantheon and by religious doctrines in which the subordination of women is said to be divinely ordained.

If It Isn't Patriarchy It Must Be Matriarchy

Applying these principles to the mounting evidence that for millennia of human history the supreme deity had been female, a number of nineteenth- and early twentieth-century scholars came to a seemingly earthshaking conclusion. If prehistory was not patriarchal, it must have been matriarchal. In other words, if men did not dominate women, women must have dominated men.

Then, when the evidence did not seem to support this conclusion of female dominance, many scholars returned to the more conventionally accepted view. If there never was a matriarchate, they reasoned, male-dominance must, after all, always have been the human norm.

The evidence, however, supports neither one of these conclusions. To begin with, the archaeological data we now have indicate that in its general structure prepatriarchal society was, by any contemporary standard, remarkably equalitarian. In the second place, although in these societies descent appears to have been traced through the mother, and women as priestesses and heads of clans seem to have played leading roles in all aspects of life, there is little indication that the position of men in this social system was in any sense comparable to the subordination and suppression of women characteristic of the male-dominant system that replaced it.

From his excavations of Catal Huyuk, where the systematic reconstruction of the life of the city's inhabitants was the primary archaeological goal, Mellaart concluded that though some social inequality is suggested by sizes of buildings, equipment, and burial gifts, this was "never a glaring one."[23] For example, there are in Catal Huyuk no major differences between houses, most of which show a standardized rectangular plan covering about twenty-five square meters of floor space. Even shrines are not structurally different from houses, nor are they necessarily larger in size. Moreover, they are intermingled with the houses in considerable numbers, once again indicating a communally based rather than a centralized, hierarchic social and religious structure.[24]

The same general picture emerges from an analysis of Catal Huyuk burial customs. Unlike the later graves of Indo-European chieftains, which clearly bespeak a pyramidal social structure ruled by a feared and fearful strongman on the top, those of Catal Huyuk indicate no glaring social inequalities.[25]

As for the relationship between men and women, it is true, as Mellaart points out, that the divine family of Catal Huyuk is represented "in order of importance as mother, daughter, son, and father,"[26] and that this probably mirrored the human families of the city's inhabitants, which were evidently matrilineal and matrilocal. It is also true that in Catal Huyuk and other Neolithic societies the anthropomorphic representations of the Goddess—the young Maid, the mature Mother, and the old Grandmother or Ancestress, all the way back to the original Creatrix—are, as the Greek philosopher Pythagoras later noted, projections of the various stages of the life of woman.[27] Also suggesting a matrilineal and matrilocal social organization is that in Catal Huyuk the sleeping platform where the woman's personal possessions and her bed or divan were located is always found in the same place, on the east side of the living quarters. That of the man shifts, and is also somewhat smaller.[28]

But despite such evidence of the preeminence of women in both religion and life, there are no indications of glaring inequality between women and men. Nor are there any signs that women subjugated or oppressed men.

In sharp contrast to the male-dominated religions of our time, in which in almost all cases until quite recently only men could become members of the religious hierarchy, there is here evidence of both priestesses and priests. For instance, Mellaart points out that although it seems likely that it was primarily priestesses who officiated at the worship of the Goddess in Catal Huyuk, there is also evidence pointing to the participation of priests. He reports that two groups of objects found only in burials in shrines were mirrors of obsidian and fine bone belt fasteners. The former were found only with the bodies of women, the latter only with men. This led Mellaart to conclude that these were "attributes of certain priestesses and priests, which would explain both their rarity and their discovery in shrines."[29]

It is also revealing that sculptures of elderly men, sometimes fashioned in a position reminiscent of Rodin's famous *The Thinker*, suggest that old men as well as old women had important and respected roles.[30] Equally revealing is that the bull and the bucranium, or horns of consecration, which have a central place in the shrines of Neolithic Anatolia, Asia Minor, and Old Europe and later in Minoan and Mycenaean imagery, are symbols of the male principle, as are the images of phalluses and boars, which make their appearance in the later Neolithic, particularly in Europe. Moreover, some of the earlier Goddess figurines are not only hybrids of human and animal features, but often also have features, such as exaggerated long necks, that can be interpreted as androgynous.[31] And of course the young god, the son-consort of the Goddess, plays a recurring part in the central miracle of pre-patriarchal religion, the mystery of regeneration and rebirth.

Clearly, then, while the feminine principle as the primary symbol of the miracle of life permeated Neolithic art and ideology, the male principle also played an important role. The fusion of these two principles through the myths and rituals of the Sacred Marriage was in fact still celebrated in the ancient world well into patriarchal times. For example, in Hittite Anatolia, the great shrine of Yazilikaya was dedicated to this purpose. And even later, in Greece and Rome, the ceremony survived as the *hieros gamos*.[32]

It is interesting in this connection that there is Neolithic imagery indicating an understanding of the joint roles of women and men in procreation. For example, a small stone plaque from Catal Huyuk shows a woman and man in a tender embrace; immediately next to them is the relief of a mother holding a child, the offspring of their union.[33]

All this imagery reflects the markedly different attitudes prevailing in the Neolithic about the relationship between women and men—attitudes in which linking rather than ranking appears to have been predominant. As Gimbutas writes, here "the world of myth was not polarized into female and male as it was among the Indo-Europeans and many other nomadic and pastoral peoples of the steppes. Both principles were manifest side by side. The male divinity in the shape of a young man or male animal appears to affirm and strengthen the forces of the creative and active female. Neither is subordinate to the other: by complementing one another, their power is doubled."[34]

Again and again we find that the debate about whether there once was or was not a matriarchate, which still periodically erupts in academic and popular works, seems to be more a function of our prevailing paradigm than of any archaeological evidence.[35] That is, in our culture built on the ideas of hierarchy and ranking and in-group versus out-group thinking, rigid differences or polarities are emphasized. Ours is characteristically the kind of if-it-isn't-this-it-has-to-be-that, dichotomized, either/or thinking that philosophers from earliest times have cautioned can lead to a simplistic misreading of reality. And, indeed, psychologists today have discovered it is the mark of a *lower* or less psychologically evolved stage of cognitive and emotional development.[36]

Mellaart apparently tried to overcome this either/or, if-it-isn't-patriarchy-it-has-to-be-matriarchy tangle when he wrote the following passage: "If the Goddess presided over all the various activities of the life and death of the Neolithic population of Catal Huyuk, so in a way did her son. Even if his role is strictly subordinate to hers, the males' role in life seems to have been fully realized."[37] But in the contradiction between a "fully realized" and a "strictly subordinate" role we again find ourselves tangled up in the cultural and linguistic assumptions inherent in a dominator paradigm: that human relations must fit into some kind of superior-inferior pecking order.

However, looked at from a strictly analytical or logical viewpoint, the primacy of the Goddess—and with this the centrality of the values symbolized by the nurturing and regenerating powers incarnated in the female body—does not justify the inference that women here dominated men. This becomes more apparent if we begin by analogizing from the one human relationship that even in male-dominant societies is not generally conceptualized in superiority-inferiority terms. This is the relationship between mother and child—and the way we perceive it may actually be a remnant of the prepatriarchal conception of the world. The larger, stronger adult mother is clearly, in hierarchic terms, superior to the smaller, weaker child. But this does not mean we normally think of the child as inferior or less valued.

Analogizing from this different conceptual framework, we can see that the fact that women played a central and vigorous role in prehistoric religion and life does not have to mean that men were perceived and treated as subservient. For here both men and women were the children of the Goddess, as they were the children of the women who headed the families and clans. And while this certainly gave women a great deal of power, analogizing from our present-day mother-child relationship, it seems to have been a power that was more equated with responsibility and love than with oppression, privilege, and fear.

In sum, in contrast to the still prevailing view of power as the power symbolized by the Blade—the power to take away or to dominate—a very different view of power seems to have been the norm in these Neolithic Goddess-worshiping societies. This view of power as the "feminine" power to nurture and give was undoubtedly not always adhered to, for these were societies of real flesh-and-blood people, not make-believe utopias. But it was still the normative ideal, the model to be emulated by both women and men.

The view of power symbolized by the Chalice—for which I propose the term *actualization power* as distinguished from *domination power*—obviously reflects a very different type of social organization from the one we are accustomed to.[38] We may conclude from the evidence of the past examined so far that it cannot be called matriarchal. As it cannot be called patriarchal either, it does not fit into the conventional dominator paradigm of social organization. However, using the perspective of Cultural Transformation theory we have been developing, it does fit the other alternative for human organization: a partnership society in which neither half of humanity is ranked over the other and diversity is not equated with inferiority or superiority.

As we will see in the chapters that follow, these two alternatives have profoundly affected our cultural evolution. Technological and social evolution tend to become more complex regardless of which model prevails. But the *direction* of cultural evolution—including whether a social system is warlike or peaceful—depends on whether we have a partnership or a dominator social structure.

CHAPTER 3

The Essential Difference: Crete

Prehistory is like a giant jigsaw puzzle with more than half its pieces destroyed or lost. It is impossible to reconstruct completely. But the greatest obstacle to the accurate reconstruction of prehistory is not that we are lacking so many pieces; it is that the prevailing paradigm makes it so hard to accurately interpret the pieces we have and to project the real pattern into which they fit.

For example, when Sir Flinders Petrie first reported on the excavations of the tomb of Meryet-Nit in Egypt, he automatically assumed Meryet-Nit was a king. Later research, however, established that Meryet-Nit was a woman and, judging from the richness of her tomb, a queen. The same mistake was made about the gigantic tomb discovered at Nagadeh by Professor de Morgan. It too was assumed to be the burial place of a king, Hor-Aha of the First Dynasty. But as the Egyptologist Walter Emery writes, later research showed that this was the sepulcher of Nit-Hotep, Hor-Aha's mother.[1]

These examples of how cultural bias has led to mistakes are only exceptional, as the art historian Merlin Stone notes, in that they were later corrected. Stone traveled all over the world, looking at excavation after excavation, archive after archive, and object after object, reexamining primary sources and then checking how they had been interpreted. And what she found was that, by and large, when there was evidence of an earlier time when women and men lived as equals, it was simply ignored.[2]

In the pages that follow, as we examine the remarkable ancient civilization discovered at the turn of the twentieth century on the Mediterranean island of Crete, we will see how this bias has led to an incomplete and, in fact, greatly distorted view not only of our cultural evolution but also of the development of higher civilization.

The Archaeological Bombshell

The discovery of the technologically advanced and socially complex ancient culture of Minoan Crete—so named by archaeologists after the legendary King Minos—was something of a bombshell. As the archaeologist Nicolas Platon, who by 1980 had been excavating the island for over fifty years, put it: "Archaeologists were dumbfounded. They could not understand how the very existence of such a highly developed civilization could have remained unsuspected until then."[3]

"From the start," writes Platon, who for many years was Superintendent of Antiquities in Crete, "amazing discoveries were made." As work progressed, "vast multi-storied palaces, villas, farmsteads, districts of populous and well-organized cities, harbor installations, networks of roads crossing the island from end to end, organized places of worship and planned burial grounds were brought to light."[4] As archaeologists continued their excavations, four scripts (Hieroglyphic, Proto-Linear, Linear A, and Linear B) were discovered, bringing Cretan civilization, by archaeological definition, into the historic or literate period. Much was learned about the social structure and values of both the earlier Minoan and later Mycenaean phases. And perhaps most strikingly, as excavations progressed and more and more frescoes, sculptures, vases, carvings, and other works of art were unearthed, there came the realization that here were the remains of an artistic tradition unique in the annals of civilization.

The story of Cretan civilization begins around 6000 B.C.E., when a small colony of immigrants, probably from Anatolia, first arrived on the island's shores. It was they who brought the Goddess with them, as well as an agrarian technology that classifies these first settlers as Neolithic. For the next four thousand years there was slow and steady technological progress, in pottery making, weaving, metallurgy, engraving, architecture, and other crafts, as well as increasing trade and the gradual evolution of the lively and joyful artistic style so characteristic of Crete. Then, in approximately 2000 B.C.E., Crete entered what archaeologists call the Middle Minoan or Old Palace period.[5]

This was already well into the Bronze Age, a time when in the rest of the then civilized world the Goddess was steadily being displaced by warlike male gods. She was still revered—as Hathor and Isis in Egypt, as Astarte or Ishtar in Babylon, or as the sun Goddess of Arinna in Anatolia. But it was now only as a secondary deity, described as the consort or mother of more powerful male gods. For this was increasingly a world where the power of women was also on the decline, a world where male dominance and wars of conquest and counterconquest were everywhere becoming the norm.

In the island of Crete where the Goddess was still supreme, there are no signs of war. Here the economy prospered and the arts flourished. And even when in the fifteenth century B.C.E. the island finally came under Achaean dominion—when archaeologists no longer speak of Minoan but rather of a Minoan-Mycenaean culture—the Goddess and the way of thinking and living she symbolized still appear to have held fast.

Under the older Minoan influence—also seen on the Greek mainland, which now likewise entered its Mycenaean period—the new Indo-European overlords of the island seem to have adopted much of the Minoan culture and religion. For example, in the pictures on the famous Hagia Triada sarcophagus of the fifteenth century B.C.E., already more stiff and stylized but still unmistakably Cretan, it is still the Goddess who rides her griffin-drawn chariot to bear the dead man to his new life. And it is still the priestesses of the Goddess, not the priests in long women's robes, who play the central role in the rituals depicted on its plastered limestone frescoes. It is they who lead the procession and who extend their hands to touch the altar.

As the cultural historian Jacquetta Hawkes remarks in the quaint language so typical of scholars: "If this was still true in the fourteenth century, its prevalence in earlier days must be as nearly as possible certain."[6] Thus, at the great palace of Knossos it is a woman—the Goddess, her high priestess, or perhaps, as Hawkes believes, the Cretan queen—who stands at the center while two approaching processions of men bear tribute to her.[7] And everywhere one finds female figures, many of them with their arms raised in a gesture of blessing, some of them holding serpents or double axes as symbols of the Goddess.

The Love of Life and Nature

These gestures of reverent blessing seem in many ways to capture the essence of Minoan culture. For, as Platon puts it, this was a society in which "the whole of life was pervaded by an ardent faith in the goddess Nature, the source of all creation and harmony." In Crete, for the last time in recorded history, a spirit of harmony between women and men as joyful and equal participants in life appears to pervade. It is this spirit that seems to shine through Crete's artistic tradition, a tradition that, again in Platon's words, is unique in its "delight in beauty, grace, and movement" and in its "enjoyment of life and close-ness to nature."[8]

Some scholars have described Minoan life as "perfectly expressive of the idea of *homo ludens*"—of "man" expressing our higher human impulses through joyful and at the same time mythically meaningful ritual and artistic play. Others have tried to sum up Cretan culture with words and phrases like "sensitivity," "grace of life," and "love of beauty and nature." And even though there are a few (e.g., Cyrus Gordon) who try to derogate or somehow redefine the Cretan phe-nomenon to make it fit such commonly accepted preconceptions as antiquity being more warlike and (except for the Hebrews) less spir-itually evolved than we, the great majority of scholars, and certainly those who have done any extensive fieldwork on the island, seem quite unable to contain their admiration, and even astonishment, in describ-ing their finds.[9]

For here we have a rich technologically and culturally advanced civilization in which, as archaeologists Hans-Günther Buchholtz and Vassos Karageorghis write, "all the artistic media—in fact, life in its totality as well as death—were deeply entrenched in an all-pervasive, ubiquitous religion." But in marked contrast to other high civilizations of the time, this religion—centering on the worship of the Goddess—seems to have both reflected and reinforced a social order in which, to quote Nicolas Platon, "the fear of death was almost obliterated by the ubiquitous joy of living."[10]

Sober scholars like Sir Leonard Woolley have described Minoan art as "the most inspired in the ancient world."[11] Archaeologists and art historians from all over the world have used phrases like "the en-chantment of a fairy world" and "the most complete acceptance of the grace of life the world has ever known."[12] And it is not only Cretan art—the magnificent frescoes of multicolored partridges, whimsical griffins, and elegant women, the exquisite golden miniatures, fine jew-elry, and gracefully molded statuettes—but also Cretan society that has struck scholars as unique.

For example, one remarkable feature of Cretan society, sharply dis-tinguishing it from other ancient high civilizations, is that there seems to have been here a rather equitable sharing of wealth. "The standard of living—even of peasants—seems to have been high," reports Platon. "None of the homes found so far have suggested very poor living con-ditions."[13]

This is not to say that Crete was richer than, or even as rich as,

Egypt or Babylon. But in view of the economic and social gulf between those on top and bottom that characterized other "high" civilizations, it is important to note that the way Crete used and distributed its wealth was apparently from the beginning markedly different.

From the first settlements, the island's economy was basically agrarian. As time passed, stock breeding, industry, and particularly trade—through a large mercantile fleet that sailed, and apparently commanded, the entire Mediterranean—assumed increasing importance, greatly contributing to the economic prosperity of the country. And although the basis of social organization was at the beginning the matrilineal *genos*, or clan, somewhere around 2000 B.C.E. Cretan society became more centralized. During both what Sir Arthur Evans called the Middle and the Late Minoan and Platon calls the Old and the New Palace periods, there is evidence of centralized governmental administration at several Cretan palaces.

But here centralization did not bring with it autocratic rule. Nor did it entail the use of advanced technology only for the benefit of a powerful few or the kind of exploitation and brutalization of the masses that is so striking in other civilizations of the time. For though there was in Crete an affluent ruling class, there is no indication (other than in later Greek myths such as that of Theseus, King Minos, and the Minotaur) that it was backed up by massive armed might.

"The development of writing led to the establishment of the first bureaucracy, as is shown by a small number of tablets in Linear A," writes Platon, who then comments on how governmental revenues from the island's increasing wealth were judiciously used to improve living conditions, which were, even by Western standards, extraordinarily "modern." "All the urban centers had perfect drainage systems, sanitary installations, and domestic conveniences." He adds that "there is no doubt that extensive public works—paid for out of the royal coffers—were undertaken in Minoan Crete. Although only a very few remains have so far been cleared, these have been revealing: viaducts, paved roads, look-out posts, roadside shelters, water pipes, fountains, reservoirs, etc. There is evidence of large-scale irrigation works with canals to carry and distribute the water."[14]

Despite recurring earthquakes, which completely destroyed the old palaces and twice interrupted the development of the new palace centers, Cretan palace architecture is also unique in civilization. These palaces are a superb blend of life-enhancing and eye-pleasing features, rather than the monuments to authority and power characteristic of Sumer, Egypt, Rome, and other ancient warlike and male-dominant societies.

There were in Cretan palaces vast courtyards, majestic facades, and hundreds of rooms laid out in the organized "labyrinths" that became a catchword for Crete in later Greek legend. In these labyrinthine buildings were many apartments laid out over several stories, at different heights, arranged asymmetrically round a central courtyard. There were special rooms for religious worship. The courtiers had their own quarters in the palace or occupied attractive houses nearby. There were also quarters for the domestic staff of the palace. Long lines of storerooms with connecting corridors were used for the orderly safekeeping of food reserves and treasures. And vast halls with rows of elegant columns were used for audiences, receptions, banquets, and council meetings.[15]

Gardens were an essential feature of all Minoan architecture. So was the design of buildings for privacy, good natural light, and domestic convenience and, perhaps above all, the attention to detail and beauty. "Both local and imported materials were used," writes Platon, "all worked with meticulous care: gypsum and tufa pilasters and tiles, perfectly bonded composed facades, walls, light-wells and courtyards. Partitions were decorated with plaster, with murals in many cases, and with marble facings. . . . Not only the walls but often the ceilings and floors were decorated with paintings, even in villas and country houses and simple town dwellings. . . . The subjects were drawn mainly from marine and land plants, religious ceremonies, and the gay life of the court and the people. The worship of nature pervaded everything."[16]

A Unique Civilization

The great palace of Knossos, famous for its grand stone staircase, its colonnaded verandas, and splendid reception suite, is also typical of Minoan culture in the aesthetic rather than monumental emphasis of its throne room and royal apartments, perhaps expressive of what the cultural historian Jacquetta Hawkes calls the "feminine spirit" of Cretan architecture.[17]

Knossos, which may have had a hundred thousand inhabitants, was connected to the south coast ports by a fine paved highway, the first of its kind in Europe. Its streets, like those of other palace centers such as Mallia and Phaistos, were paved and drained, fronted with neat two- or three-floor houses, flat-roofed, sometimes with a penthouse for use on hot summer nights.[18]

Hawkes describes the inner towns surrounding the palaces as "well designed for civilized living," and Platon characterizes the "private life" of the period as having "attained a high degree of refinement and comfort." As Platon sums it up: "The houses were adapted to all practical needs of life, and an attractive environment was created around them. The Minoans were very close to nature, and their architecture was designed to let them enjoy it as freely as possible."[19]

Cretan clothing was also typically designed for both aesthetic effect and practicality, allowing freedom of movement. Physical exercise and sports involved both men and women and were enjoyed as entertainment. As for food, a wide range of crops were cultivated, which along with stock breeding, fishing, beekeeping, and wine pressing made available a healthy and varied diet.[20]

Entertainment and religion were often intertwined, making Cretan leisure activities both pleasurable and meaningful. "Music, singing, and dancing added to the pleasures of life," writes Platon. "There were frequent public ceremonies, mostly religious, accompanied by processions, banquets, and acrobatic displays performed in theaters built for the purpose or in wooden arenas," among them the famous Cretan *taurokatharpsia,* or bull-games.[21]

Another scholar, Reynold Higgins, sums up this aspect of Cretan life as follows: "Religion for the Cretans was a happy affair, and was celebrated in palace-shrines, or else in open-air sanctuaries on the tops of mountains and in sacred caves. . . . Their religion was closely bound up with their recreation. First in importance were the bull-sports, which probably took place in the central courts of palaces. Young men and women working in teams would take it in turn to grasp the horn of a charging bull and somersault over its back."[22]

The equal partnership between women and men that seems to have characterized Minoan society is perhaps nowhere so vividly illustrated as in these sacred bull-games, where young women and men performed together and entrusted their lives to each other. These rituals, which combined excitement, skill, and religious fervor, also appear to have been characteristic of the Minoan spirit in another important respect; they were designed not only for individual pleasure or salvation but to invoke the divine power to bring well-being to the entire society.[23]

Once again, it is important to stress that Crete was not an ideal society or utopia but a real human society, complete with problems and imperfections. It was a society that developed thousands of years ago, when there was still nothing like science as we know it, when the processes of nature were still generally explained—and dealt with—through animistic beliefs and propitiatory rites.[24] Moreover, it was a society functioning in the midst of an increasingly male-dominated and warlike world.

We know, for example, that the Cretans had weapons—some, like their beautifully adorned daggers, of great technical excellence. Probably as warfare and piracy increased in the Mediterranean they also fought sea battles, both to preserve their vast maritime commerce and to protect their shores. But in contrast to other high civilizations of the time, Cretan art does not idealize warfare. As already mentioned, even the Goddess's famous double axe symbolized the bounteous fruitfulness of the earth. Shaped like the hoe axes used to clear land for the planting of crops, it was also a stylization of the butterfly, one of the Goddess's symbols of transformation and rebirth.

Neither are there any indications that Crete's material resources were—as they are in our modern world, and daily more overwhelmingly so—heavily invested in technologies of destruction. On the contrary, the evidence is that Cretan wealth was primarily invested in living harmoniously and aesthetically.

As Platon writes: "The whole of life was pervaded by an ardent faith in the goddess Nature, the source of all creation and harmony. This led to a love of peace, a horror of tyranny, and a respect for the law. Even among the ruling classes personal ambition seems to have been unknown; nowhere do we find the name of an author attached to a work of art nor a record of the deeds of a ruler."[25]

In our time, when "a love of peace, a horror of tyranny, and a respect for the law" may be required for our survival, the differences between the spirit of Crete and that of its neighbors are of more than academic interest. In the Cretan towns without military fortifications, the "unprotected" villas on the edge of the sea, and the lack of any sign that the various city-states within the island fought one another or embarked on aggressive wars (in sharp contrast to the walled cities and chronic warfare that were elsewhere already the norm), we find this firm confirmation from our past that our hopes for peaceful human coexistence are not, as we are so often told, "utopian dreams." And in the mythical images of Crete—the Goddess as Mother of the universe, and humans, animals, plants, water, and sky as her manifestations here on earth—we find the recognition of our oneness with nature, a theme that is today also reemerging as a prerequisite for ecological survival.

But what is perhaps most noteworthy in terms of the relationship of society and ideology is that, particularly in its earlier Minoan period, Cretan art appears to reflect a society in which power is not equated with dominance, destruction, and oppression. In the words of Jacquetta Hawkes, one of the few women to write of Crete, "the idea of a warrior monarch triumphing in the humiliation and slaughter of the enemy" is here absent. "In Crete, where hallowed rulers commanded wealth and power and lived in splendid palaces, there was hardly a trace of these manifestations of manly pride and unthinking cruelty."[26]

A remarkable feature of Cretan culture is that there are here no statues or reliefs of those who sat on the thrones of Knossos or of any of the palaces. Besides the fresco of the Goddess—or perhaps a queen/priestess—at the center of a gift-bearing procession, there seem to be no royal portrayals of any kind until the latest phase. Even then, the sole possible exception, the painted relief sometimes identified as the young prince, shows a long-haired youth, unarmed, naked to the waist, crowned with peacock plumes and walking among flowers and butterflies.

Equally striking, and revealing, is the absence in the art of Minoan Crete of any grandiose scenes of battle or of hunting. "The absence of these manifestations of the all-powerful male ruler that is so widespread at this time and at this stage of cultural development as to be almost universal," Hawkes comments, "is one of the reasons for supposing that the occupants of Minoan thrones may have been queens."[27]

This too is the conclusion of the cultural anthropologist Ruby Rohrlich-Leavitt. Writing of Crete from a feminist perspective, she points out that it is modern archaeologists who have dubbed the young man just described the "young prince" or the "priest-king," when in fact, no single representation of a king or a dominant male god has yet been found. She also observes that the absence of idealizations of male violence and destructive power in Cretan art goes hand in hand with the fact that this was a society where "peace endured for 1,500 years both at home and abroad in an age of incessant warfare."[28]

Platon, who also characterizes the Minoans as an "exceptionally peace-loving people," does write of the occupants of the Minoan thrones as kings. However, he too is struck by how, as he puts it, "each king ruled his own domain in close harmony and 'peaceful co-existence' with the others." Platon comments on the close links between government and religion, a typical feature of ancient political life. But he points out that here, once again in sharp contrast to other contemporary city-states, "the authority of the king was probably limited by councils of high officials on which other social classes may have been represented."[29]

These still largely ignored data about the prepatriarchal civilization of ancient Crete provide us with some fascinating clues, which we will pursue later, on the origins of much that we value in Western civilization. Especially fascinating is how our modern belief that government should be representative of the interests of the people seems to have been foreshadowed in Minoan Crete long before the so-called birth of democracy in classical Greek times. Moreover, the emerging modern conceptualization of power as responsibility rather than domination likewise seems to be a reemergence of earlier views.

For what the evidence indicates is that in Crete power was primarily equated with the responsibility of motherhood rather than with the exaction of obedience to a male-dominant elite through force or the fear of force. This is the definition of power characteristic of the partnership model of society, in which women and traits associated with women are not systematically devalued. And this is the definition of power that still prevailed in Crete as its social and technological evolution became more complex, profoundly affecting its cultural evolution.

Of particular interest is that long after Crete enters the Bronze Age, at the same time that the Goddess, as the giver and provider of all life in nature, is still venerated as the supreme embodiment of the mysteries of this world, women continue to maintain their prominent position in Cretan society. Here, as Rohrlich-Leavitt writes, women are "the central subjects, the most frequently portrayed in the arts and crafts. And they are shown mainly in the public sphere."[30]

The assertion that the city-state, or what some modern scholars call "statism," structurally requires warfare, hierarchism, and the subjugation of women is thus not borne out. In the city-states of Crete, legendary for their wealth, superb arts and crafts, and flourishing trade, it is notable that new technologies, and with them a larger and more complex scale of social organization including increasing specialization, did *not* bring about any deterioration in the status of women.

On the contrary, in Minoan Crete role redistributions accompanying technological change appear to have strengthened rather than weakened the status of women. Because here there was no fundamental social and ideological change, the new roles required by technological advances did not bring about the kind of historical discontinuity we see elsewhere. In the societies of southern Mesopotamia we find rigid social stratification and constant warfare by about 3500 B.C.E., along with the declining status of women. In Minoan Crete, although urbanization and social stratification existed, warfare was absent and the status of women did *not* decline.[31]

The Invisibility of the Obvious

Under the prevailing paradigm, where ranking is the primary organizational principle, if women have high status the inference is that men's status must be lower. Earlier we saw how evidence of matrilineal inheritance and descent, a woman as supreme deity, and priestesses and queens with temporal power is interpreted as indicating a "matriarchal" society. But this conclusion is wholly unwarranted by the archaeological evidence. Nor does it follow from the high status of Cretan women that Cretan men had a status comparable to that of women in male-dominant social systems.

In Minoan Crete the entire relationship between the sexes—not only definitions and valuations of gender roles but also attitudes toward sensuality and sex—was obviously very different from ours. For example, the bare-breasted style of dress for women and the skimpy clothes emphasizing the genitals for men demonstrate a frank appreciation of sexual differences and the pleasure made possible by these differences. From what we now know through modern humanistic psychology, this "pleasure bond" would have strengthened a sense of mutuality between women and men as individuals.[32]

The Cretans' more natural attitudes toward sex would also have had other consequences equally difficult to perceive under the prevailing paradigm, wherein religious dogma often views sex as more sinful than violence. As Hawkes writes, "The Cretans seem to have reduced and diverted their aggressiveness through a free and well-balanced sexual life."[33] Along with their enthusiasm for sports and dancing and their creativity and love of life, these liberated attitudes toward sex seem to have contributed to the generally peaceful and harmonious spirit predominant in Cretan life.

As we have seen, it is this matter of spirit that sets Crete apart from the other high civilizations of its time. As Arnold Hauser put it, "Minoan culture is exceptional in the essential differences of its spirit from that of its contemporaries."[34]

But now comes the eternal blockage, the point where scholars encounter the information that is automatically excluded under the prevailing worldview. For when it comes to linking this essential difference with the fact that Minoan Crete was the last, and most technologically advanced, society in which male dominance was *not* the norm, the vast majority of scholars suddenly go blank or quickly head in another direction. At best, they get around the difficulty with a peripheralizing strategy. They may note that, in sharp contrast to other ancient *and* contemporary civilizations, in Crete the "feminine" virtues of peaceableness and sensitivity to the needs of others were given social priority. And they may also note that in contrast to other societies, Cretan women had high social, economic, political, and religious positions. *But* they do so only in passing, with no emphasis, thus signaling to the reader receptive to their authority that this is an ancillary or peripheral matter.

In going through most of the literature on Crete, one is chronically reminded of Charles Darwin's curious footnote to *The Descent of Man*. When writing a section on racial differences for this scientific classic, Darwin recalled that when he was in Egypt he had thought that the features of a statue of the pharaoh Amunoph III were remarkably negroid. But having said this, even in a mere footnote, he immediately qualified what he had seen with his own eyes—and which has since been firmly established—that there were in Egypt black pharaohs. Though by his own account his observations were further verified by two people who were with him at the time, he felt compelled to cite two well-known authorities on the subject, J. C. Nott and George R. Gliddon, who in their book *Types of Mankind* had described the features of pharaohs as "superbly European" and maintained that the statue in question was definitely not of "Negro intermixture."[35]

At the start of this chapter we remarked similar incidents of this kind relating to the evidence for women pharaohs, for example, Meryet-Nit and Nit-Hotep. But while in Egyptology one finds this kind of authoritative blindness here and there, in most of the scholarly literature about Crete it is all-pervasive, at every turn deflecting, rendering invisible or at best trivializing the exceptionally clear message of Cretan art. Long after Darwin, when more statues and much more clear visual evidence of the historical existence of black rulers was discovered, the experts (overwhelmingly white males, of course) still asserted there definitely could be no "Negro intermixture."[36] In the same way, the striking evidence of the essential difference that sets Crete apart from other societies is still regularly either denied or glossed over by most scholars.

The central role played by women in Cretan society is so striking that from the very first discovery of Minoan culture scholars have been unable to ignore it completely. Like Darwin, however, they have felt compelled to fit what they saw with their own eyes into the prevailing ideology. For example, when Sir Arthur Evans began excavating on the island in the early 1900s he recognized that the Cretans worshiped a female deity. He also saw that Cretan art portrayed what he called "scenes of feminine confidence." But in commenting on these scenes, Evans felt compelled to immediately equate them with nothing more than what he termed the feminine "tittle-tattle" of "society scandals."[37]

The posture of Hans-Günther Buchholtz and Vassos Karageorghis, on the one hand, tends to be a caricature of the stereotypically Germanic attitude toward women. On the other hand, even they comment that feminine "pre-eminence in every sphere of life was reflected in the Pantheon," and that, even later on, "the high esteem of the female is also discernible in the religion of the more masculine Mycenaean civilization."[38] Only a woman, Jacquetta Hawkes, forthrightly characterizes Minoan civilization as "feminine"—but even she stops short of pursuing the full implications of this important insight.

Platon specifically notes that "the important part played by women is discernible in every sphere." He further writes that "there is no doubt that women—or at least the influence of feminine sensitivity—made a notable contribution to Minoan art." He writes that "the dominant role played by women in society is shown by the fact that they took an active part in all aspects of New Palace life." But then, having acknowledged women's high status and active participation in all aspects of life to be an essential characteristic of Cretan culture, even Platon feels compelled to add that "this may have been due to the absence of men on long sea journeys." *This* in an otherwise exceptionally fine scholarly work in which he specifically notes that "although it would be misleading to describe it [Crete] as a matriarchy, there is a great deal of evidence—even from later Hellenic times—that the succession passed through the female line."[39]

So again and again we see how under the prevailing paradigm our real past—and the original thrust of our cultural evolution—can only be seen as through a glass darkly. But once we are face to face with the full import of what this past foreshadowed—what we, at our level of technological and social development, could have been and still can be—we confront a haunting question. What brought about the radical change in cultural direction, the shift that plunged us from a social order upheld by the Chalice to one dominated by the Blade? When and how did this happen? And what does this cataclysmic change tell us about our past—and our future?

CHAPTER 4

Dark Order Out of Chaos: From the Chalice to the Blade

We measure the time we have been taught is human history in centuries. But the span for the earlier segment of a much different kind of history is measured in millennia, or thousands of years. The Paleolithic goes back over 30,000 years. The Neolithic age agricultural revolution was over 10,000 years ago. Catal Huyuk was founded 8500 years ago. And the civilization of Crete fell only 3200 years ago.

For this span of millennia—many times as long as the history we measure on our calendars from the birth of Christ—in most European and Near Eastern societies the emphasis was on technologies that support and enhance the quality of life. During the thousands of years of the Neolithic great strides were made in the production of food through farming, as well as in hunting, fishing, and the domestication of animals. Housing was advanced through innovations in construction, the making of rugs, furniture, and other household articles, and even (as in Catal Huyuk) town planning.[1] Clothing had left the time of skins and furs far behind with the invention of weaving and sewing. And, as both materially and spiritually the foundations for higher civilization were being laid, the arts also flourished.

As a general rule, descent was probably traced through the mother. The elder women or heads of clans administered the production and distribution of the fruits of the earth, which were seen as belonging to all members of the group. Along with common ownership of the principal means of production and a perception of social power as responsibility or trusteeship for the benefit of all came what seems to have been a basically cooperative social organization. Both women and men—even sometimes, as in Catal Huyuk, people of different racial stocks—worked cooperatively for the common good.[2]

Greater male physical strength was here not the basis for social oppression, organized warfare, or the concentration of private property in the hands of the strongest men. Neither did it provide the basis for supremacy of males over females or of "masculine" over "feminine" values. On the contrary, the prevailing ideology was gynocentric, or woman-centered, with the deity represented in female form.

Symbolized by the feminine Chalice or source of life, the generative, nurturing, and creative powers of nature—not the powers to destroy— were, as we have seen, given highest value. At the same time, the function of priestesses and priests seems to have been not to serve and give religious sanction to a brutal male elite but to benefit all the people in the community in the same way that the heads of the clans administered the communally owned and worked lands.[3]

But then came the great change—a change so great, indeed, that nothing else in all we know of human cultural evolution is comparable in magnitude.

The Peripheral Invaders

At first it was like the proverbial biblical cloud "no bigger than a man's hand"—the activities of seemingly insignificant nomadic bands roaming the less desirable fringe areas of our globe seeking grass for their herds. Over millennia they were apparently out there in the harsh, unwanted, colder, sparser territories on the edges of the earth, while the first great agricultural civilizations spread out along the lakes and rivers in the fertile heartlands. To these agricultural peoples, enjoying humanity's early peak of evolution, peace and prosperity must have seemed the blessed eternal state for humankind, the nomads no more than a peripheral novelty.

We have nothing to go by but speculation on how these nomadic bands grew in numbers and in ferocity and over what span of time.[4] But by the fifth millennium B.C.E., or about seven thousand years ago, we begin to find evidence of what Mellaart calls a pattern of disruption of the old Neolithic cultures in the Near East.[5] Archaeological remains indicate clear signs of stress by this time in many territories. There is evidence of invasions, natural catastrophes, and sometimes both, causing large-scale destruction and dislocation. In many areas the old painted pottery traditions disappear. Bit by devastating bit, a period of cultural regression and stagnation sets in. Finally, during this time of mounting chaos the development of civilization comes to a standstill. As Mellaart writes, it will be another two thousand years before the civilizations of Sumer and Egypt emerge.[6]

In Old Europe the physical and cultural disruption of the Neolithic societies that worshiped the Goddess also seems to begin in the fifth millennium B.C.E., with what Gimbutas calls Kurgan Wave Number One. "Thanks to the growing number of radiocarbon dates, it is now possible to trace several migratory waves of steppe pastoralists or 'Kurgan' people that swept across prehistoric Europe," reports Gimbutas. These repeated incursions and ensuing culture shocks and population shifts were concentrated in three major thrusts: Wave No. 1, at c. 4300–4200 B.C.E.; Wave No. 2, c. 3400–3200 B.C.E.; and Wave No. 3, c. 3000–2800 B.C.E. (dates are calibrated to dendrochronology).[7]

The Kurgans were of what scholars call Indo-European or Aryan language–speaking stock, a type that was in modern times to be idealized by Nietzsche and then Hitler as the only pure European race. In fact, they were not the original Europeans, as they swarmed down on that continent from the Asiatic and European northeast. Nor were they even originally Indian, for there was another people, the Dravidians, who lived in India before the Aryan invaders conquered them.[8]

But the term *Indo-European* has stuck. It characterizes a long line of invasions from the Asiatic and European north by nomadic peoples. Ruled by powerful priests and warriors, they brought with them their male gods of war and mountains. And as Aryans in India, Hittites and Mittani in the Fertile Crescent, Luwians in Anatolia, Kurgans in eastern Europe, Achaeans and later Dorians in Greece, they gradually imposed their ideologies and ways of life on the lands and peoples they conquered.[9]

There were other nomadic invaders as well. The most famous of these are a Semitic people we call the Hebrews, who came from the deserts of the south and invaded Canaan (later named Palestine for the Philistines, one of the peoples who lived in the area). The moral precepts we associate with both Judaism and Christianity and the stress on peace in many modern churches and synagogues now obscures the historical fact that originally these early Semites were a warring people ruled by a caste of warrior-priests (the Levite tribe of Moses, Aaron, and Joshua). Like the Indo-Europeans, they too brought with them a fierce and angry god of war and mountains (Jehovah or Yahweh). And gradually, as we read in the Bible, they too imposed much of their ideology and way of life on the peoples of the lands they conquered.

These striking similarities between the Indo-Europeans and the ancient Hebrews have led to some conjecture that there may here be some common origins, or at least some elements of cultural diffusion.[10] But it is not the bloodlines or cultural contacts that cannot be found that are of such interest. It is what seems most definitely to unite these peoples of so many different places and times: the structure of their social and ideological systems.

The one thing they all had in common was a dominator model of social organization: a social system in which male dominance, male violence, and a generally hierarchic and authoritarian social structure was the norm. Another commonality was that, in contrast to the societies that laid the foundations for Western civilization, the way they characteristically acquired material wealth was not by developing technologies of production, but through ever more effective technologies of destruction.

Metallurgy and Male Supremacy

In that classic Marxist work *The Origin of the Family, Private Property, and the State,* Friedrich Engels was one of the first to link the emergence of hierarchies and social stratification based on private property with male domination over women. Engels further linked the shift from matriliny to patriliny with the development of copper and bronze metallurgy.[11] However, though this was a pioneering insight, it was only crudely on the mark. For it is only in light of recent research that we can see the specific—and sociologically fascinating—ways copper and bronze metallurgy radically redirected the course of cultural evolution in Europe and Asia Minor.

What brought about these radical changes does not seem to relate to the discovery of these metals. Rather it relates to a fundamental point about technology we have been making: the *uses* to which these metals were put.

The assumption under the prevailing paradigm is that all important early technological discoveries must have been made by "man the hunter" or "man the warrior" for the purpose of more effective killing. In college courses and popular modern epics like Arthur C. Clarke's film *2001,* we are taught this has been so starting with the very first crude wood and stone implements, which by this logic were clubs and knives for killing others.[12] Hence it has also been assumed that metals were first and foremost used for weapons. However, the archaeological evidence shows that such metals as copper and gold had long been known to the people of the Neolithic. But they used them for ornamental and religious purposes and for the manufacture of tools.[13]

New dating techniques not available in Engels's time indicate that metallurgy in Europe first appears in the sixth millennium B.C.E. among people living south of the Carpathian Mountains and in the region of the Dinaric and Transylvanian alps. These first metal finds are in the form of jewelry, statuettes, and ritual objects. By the fifth and early fourth millennium copper also seems to have come into general use for manufacturing flat axes and shaft-hoe axes, wedge-shaped tools, fishhooks, awls, needles, and double-spiral pins. But as Gimbutas points out, the copper axes of Old Europe "were wood-working tools, not battle axes or symbols of divine power as they were known to be in proto- and historic Indo-European cultures."[14]

The archaeological evidence thus supports the conclusion that it was not metals per se, but rather their use in developing ever more effective technologies of destruction, that played such a critical part in what Engels termed "the world historical defeat of the female sex."[15] Nor did male dominance become the norm in Western prehistory, as Engels implies, when gathering-hunting peoples first begin to domesticate and breed animals (in other words, when herding became their main technology of production). Rather, it happened much later, during the millennia-long incursions of pastoral hordes into the more fertile lands where farming had become the main technology of production.

As we have seen, technologies of destruction were *not* important social priorities for the farmers of the European Neolithic Age. But for the warlike hordes that came pouring down from the arid lands of the north, as well as up from the deserts of the south, they were. And it is at this critical juncture that metals played their lethal part in forging human history: not as a general technological advance, but as weapons to kill, plunder, and enslave.

Gimbutas has painstakingly reconstructed this process in Old Europe. She begins with the fact there was no copper in the regions where the pastoralists came from, the arid steppes north of the Black Sea. "This leads to the hypothesis," she writes, "that the horse-riding Kurgan people of the steppe were aware of the metal technology which existed in the fifth and fourth millennia B.C.E. south of the Caucasus Mountains. Probably by no later than 3500 B.C.E. they had learned metallurgical techniques from the Transcaucasians, and soon afterward, they were exploiting the ores of the Caucasus."[16] Or more specifically, soon afterward they were forging more lethally effective weapons out of metal.[17]

Gimbutas's data are based on large-scale post–World War II excavations as well as on the introduction of new dating techniques. To condense radically, they indicate that the transition from the Copper to the Bronze Age (when copper-arsenic or copper-tin alloys first made their appearance) occurred in the period between 3500 and 2500 B.C.E. This is considerably earlier than the date of circa 2000 B.C.E. traditionally given by earlier scholars. Moreover, the rapid spread of bronze metallurgy over the European continent is linked with the evidence of now increasingly massive incursions of the extremely mobile, warlike, hierarchic, and male-dominated pastoralist peoples from the northern steppes whom Gimbutas calls the Kurgans. "The appearance of bronze weapons—daggers and halberds—together with thin and sharp axes of bronze and maceheads and battle-axes of semi-precious stone and flint arrowheads, coincides with the routes of dispersal of the Kurgan people," writes Gimbutas.[18]

The Shift in Cultural Evolution

This is by no means to say that the radical change in the cultural evolution of Western society was simply a function of wars of conquest. As we shall see, the process was far more complex. However, there seems little question that from the very beginning warfare was an essential instrument for replacing the partnership model with the dominator model. And war and other forms of social violence continued to play a central role in diverting our cultural evolution from a partnership to a dominator direction.

As we will see, the shift from a partnership to a dominator model of social organization was a gradual, and after a while predictable, process. However, the events that triggered this change were relatively sudden, and at the time, unpredictable. What the archaeological record tells us is startlingly congruent with the new scientific thinking about unpredictable change—or how long-established states of systems equilibrium and near equilibrium can with relative rapidity shift to a far from equilibrium, or chaotic, state. Even more remarkable is how this radical change in our cultural evolution in certain respects fits the nonlinear evolutionary model of "punctuated equilibria" proposed by Eldredge and Gould, with the appearance of "peripheral isolates" at critical "bifurcation points."[19]

The "peripheral isolates" that now emerged from what are literally the fringes of our globe (the barren steppes of the north and the arid deserts of the south) were not a different species. But, interrupting a long stretch of stable development guided by a partnership model of society, they brought with them an entirely different system of social organization.

At the core of the invaders' system was the placing of higher value on the power that takes, rather than gives, life. This was the power symbolized by the "masculine" Blade, which early Kurgan cave engravings show these Indo-European invaders literally worshiped.[20] For in their dominator society, ruled by gods—and men—of war, this was the supreme power.

With the appearance of these invaders on the prehistoric horizon— and not, as is sometimes said, with men's gradual discovery that they too played a part in procreation—the Goddess, and women, were reduced to male consorts or concubines. Gradually male dominance, warfare, and the enslavement of women and of gentler, more "effeminate" men became the norm.

How fundamentally different these two social systems were, and how cataclysmic were the norm-changes forced by these "peripheral isolates"—now become "peripheral invaders"—is summarized in the following passage from Gimbutas's work:

"The Old European and Kurgan cultures were the antithesis of one another. The Old European were sedentary horticulturalists prone to live in large well-planned townships. The absence of fortifications and weapons attests the peaceful coexistence of this egalitarian civilization that was probably matrilinear and matrilocal. The Kurgan system was composed of patrilineal, socially stratified, herding units which lived in small villages or seasonal settlements while grazing their animals over vast areas. One economy based on farming, the other on stock breeding and grazing, produced two contrasting ideologies. The Old European belief system focused on the agricultural cycle of birth, death, and regeneration, embodied in the feminine principle, a Mother Creatrix. The Kurgan ideology, as known from comparative Indo-European mythology, exalted virile, heroic warrior gods of the shining and thunderous sky. Weapons are nonexistent in Old European imagery; whereas the dagger and battle-axe are dominant symbols of the Kurgans, who like all historically known Indo-Europeans, glorified the lethal power of the sharp blade."[21]

Warfare, Slavery, and Sacrifice

Perhaps most significant is that in the representations of weapons engraved in stone, stelae, or rocks, which also only begin to appear *after* the Kurgan invasions, we now find what Gimbutas describes as "the earliest known visual images of Indo-European warrior gods."[22] Some figures are "semi-anthropomorphic," reports Gimbutas about the excavations of a series of rock carvings in the Italian and Swiss alps; they have heads and arms. But the majority are abstract images "in which the god is represented by his weapons alone, or by weapons in combination with a belt, necklace, double-spiral pendant, and the divine animal—a horse or stag. In several of the compositions a sun or stag antlers occur in the place where the god's head should be. In others, the god's arms are represented as halberds or axes with long shafts. One, three, seven, or nine daggers are placed in the center of the composition, most frequently above or below the belt."[23]

"Weapons obviously represented the god's functions and powers," writes Gimbutas, "and were worshipped as representations of the god himself. The sacredness of the weapon is well evidenced in all Indo-European religions. From Herodotus we know the Scythians made sacrifices to their sacred dagger, Akenakes. No previous engravings or images of weapon-carrying divinities are known in the Neolithic Alpine region."[24]

This glorification of the lethal power of the sharp blade accompanied a way of life in which the organized slaughter of other human beings, along with the destruction and looting of their property and the subjugation and exploitation of their persons, appears to have been normal. Judging from the archaeological evidence, the beginnings of slavery (the ownership of one human being by another) seem to be closely linked to these armed invasions.

For instance, these findings indicate that in some Kurgan camps the bulk of the female population was *not* Kurgan, but rather of the Neolithic Old European population.[25] What this suggests is that the Kurgans massacred most of the local men and children but spared some of the women, whom they took for themselves as concubines, wives, or slaves. Evidence that this was standard practice is found in Old Testament accounts from several millennia later, when the nomadic Hebrew tribes invaded Canaan. In Numbers 31:32–35, for example, we read that among the spoils of war taken by the invaders in their battle against the Midianites, there were, in this order, sheep, cattle, asses, and thirty-two thousand girls who had had no intercourse with a man.

The violent reduction of women, and thus also of both their female and male children, to the status of mere male possessions is also documented in Kurgan burial practices. As Gimbutas notes, among the first known evidences of "Kurganization" are a number of graves dating from sometime before the fourth millennium B.C.E.—in other words, shortly after the first wave of Kurgan invaders swept into Europe.[26]

These are the "chieftain graves" characteristic of Indo-European dominator rankings, indicating a radical shift in social organization, with a strongman elite at the top. In these graves—in Gimbutas's words clearly an "alien cultural phenomenon"—a marked change in burial rites and practices is also evident. In contrast to Old European burials, which showed little indication of social inequality, there are here marked differences in the size of the graves as well as in what archaeologists call "funerary gifts": the contents found in the tomb other than the deceased.[27]

Among these contents, for the first time in European graves, we find along with an exceptionally tall or large-boned male skeleton the skeletons of sacrificed women—the wives, concubines, or slaves of the men who died. This practice, which Gimbutas describes as *suttee* (a term borrowed from the Indian name for the immolation of widows, which continued there into the twentieth century), was apparently introduced by the Indo-European Kurgans into Europe. It appears for the first time west of the Black Sea at Suvorovo in the Danube delta.[28]

These radical innovations in burial practices are, moreover, characteristic of all three of the Kurgan invasions. For example, in the so-called Globular Amphora culture that dominated in northern Europe almost a thousand years after the first wave of Kurgans arrived, the same brutal burial practices, reflecting the same type of social and cultural organization, prevail. As Gimbutas writes, "The possibility of co-incidental deaths is over-ruled by the frequency of these multiple burials. Generally, the male skeleton is buried with his gifts at one end of the cist grave, while two or more individuals are grouped at the other end. . . . Male dominance is confirmed by Globular Amphora tombs. Polygyny is documented by the cist grave at Vojtsekhivka in Volynia, where a male skeleton was flanked in heraldic order by two women and four children, a young man and a young woman lay at his feet."[29]

These high-status graves are also repositories of other articles deemed important to these ruling-class men not only in life but in death. "A warrior-consciousness previously unknown in Old Europe," reports Gimbutas, "is evidenced in equipment recovered from Kurgan graves: bows, and arrows, spears, cutting and thrusting 'knives' (proto-daggers), antler-axes, and horse bones."[30] Also found in these graves are symbolic objects such as pig or boar mandibles and tusks, dog skeletons, and auroch or cattle scapulae, providing further archaeological evidence that there has been not only a radical social shift but a radical ideological shift as well.

These burials show the great social value now placed on technologies for destruction and domination. They also contain evidence of a strategy for ideological obliteration and takeover we are to see more and more of: the appropriation by men of important religious symbols that their subject peoples once associated with women in the worship of the Goddess.

"The tradition of placing boar and pig mandibles, dog burials, and aurochs or cattle scapulae exclusively in male graves," notes Gimbutas, "can be traced to Kurgan I–II (Srednij Stog) graves in the Pontic steppe. The economic importance attached to pigs and boars as a food source is overshadowed by religious implications of the bones of these animals found solely in association with high-ranking males of the community. The symbolic ties now evidenced between men and the boar, pig, and dog are a *reversal* of the religious significance these animals held in Old Europe, where the pig was the sacred companion of the Goddess of Regeneration."[31]

The Truncation of Civilization

Spreading westward and southward, the archaeological landscape of Old Europe is now traumatically altered. "Millennial traditions were truncated," writes Gimbutas, "towns and villages disintegrated, magnificent painted pottery vanished; as did shrines, frescoes, sculptures, symbols, and script."[32] At the same time there now comes into play a new living war machine, the armed man on a horse—which in its time must have had the impact a tank or an airplane has among primitives in ours. And in the wake of the Kurgan devastation, we find their typical warrior-chieftain graves, with their human sacrifices of women and children, their animal sacrifices, and their caches of weapons surrounding the dead chiefs.[33]

Writing before the excavations of the 1960s and 70s, and before Gimbutas systematically organized both the old and new data using the latest carbon and dendrochronology dating techniques, the European prehistorian V. Gordon Childe describes the same general pattern. Childe characterizes the culture of early Europeans as "peaceful" and "democratic," with no hint of "chiefs concentrating the communities' wealth."[34] But then he notes how all this gradually changed, as warfare, and particularly the use of metal weapons, is introduced.

Like Gimbutas, Childe observes that as weapons increasingly appear in the excavations, so do chief's tombs and houses that clearly evidence social stratification, with strongman rule becoming the norm. "Settlements were often planted on hill tops," writes Childe. Both there and in the valleys they are now "frequently fortified." Moreover, he too emphasizes that, as "competition for land assumed a bellicose character, and weapons such as battle-axes became specialized for warfare," not only the social, but also the ideological organization of European society underwent a fundamental alteration.[35]

Even more specifically, Childe notes how as warfare becomes the norm "the consequent preponderance of the male members of the communities may account for the general disappearance of female figurines." He remarks how these female figurines, so ubiquitous in the earlier levels, are now "no more in evidence" and then concludes: "The old ideology has been changed. That may reflect a change from a matrilineal to patrilineal organization of society."[36]

Gimbutas is even more specific. Based on the systematic study of Old European chronologies, drawing from her own work and that of other archaeologists, she painstakingly describes how in the wake of each new wave of invasions there is not only physical devastation but what historians call cultural impoverishment. Already in the wake of Wave Number One the destruction is so massive that only pockets of Old European settlement survive—for example, the Cotofeni complex of the Danube valley of Oltenia, western and northwestern Muntenia, and the south of Banat and Transylvania. But even here there are signs of significant change, notably the appearance of defense mechanisms such as trenches and ramparts.[37]

For the majority of Old European settlements, such as the Karanovo farmers of the lower Danube basin, the Kurgan invasions were, in Gimbutas's words, catastrophic. There is wholesale material destruction of houses, of shrines, of finely crafted artifacts and works of art, which have no meaning or value to the barbarian invaders. Masses of people are massacred, enslaved, or put to flight. As a result, chain reactions of population shifts are set in motion.[38]

Now what Gimbutas calls "hybrid cultures" begin to appear. These cultures were based on "the subjugation of remaining Old European groups and their rapid assimilation into the Kurgan pastoral economy and agnatically-linked [patrilinear], stratified societies."[39] But these new hybrid cultures are far less technologically and culturally advanced than the cultures they replaced. The economy is now based primarily on stock breeding. And though some of the Old European techniques are still in evidence, the pottery is now strikingly uniform and inferior. For example, in the Cernavoda III settlements that appear in Romania after Kurgan Wave Number Two, there is no trace of pottery painting or of the Old European symbolic designs. In east Hungary and western Transylvania the pattern is similar. "The diminished size of communities—no larger than 30 to 40 individuals—indicates a restructured social system of small herding units," writes Gimbutas.[40] And fortifications now begin to appear everywhere, as gradually the acropolis or hill fort replaces the old unwalled settlement.

And so, as prehistoric excavations evidence, the archaeological landscape of Old Europe is transformed. Not only do we find increasing signs of physical destruction and cultural regression in the wake of each wave of invasions; the direction of cultural history is also profoundly altered.

Slowly, as the Old Europeans, for the most part unsuccessfully, try to protect themselves from their barbaric invaders, new definitions of what is normal for both society and ideology begin to emerge. Everywhere now we see the shift in social priorities that is like an arrow shot through time to pierce our age with its nuclear tip: the shift toward more effective technologies of destruction. This is accompanied by a fundamental ideological shift. The power to dominate and destroy through the sharp blade gradually supplants the view of power as the capacity to support and nurture life. For not only was the evolution of the earlier partnership civilizations truncated by armed conquests; those societies that were not simply wiped out were now also radically changed.

Now everywhere the men with the greatest power to destroy—the physically strongest, most insensitive, most brutal—rise to the top, as everywhere the social structure becomes more hierarchic and authoritarian. Women—who as a group are physically smaller and weaker than men, and who are most closely identified with the old view of power symbolized by the life-giving and sustaining chalice—are now gradually reduced to the status they are to hold hereafter: male-controlled technologies of production and reproduction.

At the same time the Goddess herself gradually becomes merely the wife or consort of male deities, who with their new symbolizations of power as destructive weapons or thunderbolts are now supreme. In sum, through the gradual process of both social and ideological transformation we will examine in more detail in the chapters that follow, the story of civilization, of the development of more advanced social and material technologies, now becomes the familiar bloody span from Sumer to ourselves: the story of violence and domination.

The Destruction of Crete

The violent end of Crete is particularly haunting—and instructive. Because it was an island to the south of the European mainland, Crete was walled off for a time from the warlike hordes by the mothering sea. But at last here too the end came, and the last civilization based on a partnership rather than a dominator model of social organization fell.

The beginning of the end followed the mainland pattern. During the Mycenaean period, controlled by the Indo-European Achaeans, Cretan art becomes less spontaneous and free. And now clearly visible in the Cretan archaeological record is a much greater concern with, and emphasis on, death. "Before they came under Achaean influence the Cretans characteristically did not make much of death and funerary rites," notes Hawkes. "The attitude of the Achaean elite was quite otherwise."[41] Now we find evidence of great expenditures of wealth and labor on provisions for the royal and noble dead. And, most tellingly, due partly to the Achaean influence and partly to the mounting threat of another wave of invasions from the European continent, there are clear signs of a growing martial spirit.

Just when and how the Mycenaean period began and ended in Crete is still the subject of much controversy. One theory is that the Achaean takeover, both of Crete itself and of what appear to have been Minoan settlements on the Greek mainland, came in the wake of a series of earthquakes and tidal waves that so weakened Minoan civilization it could no longer resist the barbarians pressing down from the north. The difficulty is that the time usually assigned to these disasters is circa 1450 B.C.E., and there is at that time no evidence of an armed invasion of Crete.[42] Nevertheless, whether it was by actual conquest following earthquakes, by a coup brought about by military pressures, or by Achaean chieftains marrying Cretan queens, we do know that during the final centuries of Cretan civilization the island came under the rule of Greek-speaking Achaean kings. And although those men adopted many of the more civilized Minoan ways, they also brought with them a social and ideological organization oriented more toward death than life.

Some of our knowledge about the Mycenaean period comes to us from the so-called Linear-B tablets found in both Crete and the Greek mainland, which have now been deciphered. In the tablets found in both Knossos and Pylos (a Mycenaean settlement on the southern tip of Greece) names of divinities are listed. To the profound satisfaction of those who had long contended there was continuity between Crete and classical Greece, these reveal that the deities of the later Olympian pantheon (Zeus, Hera, Athena, Artemis, Hermes, etc.) were already worshiped, albeit in different forms and contexts, centuries before we next hear of them in Hesiod and Homer.[43] In conjunction with the archaeological evidence, these tablets also reveal, as Hawkes put it, "a well-balanced marriage between the Cretan and Achaean divinities."[44]

But this Mycenaean marriage of Minoan and Achaean culture was to be short-lived. From the Pylos tablets, many of which were, in Hawkes's words, "drawn up during the last days of peace as part of a vain effort to avert catastrophe," we learn that the Mycenaean wanax, or king, had received advance warning that Pylos was to be attacked. "The emergency was faced without panic," writes Hawkes. "The clerks remained at their benches patiently recording all that was done." Dispositions of rowers were made to provide a defensive fleet. Masons were sent out, presumably to begin to build fortifications along the long unfortified coastline. To equip the soldiers, about a ton of bronze was collected, and nearly two hundred bronzesmiths assembled. Even bronze belonging to sanctuaries of the Goddess was requisitioned in what Hawkes calls "a moving testimony to the crisis of turning from peace to war."[45]

But it was all to no avail. "There is no sign that the much-needed walls ever went up at Pylos," writes Hawkes. "From the tablets that record the effort to save the kingdom one must turn to the fabric of the royal hall to discover that it failed. The barbarian warriors broke in. They must have been astonished by the painted rooms and the treasure they contained. . . . When they had finished looting they cared nothing for the building with its unwarlike foreign embellishments. They set fire to it and it burned furiously. . . . The heat was so great that some of the pottery vessels in the pantries melted into vitreous lumps, while stone was reduced to lime. . . . In the storerooms and the tax office by the entrance the abandoned tablets were fired to a hardness that was to preserve them for all time."[46]

And so, one by one, both on the Greek mainland and islands and in Crete, the achievements of this civilization that reached an early high point for cultural evolution were destroyed. "Probably the story was everywhere much the same, as Mycenae, Tiryns and all the other royal

strongholds except Athens were engulfed by the barbarian tide," writes
Hawkes. "Dorians in time took all the Peloponnese except Arcadia and
went on to dominate Crete, Rhodes and all the adjacent islands. The
most venerable of all the royal houses, Knossos, may have been among
the last to fall."[47]

By the eleventh century B.C.E. it was all over. After taking to the
mountains, from where for a time they waged guerrilla war against the
Dorian settlements, the last pockets of Cretan resistance collapsed.[48]
Along with masses of immigrants, the spirit that had once made Crete,
in Homer's words, "a rich and lovely land" now fled the island that
had for so long been its home.[49] With time even the existence of the
self-confident women—and men—of Minoan Crete was to be forgotten, as was peace, creativity, and the life-sustaining powers of the Goddess.

A Disintegrating World

The fall of Crete approximately three thousand years ago can be
said to mark the end of an era. It was an end that, as we have seen,
began millennia earlier. Beginning in Europe somewhere around 4300
or 4200 B.C.E., the ancient world was battered by wave after wave of
barbarian invasions. After the initial period of destruction and chaos,
gradually there emerged the societies that are celebrated in our high
school and college textbooks as marking the beginnings of Western
civilization.

But concealed within this purportedly grand and glorious beginning
was the flaw that has widened into the most dangerous of chasms in
our time. After millennia of upward movement in our technological,
social, and cultural evolution, an ominous split was now underway.
Like the deep cracks left by violent movements of the earth in that
time, the breach between our technological and social evolution on the
one hand and our cultural evolution on the other would steadily widen.
The technological and social movement toward greater complexity of
structure and function resumed. But the possibilities for cultural development were now to be stunted—rigidly caged in a dominator society.[50]

Everywhere society was now becoming male dominant, hierarchic,
and warlike. In Anatolia, where the people of Catal Huyuk had lived
in peace for thousands of years, the Hittites, an Indo-European people
mentioned in the Bible, took over. And although their archaeological
remains, such as the great sanctuary at Yazilikaya, show the Goddess

was still worshiped, she was increasingly relegated to the status of the wife or mother of new male gods of war and thunder. The pattern was similar in Europe, Mesopotamia, and Canaan. Not only was the Goddess no longer supreme, she was also being transformed into a patroness of war.

Indeed, to the people living through these terrifying times, it must have seemed as though the very heavens, once thought to be the abode of a bountiful Goddess, had been captured by antihuman supernatural forces allied with their brutal representatives on earth. Not only was "divinely-ordained" strongman rule and chronic warfare everywhere becoming the norm; there is also considerable evidence that the period from c. 1500 to 1100 B.C.E. was one of uncommonly intense physical as well as cultural chaos.

It was during this time that a series of violent volcanic eruptions, earthquakes, and tidal waves rocked the Mediterranean world. Indeed, so profoundly was the physical environment shaken and rearranged that what happened may account for the tale of Atlantis, an entire continent that supposedly sank during an inconceivably vast and devastating natural disaster.

Coupled with these natural terrors came still further man-made terror. From the north the Dorians were pushing deeper and deeper into Europe. Finally Greece and even Crete fell under the onslaught of their iron weapons. In Anatolia, the warlike Hittite empire collapsed under the pressure of new invaders. This move in turn drove the Hittites southward into Syria. The lands of the Levant were also invaded during this period, by both land and sea, by displaced peoples, including the Philistines we read about in biblical accounts.

Farther south, Assyria now suddenly became a world power, pushing into Phrygia, Syria, Phoenicia, and even as far as Anatolia and the Zagros Mountains to the east. The extent of their barbarity can still be seen today in the bas reliefs commemorating the "heroic" exploits of a later Assyrian king, Tiglath-pileser. Here what look like the populations of whole cities are stuck alive on stakes running through the groin and out the shoulders.

Even as far south as Egypt there were repercussions, as invaders called in hieroglyphics the People from the Sea (believed by many scholars to be Mediterranean refugees) tried to take over the Nile Delta at the beginning of the eleventh century B.C.E. They were defeated by Ramses III, but we can still see them today on the murals of his funerary temple in Thebes, where they stream past us in ships, chariots, and on foot with families and ox carts.

In Canaan, in what biblical scholars believe were three migratory waves, the Hebrew tribes, now consolidated under the rule of the Levitic warrior-priests, began a series of wars of conquest.[51] As we can still read in the Bible, despite their war god Jehovah's promises of victory, it took them hundreds of years to overcome the Canaanite resistance— which is variously explained in the Bible as decreed by God to provide his people practice in warfare, to test and punish them, or to keep cultivated areas from desolation until the invaders' numbers would be sufficiently increased.[52] As we can also still read in the Bible, for example in Deuteronomy 3:3–6, the practice of these "divinely inspired" invaders was of "utterly destroying the men, women, and children of every city."

All over the ancient world populations were now set against populations, as men were set against women and against other men. Wandering over the width and breadth of this disintegrating world, masses of refugees were everywhere fleeing their homelands, desperately searching for a haven, for a safe place to go.

But there was no such place left in their new world. For this was now a world where, having violently deprived the Goddess and the female half of humanity of all power, gods and men of war ruled. It was a world in which the Blade, and not the Chalice, would henceforth be supreme, a world in which peace and harmony would be found only in the myths and legends of a long lost past.

CHAPTER 5

Memories of a Lost Age: The Legacy of the Goddess

The fall of the Roman Empire, the Dark Ages, the Plague, World Wars I and II—all other times of seeming chaos we know of are dwarfed by comparison with what happened at a time about which we have until now known so little: the evolutionary crossroads in our prehistory when human society was violently transformed. Now, thousands of years later, when we are nearing the possibility of a second social transformation—this time a shift from a dominator society to a more advanced version of a partnership society—we need to understand everything we can about this astonishing piece of our lost past. For at stake at this second evolutionary crossroads, when we possess the technologies of total destruction once attributed only to God, may be nothing less than the survival of our species.

Yet even when confronted with the authority of new research, with new archaeology, and the corroboration from social science, this truly huge block of new knowledge about millennia of human history so contradicts all we have been taught that its hold on our minds is like a message written in sand. The new knowledge may linger there for a day, or even a week. But relentlessly the force of the teaching of centuries works to undermine it, until what is left is merely a fleeting impression of a time of great excitement and hope. Only through reinforcement from other sources—both familiar and unfamiliar—can we hope to retain this knowledge long enough to make it our own.

Evolution and Transformation

One source of reinforcement, as we have seen, comes from the new scientific findings about both systems stability and systems change.

This recently emerging body of knowledge, popularly identified with the "new physics" and sometimes called "self-organizing" theory and/ or "chaos" theory, for the first time provides an adequate framework for beginning to understand what happened to us during our prehistory—and what may, in a different direction, happen to us again now.

Within the perspective of this new conceptual framework, as incorporated in Cultural Transformation theory, what we have been examining are two aspects of social dynamics. The first relates to social stability—how for thousands of years there were human societies that were organized in a way that is different from the way we have been taught all human systems are organized. The second relates to how social systems, like other systems, can, and do, undergo fundamental change.

In the last chapter we saw the dynamics of the first great social shift in our cultural evolution: how after a period of systems disequilibrium, or chaos, there was a critical bifurcation point out of which an entirely different social system emerged. Everything we can find out about this first systems transformation, by providing us with insight into what happens during periods of fundamental or "chaotic" change, illuminates not only our past but also our present and future.

Still, one may ask, if the shift from a partnership to a dominator society ushered in a later period in our species' history, does this not mean that a dominator system is, after all, an evolutionary step up? Here we return to two points mentioned in the Introduction. The first is the confusing use of the term *evolution* as both descriptive and normative, both as a word for describing what happened in the past and a term connoting movement from "lower" to "higher" levels (with the implicit judgment that what came later must be better). The second point is that not even our technological evolution has been a linear upward movement, but rather a process interrupted by massive regressions.

We also return to another, equally important point: the essential difference between cultural and biological evolution. Biological evolution entails what scientists call speciation: the emergence of a wide variety of progressively more complex forms of life. By contrast, human cultural evolution relates to the development of *one* highly complex species—ours—that has two different forms: the female and the male.

This human dimorphism, or difference in form, as we have seen, acts as a fundamental constraint on possibilities for our social organization, which may be founded on either the ranking or linking of the two halves of humanity. The critical difference that must again be stressed is that each of the two resultant models has a characteristic type of technological and social evolution. Consequently, the *direction* of our cultural evolution—particularly whether it will be peaceful or warlike—depends on which of these two possible models is the guide for evolution.

Our social and technological evolution can—and, as we saw, did—move from simpler to more complex levels under first a partnership society and later a dominator society. However, our cultural evolution, which directs the *uses* we make of greater technological and social complexity, is radically different for each model. And this direction of cultural evolution in turn profoundly affects the direction of our social and technological evolution.

The most obvious example is technology. Under the cultural guidance of the partnership paradigm the emphasis was on technologies for peaceful purposes. But with the rise of the dominator paradigm, there was the vast shift to the development of technologies of destruction and domination that has steadily escalated over the centuries into our own endangered time.

Because we are not accustomed to look at history in terms of a dominator or partnership model of society that shapes our past, present, and future, it is difficult for us to see the profound effect these two models have had on our cultural evolution. This is why another corroborating source for the change in our cultural direction about five thousand years ago is so important. Unlike "chaos" theory, this second source is not at all new. In fact, it is something we already know, something long implanted within our minds: the storehouse of the sacred, secular, and scientific mythology of Western civilization, which can only now be seen to reveal the reality of an earlier and better past.

A Golden Race and the Legend of Atlantis

Writing toward the end of the period Western historians call the Greek Dark Age—the three or four hundred years following the Dorian invasions—the ancient poet Hesiod tells us there once was a "golden race." "All good things," Hesiod writes, "were theirs. The fruitful earth poured forth her fruits unbidden in boundless plenty. In peaceful ease they kept their lands with good abundance, rich in flocks and dear to the immortals."[1]

But after this race, which Hesiod calls "pure spirits" and "defenders from evil," came a lesser "race of silver," who were in turn replaced by "a race of bronze, in no way like the silver, dreadful and mighty,

sprung from shafts of ash." Hesiod goes on to explain how this people—obvious to us now, the Bronze Age Achaeans—brought with
them war. "The all-lamented sinful works of Ares were their chief
care." Unlike the two earlier peoples, they were not peaceful agrarians:
"they ate no grain, but hearts of flint were theirs, unyielding and un-
conquered."[2]

In commenting on Hesiod's third "race of men," the historian John
Mansley Robinson writes: "We know who these men were. They came
out of the north, about 2000 B.C.E., bearing weapons of bronze. They
settled the mainland, built the great Mycenaean fortresses, and left
behind them the documents in Linear B which we now know to be an
early form of Greek. . . . We can trace the extension of their power
southward to Crete and eastwards to the coast of Asia Minor, where
they sacked the city of Troy toward the beginning of the twelfth century
B.C.E."[3]

But for Hesiod, the Mycenaean descendants of the Achaeans and
the peoples they conquered were a fourth and separate "race." "This
was more just, and nobler than the last," writes Hesiod.[4] Like Homer,
he idealizes these people, who had shed some of their barbarity and
adopted many of the more civilized customs of the Old Europeans.

But then there appeared on the historical horizon of Europe a "fifth
race of men." These were the people who in Hesiod's time still ruled
Greece and from whom Hesiod himself was descended. "Would I had
no share in this fifth race of men," he writes. "Would that I had died
before or afterwards been born." For now "one man will sack another's
city. . . . Right shall depend on might and piety shall cease to be."[5] As
Robinson notes, the people of this "fifth race" were the Dorians, "who,
with their iron weapons, destroyed the Mycenaean strongholds and
took the land for themselves."[6]

The historicity of Hesiod's bronze and iron races as the Achaean
and Dorian Indo-European invaders of Greece is generally recognized
by scholars. But Hesiod's description of the "golden age" of peaceful
agrarians, still remembered in his time, who did not yet worship Ares,
the god of war, has been consistently interpreted as no more than fantasy.

For a long time this was also true of what is probably the best-
known Greek myth about an earlier and better time: the legend of
Atlantis, where, according to Plato, there once flourished a great and
noble civilization that was engulfed by the sea.

Plato located his lost civilization of Atlantis in the Atlantic Ocean,
presumably based on Solon's Egyptian informants, who said it lay in

the "far west" and also assigned it a much later date. However, as J. V. Luce writes in the *The End of Atlantis,* some of the elements of Plato's Atlantis are a "startlingly accurate sketch of the Minoan empire in the sixteenth century B.C.E."[7] Or as the Greek archaeologist Nicolas Platon writes, "the legend handed down by Plato of the submerged Atlantis may be a reference to the history of Minoan Crete and its sudden destruction." For, according to Plato, Atlantis is destroyed by "violent earthquakes and floods," just as Minoan civilization is now believed by scholars to have been given the death blow that made possible the Achaean takeover of both Crete and the Minoan settlements in Greece.[8]

This theory was first proposed in 1939 by Professor Spyridon Marinatos, director of the Greek Archaeological Service. More recently it has found support in geological evidence that in about 1450 B.C.E. there was in the Mediterranean a series of volcanic eruptions of such severity that they caused part of the island of Thera (now a tiny strip of land sometimes called Santorini) to collapse into the sea. These eruptions also set in motion enormous earthquakes and tidal waves. The occurrence and severity of these natural disasters, which seem the basis for folk memories of the sunken land mass Plato called Atlantis, is also verified by archaeological excavations in Thera as well as Crete. Here there is evidence of severe earthquake damage and massive coastal destruction caused by tidal waves during the same period.[9]

As Luce puts it, it now seems that "tidal waves were the real 'bull from the sea' which was sent to plague the rulers of Knossos."[10] And it also seems that the story of Atlantis is actually the garbled folk memory, not of a lost Atlantic continent, but of the Minoan civilization of Crete.[11]

The Garden of Eden and the Tablets of Sumer

An earlier time when humans led more harmonious lives is also a recurrent theme in the legends of Mesopotamia. Here there are repeated references to a time of plenty and peace, a time before a great flood, when women and men lived in an idyllic garden. These are the stories from which biblical scholars now believe the Old Testament myth of the Garden of Eden in part derives.

Viewed in light of the archaeological evidence we have been examining, the story of the Garden of Eden is also clearly based on folk memories. The Garden is an allegorical description of the Neolithic, of when women and men first cultivated the soil, thus creating the first "garden." The story of Cain and Abel in part reflects the actual confrontation of a pastoral people (symbolized by Abel's offering of his slaughtered sheep) and an agrarian people (symbolized by Cain's offering of "the fruits of the ground" rejected by the pastoral god Jehovah). Likewise, the Garden of Eden and Fall from Paradise myths in part draw from actual historical events. As will be detailed in succeeding chapters, these stories reflect the cataclysmic cultural change we have been examining: the imposition of male dominance and the accompanying shift from peace and partnership to domination and strife.

In Mesopotamian legends we also find recurring references to a Goddess as the supreme deity or "Queen of Heaven"—an appellation that is also later found in the Old Testament, but now in the context of prophets railing against the resurgence of earlier religious beliefs. Indeed, the earliest Mesopotamian inscriptions abound with references to a Goddess. A Sumerian prayer exalts the glorious Queen Nana (a name of the Goddess) as "the Mighty Lady, the Creatress." Another tablet refers to the Goddess Nammu as "the Mother who gave birth to heaven and earth."[12] In both Sumerian and later Babylonian legends we find accounts of how women and men were created simultaneously or in pairs by the Goddess[13]—stories that in an already male-dominated society would seem to hark back to a time when women were not seen as inferior to men.

That there was in this region, so long regarded as the cradle of civilization, an earlier time when descent was still matrilineal and women were not yet male-controlled can also be inferred from other tablets. For example, even as late as 2000 B.C.E. we read in a legal document from Elam (a city-state slightly east of Sumer) that a married woman, refusing to make her bequest jointly with her husband, passed her entire property on to her daughter. Here too we find that only in later periods did the Goddess of Elam become known as "the Great Wife" and become relegated to a position secondary to that of her husband Humbam. Even in later Babylon, already harshly male dominant, there is documentary evidence that some women were still holding and managing their own property, particularly priestesses, who also traded extensively.[14]

Moreover, as Professor H. W. F. Saggs writes, "in early Sumerian religion a prominent position is occupied by Goddesses who afterward virtually disappeared, save—with the one exception of Ishtar—as consorts to particular gods." This supports the conclusion that, again in Saggs's words, "the status of women was certainly much higher in the early Sumerian city-state than it subsequently became."[15] That there was in the lands of the Fertile Crescent an earlier time before male dominance and the supremacy of fearful, armed male deities became the norm is also indicated by tombs like that of Queen Shub-Ad from the First Dynasty of Ur. For here—although archaeologists assert that the grave next to her, containing a male skeleton, was that of the king—only her name is inscribed. And her tomb is the more splendid and opulent one.[16] Similarly, although Sumerian histories generally speak of the "reigns" of Lugalanda and Urukagina and refer to their wives Baranamtarra and Shagshag only in passing, a look at official documents reveals they were actually dated in the names of the two queens.[17] This raises the question of whether these women were really merely "consorts" under the rule and dominance of men.

This question is also raised if we take a close look at the text of the so-called Urukagina reforms of Sumeria, dated circa 2300 B.C.E. Here we read how henceforth the fruit trees and the food grown on temple lands were to be used for those in need, rather than, as had become the custom, solely for the priests—and how this practice dated back to the way things were done in earlier times. But it is not only that these reforms took place during times when queens still (or once again) wielded power; as the art historian Merlin Stone points out, this also suggests that the earlier societies of Sumer were less hierarchical and more communally oriented.[18]

Beyond that, it tells us that more humane customs and laws, such as the requirement that those in need be helped by the community, likewise date back to the partnership societies era—and that in this respect the Urukagina reforms were simply reasserting the moral and ethical precepts of that earlier time. As Stone points out, this conclusion is confirmed by the word used to label these reforms. They are called *amargi*, which in Sumerian has the double meaning of "freedom" and "return to the mother." Once again this suggests a memory of an earlier and less oppressive time when women as heads of clans or queens still wielded power as a responsibility rather than as a means of autocratic control.[19]

It is also from Sumerian tablets that we learn that the Goddess Nanshe of Lagash was worshiped as "She who knows the orphan, knows the widow, seeks justice for the poor and shelter for the weak."[20] On New Year's Day it was she who judged all of humankind. And in tablets from nearby Erech, we read that the Goddess Nidaba was known as "The Learned of the Holy Chambers, She who teaches the Decrees."[21] Such ancient names of the Goddess as the Giver of Law, of Justice, and of Mercy, and the first Judge would also seem to indicate the existence of some earlier codification of laws, and possibly even a judicial system of some complexity, in which the Sumerian priestesses who served the Goddess perhaps adjudicated disputes and administered justice.

In Mesopotamian tablets we further read how the Goddess Ninlil was revered for giving her people an understanding of planting and harvesting methods.[22] There is, moreover, linguistic evidence pointing to the origins of agriculture. The words found in Sumerian texts for farmer, plow, and furrow are *not* Sumerian. Neither are the words for weaver, leathermaker, basketmaker, smith, mason, and potter. What this seems to indicate is that all these basic technologies of civilization were taken over by later invaders from the earlier Goddess-worshiping peoples of the area, whose language has otherwise been lost.[23]

The Gifts of Civilization

It is a widespread assumption that however bloody things have been since the days of the Sumerians and Assyrians this was just the unfortunate prerequisite for technological and cultural advance. If the "savages" who existed prior to our "earliest" civilizations were peaceable, it is reasoned they would naturally, lacking the proper motivation, have produced little of any lasting value. For the spur of war, the "man-in-the-street" and the Pentagon theorist will hold, has been necessary to bring on all technological and, by implication, cultural advance. However, the data we are now examining, as well as many other ancient myths and legends, tell us the same thing we are learning from archaeological excavations. This is that one of the best-kept historical secrets is that practically all the material and social technologies fundamental to civilization were developed before the imposition of a dominator society.

The principles of food growing, as well as of construction, container, and clothing technology were all already known by the Goddess-worshiping peoples of the Neolithic.[24] So were increasingly sophisticated uses of natural resources such as wood, fibers, leather, and later, metals in manufacturing. Our most important nonmaterial technologies, such as law, government, and religion, likewise date back to what, borrowing from Gimbutas's term Old Europe, we may call the Old Society. And so also do the related concepts of prayer, judgeship, and priesthood. Dance, ritual drama, and oral or folk literature, as well as art, architecture, and town planning are likewise pre-dominator society.[25] Trade, by both land and sea, is another legacy of this earlier era.[26] So is administration, education, and even forecasting of the future. For the first identification of oracular or prophetic power is with the priestesses of the Goddess.[27]

Religion supports and perpetuates the social organization it reflects. In many surviving ancient religious texts it is the Goddess—not any of the then already dominant male deities—who is identified as the one who gave the people the "gifts of civilization."[28] The myths attributing our major physical and spiritual inventions to a female deity may thus reflect their actual invention by women.[29]

Such a hypothesis is just about inconceivable under the prevailing paradigm. For it pictures woman as dependent and secondary to man, not only intellectually inferior, but according to our Bible, so much less spiritually developed than man that she is to blame for our fall from grace.

But in societies that conceptualized the supreme power in the universe as a Goddess, revered as the wise and just source of all our material and spiritual gifts, women would tend to internalize a very different self-image. With such a powerful role model they would tend to consider it both their right and their duty to actively participate and to take the lead in developing and using both material and spiritual technologies. They would tend to see themselves as competent, independent, and most certainly creative and inventive. Indeed, there is growing evidence of the participation and leadership of women in the development and administration of the material and nonmaterial technologies upon which a dominator order was later superimposed.

Going all the way back to the time our ancestral primates first began to change into humans, scholars are beginning to reconstruct a far more balanced view of our evolution—one in which women, not just men, play central roles. The old evolutionary model based on "man the hunter" attributes the beginnings of human society to the "male bonding" required for hunting. It also claims our first tools were developed by men to kill their prey—and also to kill competing or weaker humans. An alternative evolutionary model has now been proposed by scientists like Nancy Tanner, Jane Lancaster, Lila Leibowitz, and Adrienne Zihlman.[30]

This alternative view is that the erect posture required for the freeing of hands was not linked to hunting but rather to the shift from foraging (or eating as one goes) to gathering and carrying food so it could be both shared and stored. Moreover, the impetus for the development of our much larger and more efficient brain and its use to both make tools and more effectively process and share information was not the bonding between men required to kill. Rather, it was the bonding between mothers and children that is obviously required if human offspring are to survive. According to this theory, the first human-made artifacts were not weapons. Rather, they were containers to carry food (and infants) as well as tools used by mothers to soften plant food for their children, who needed both mother's milk and solids to survive.[31]

This theory is more congruent with the fact that primates, as well as the most primitive existing tribes, rely primarily on gathering rather than hunting. It also is congruent with the evidence that meat eating formed only a miniscule part of the diet of ancestral primates, hominids, and early humans. It is further supported by the fact that primates differ from birds and other species in that typically only mothers share food with their young. Among primates we also see the development of the first tools, *not* for killing, but for gathering and processing food. And among some of the most thoroughly observed existing primates, chimpanzees, we see females using these tools more frequently.[32]

So, as Tanner writes of the still much earlier time that provided the foundation for the Old Society we have examined, "woman the gatherer," rather than "man the hunter," seems to have played a most critical role in the evolution of our species.[33] "Offspring with mothers intelligent enough to find, gather, premasticate, and share sufficient food with them had the selective advantage," observes Tanner. "Among those surviving children, those best able to learn and improve on their mother's techniques, and those who, like their mothers, were willing to share, in turn had the children who were most likely to live long enough to reproduce."[34]

"It is highly unlikely," she continues, "that tools were used for killing animals at this time, since the prey was small and defenseless and could be caught and killed with the hands." Moreover, it is "highly probable that it was women with offspring who developed the new gathering technology"—not only the tools but the human bipedalism, or independent use of hands and feet, that is a prerequisite for gathering as against foraging. Women would be in most need of free hands to carry both food and offspring.[35]

It is also more than likely that women invented that most fundamental of all material technologies, without which civilization could not have evolved: the domestication of plants and animals.[36] In fact, even though this is hardly ever mentioned in the books and classes where we learn the history of "ancient man," most scholars today agree that this is probably how it was. They note that in contemporary gatherer-hunter societies women, not men, are typically in charge of processing food. It would thus have been more likely that it was women who first dropped seeds on the ground of their encampments, and also began to tame young animals by feeding and caring for them as they did for their own young. Anthropologists also point to the fact that in the primarily horticultural economies of "developing" tribes and nations, contrary to Western assumptions, the cultivation of the soil is to this day primarily in the hands of women.[37]

This inference is further supported by the many ancient religious myths that explicitly attribute the invention of agriculture to the Goddess. For example, in Egyptian records the Goddess Isis is repeatedly referred to as the inventor of agriculture. In Mesopotamian tablets the Goddess Ninlil is revered for teaching her people to farm.[38] There are also in both archaeology and myth numerous nonverbal associations of the Goddess and agriculture. These span a huge period of time, ranging all the way from Catal Huyuk, where offerings of grain were made in shrines of the Goddess, to classical Greek times, when similar offerings were still made to female deities like Demeter and Hera.[39]

Based on extensive research of prehistoric myths, scholars like Robert Briffault and Erich Neumann have also concluded that pottery was invented by women. It was at one time regarded as a sacred process associated with the worship of the Goddess and is generally associated with women. The weaving and spinning of cloth is likewise in most ancient mythologies associated with woman and with female deities, who, like the Greek Fates, are still said to spin the destinies of "men."[40]

There is also evidence from Egypt and Europe, as well as the Fertile Crescent, that the association of femininity with justice, wisdom, and intelligence dates back to very ancient times. Maat is the Egyptian Goddess of justice. Even after male dominance was imposed, the Egyptian Goddess Isis and the Greek Goddess Demeter were both still known as lawgivers and sages dispensing righteous wisdom, counsel, and justice. Archaeological records of the Middle Eastern city of Nimrud, where the already martial Ishtar was worshiped, show that even then some women still served as judges and magistrates in courts of law. From the pre-Christian legends of Ireland we also learn that the Celts worshiped Cerridwen as the Goddess of intelligence and knowledge.[41] The Greek Fates, the enforcers of laws, and the Greek Muses, who inspire all creative endeavor, are, of course, female. And so is the image of Sophia, or Wisdom, which prevailed well into medieval Christian times, along with the image of the Goddess as the Madonna of Mercy.[42]

There is also abundant evidence that spirituality, and particularly the spiritual vision characteristic of wise seers, was once associated with woman. From Mesopotamian archaeological records we learn that Ishtar of Babylon, successor to Innana, was still known as the Lady of Vision, She Who Directs the Oracles, and the Prophetess of Kua. Babylonian tablets contain numerous references to priestesses giving prophetic advice at the shrines of Ishtar, some of which are significant in the records of political events.[43]

From ancient Egyptian records we know that the picture of a cobra was the hieroglyphic sign for the word *Goddess* and that the cobra was known as the Eye, *uzait,* a symbol of mystic insight and wisdom. The cobra Goddess known as Ua Zit was the female deity of Lower Egypt (north) in predynastic times. Later, both the Goddess Hathor and Maat were still known as the Eye. The uraeus, a rearing serpent, is frequently found upon the foreheads of Egyptian royalty. Moreover, a prophetic sanctuary, possibly the site of an earlier shrine to the Goddess Ua Zit, stood in the Egyptian city of Per Uto, which the Greeks called Buto, the Greek name for the cobra Goddess herself.[44]

The well-known oracular shrine at Delphi also stood on a site originally identified with the worship of the Goddess. And even in classical Greek times, after it was taken over for the worship of Apollo, the oracle still spoke through the lips of a woman. She was a priestess called Pythia, who sat upon a tripod stool around which a snake called the python coiled. Moreover, we read in Aeschylus that at this holiest of shrines the Goddess was revered as the primeval prophetess. This again suggests that even as late as the classical age of Greece the partnership society tradition of seeking divine revelation and prophetic wisdom through women had not yet been forgotten.[45]

From the writings of Diodorus Siculus in the first century B.C.E., we learn that even at that late date not only justice but healing was associated with women. When he traveled in Egypt, he found that the Goddess Isis, the successor of both Ua Zit and Hathor, was still revered not only as the one who first established law and justice but also as a great healer.[46] In this connection, it is interesting that the intertwined serpents known as the caduceus are still the emblem of the modern medical profession. Legend has it that this tradition derived from the identification of snakes with priests of the Greek god Asclepius. But a case can be made for the position that the association of snakes and healing derives from a much earlier tradition: This is the association of the serpent with the Goddess, an association, which, as we have seen, probably applied to both healing and prophecy.[47]

Even the invention of writing, long assumed to date back to around 3200 B.C.E. in Sumer, appears to have much earlier, and possibly feminine, roots. In Sumerian tablets the Goddess Nidaba is described as the scribe of the Sumerian heaven as well as the inventor of both clay tablets and the art of writing. In Indian mythology the Goddess Sarasvati is credited with inventing the original alphabet.[48] And now, based on archaeological excavations of Old Europe, Gimbutas has found that the first beginnings of schematized writing go way back into the Neolithic. Moreover, these beginnings seem not to be, as in Sumer, connected with a "commercial-administrative" script designed to keep better track of material accumulations. Rather, the first use of this most powerful tool of human communication seems to have been spiritual: a sacred script associated with the worship of the Goddess.[49]

Probably the most widely known findings supporting this newer theory come from the European site of Vinca, fourteen miles east of Belgrade in Yugoslavia. As with a number of other sites, when Vinca culture was originally discovered it was believed to be much more recent than it actually is because of its high degree of artistic sophistication. Professor M. Vasic, who excavated Vinca culture between 1908 and 1932, first concluded it was a center of Aegean civilization in the second millennium B.C.E. Then he decided that it was of an even later period and must actually have been a Greek colony—conclusions which, as Gimbutas notes, continue to be cited in some modern histories of the Balkans.[50]

These theories, promulgated before archaeology had scientific dating tools such as radiocarbon and dendrochronology methods, were congruent with the then prevailing archaeological paradigm that there was no advanced indigenous culture in the early Balkans. But the calibrated radiocarbon dates that have now been obtained from eight sites of different phases of Vinca culture date it to between 5300 and 4000 B.C.E.—that is, some seven thousand years ago.[51] These data, in addition to the archaeological evidence that the Goddess was the supreme deity, put Vinca squarely in a partnership society period.

It was in Vinca that the so-called Tartara tablets and other signs inscribed on figurines and pottery were discovered. Gimbutas chronicles how these finds, coupled with "evidence of a marked intensification of spiritual life in general"[52] led to another theory, still at least somewhat congruent with the old archaeological paradigm that there was no advanced indigenous culture in the Balkans. This was that Vinca culture was an import from Anatolia, or even Mesopotamia. But Vinca culture has now been established as native to the Balkans. Thus, if the markings inscribed in the Neolithic tablets, figurines, and other objects excavated at Vinca, as well as at other Old European sites, are what they appear to be—a rudimentary form of linear script—the origins of writing are much more ancient than was formerly believed, going back well before the dominator era.[53]

There is certainly mounting evidence to support this conclusion. In 1980 Professor Gimbutas reported that "at present over sixty sites are known to have yielded inscribed objects. . . . Most of the sites are those of the Vinca and Tisza culture groups and of the Karanovo culture in central Bulgaria. Inscribed or painted signs are also known on Dimini, Cucuteni, Petresti, Lengyel, Butmir, Bukk, and Linear Pottery ceramics." These finds indicate that "it is no longer appropriate to speak of a 'Vinca script' or of the Tartara plaque," as "it now appears that the script was a universal feature of Old European civilization."[54]

Moreover, this script appears to have been an outgrowth of the earlier tradition of using art as a kind of visual shorthand to communicate important concepts. All over Old Europe are highly stylized Goddess figurines incised with symbolic signs such as meanders, chevrons, Vs, Xs, whirls, circles, and multiple lines. As Gimbutas writes, these images represented collectively approved and understood means for communicating the basic world-explaining assumptions of their time. When this form of symbolic communication was later taken one step further, what is probably the first form of human script evolved. These are ideograms in which existing symbolic signs (already present in the Paleolithic and widespread in the Neolithic) were modified by lines, curves, and dots.

Gimbutas, who is working to decipher the Old European script, also believes that some of these ideograms gradually acquired a phonetic value. "The *V*," she writes, "is one of the most frequently encountered marks on figurines and other cult objects. It is my opinion that it is used in the script with phonetic value derived from the sign-ideogram. *M*, probably an ideogram for water as in Egyptian, must have had a phonetic value from very early times, at least no later than the sixth millennium B.C.E."[55]

Through intensive study of symbols and signs first found primarily on figures and later increasingly presented on pottery, seals, disks, and plaques, Gimbutas has tried to decipher meanings through association. For example, she hypothesizes that V glyphs may have been a way of representing the Goddess in her epiphany of the bird, and that objects so marked were originally dedicated to her cult. She further observes how when later signs are inscribed in rows, as on the Gradeshika dish, the repetitive clusters of Vs (as well as of Ms, Xs, and Ys) may have represented vows, prayers, or assignments of gifts to the Goddess.[56]

Gimbutas also points to the "unquestionable similarities between Old European characters and those of Linear A, Cypro-Minoan, and classical Cypriot."[57] This raises the strong possibility that Linear A, the earliest and as yet undeciphered script found in Minoan Crete, may have been a later development of this already extant Neolithic script tradition—not, as was hitherto assumed, borrowed by the Cretans from the people they traded with in Asia Minor and Egypt.[58]

A New View of the Past

All this information about our lost past inevitably sets in motion conflict between the old and the new in our own minds. The old view was that the earliest human kinship (and later economic) relations developed from men hunting and killing. The new view is that the foundations for social organization came from mothers and children sharing.[59] The old view was of prehistory as the story of "man the hunter-warrior." The new view is of both women and men using our unique human faculties to support and enhance life.

Just as some of the most primitive existing societies, like those of the BaMbuti and !Kung, are not characterized by warlike cavemen dragging women around by the hair, it now appears that the Paleolithic was a remarkably peaceful time. And just as Heinrich and Sophia Schliemann defied the scholarly establishment of their time and proved the city of Troy was not Homeric fantasy but prehistoric fact, new archaeological findings verify legends about a time before a male god decreed woman be forever subservient to man, a time when humanity lived in peace and plenty.

In sum, under the new view of cultural evolution, male dominance, male violence, and authoritarianism are not inevitable, eternal givens. And rather than being just a "utopian dream," a more peaceful and equalitarian world is a real possibility for our future.

But our legacy from these Goddess-worshiping societies is not only the haunting memory of a time when the "tree of life" and the "tree of knowledge" were still viewed as Mother Nature's gifts to both women and men. Nor is it only the poignant sense of what might have been had humanity been permitted to come of age free to enjoy these gifts. As we have seen, the basic technologies on which all later civilization has been built are our legacy from these early partnership societies.

None of this is to say that these societies were ideal. Even though they made great contributions to human culture and were later remembered as a more innocent and better time, these were *not* utopian societies. It is important to stress that a peaceful society does not signify the absence of all violence; that these were societies made up of flesh and blood human beings, with human foibles and failings.

Moreover, for all their ingenuity and promise, the material technologies of the Neolithic were still quite primitive in comparison to what we have today. Although there is evidence of a script, there seems to have been no written literature. And even though much was known about matters ranging from agriculture to astronomy, there was probably no science as we know it today.

In fact, in the religious art of the Neolithic, we can see how, lacking our kind of scientific knowledge, our forebears tried to explain, and influence, the universe in ways that in our own time seem primitive and superstitious. And although the most massive evidence of human sacrifice is found in later dominator societies, there are a few indications the practice of ritual sacrifice may date back to this earlier time.[60]

A useful perspective on the positives and negatives is provided by what we may, from the evidence, infer of this earlier age's particular quality of mind. Neolithic art is sometimes characterized as irrational because it abounds in the kind of imagery we associate with fairy tales, horror films, and even science fiction fantasy. But if we define rational by any humane standards, as meaning the use of our minds to transcend some of nature's destructiveness and brutality, and define irrational as destructive thinking and behavior, it would be more accurate to say that Neolithic art reflects not so much an irrational as a prerational worldview.[61] As contrasted to the more empirical thinking so highly valued in our secular age, it was the product of a mind characterized by a fantasizing, intuitive, and mystical consciousness.

This is not to suggest, as was argued by the psychologist Julian Jaynes, that these earlier peoples were exclusively right-brained. Jaynes claimed that real human consciousness—which he equated with the use of our more logical or left-brain functions only—arose through the cataclysmic jolts provided by the bloody sequence of invasions and natural disasters we have examined. In fact, he contended that until then we were little more than right-brained, god-possessed automatons.[62] But we have only to look at the sanctuaries of Stonehenge and Avebury to see that already in the Neolithic period the logical, sequential, linear thinking characteristic of left-brain operation was well established. Clearly the alignment of those huge stones with the movements of the sun and moon, as well as their shaping, transport, and placement, required an advanced understanding of mathematics, astronomy, and engineering.[63] And certainly the people of Crete—who built viaducts, paved roads, designed architecturally complex palaces, and had indoor plumbing, a flourishing trade, and a great deal of knowledge about navigation—must also have made extensive use of left-brain as well as right-brain thinking. For Crete's material achievements are astonishing even by modern standards, actually surpassing those of many developing societies today.

Still more arresting, when compared to our modern world, is that in these prehistoric partnership societies technological advances were used primarily to make life more pleasurable rather than to dominate and destroy. This leads back to the fundamental distinction between the cultural evolution of dominator and partnership societies. It also points to the conclusion that, in this important respect, our earlier, technologically and socially less advanced partnership societies were more evolved than the high-technology societies of the present world, where millions of children are condemned to die of hunger each year while billions of dollars are poured into ever more sophisticated ways to kill.

From this perspective, the modern search for a lost ancient spirituality can be seen in a new and extremely useful light. In essence, the search of so many people today for the mystical wisdom of an earlier time is the search for the kind of spirituality characteristic of a partnership rather than a dominator society.

Both the mythical and archaeological evidence indicate that perhaps the most notable quality of the pre-dominator mind was its recognition of our oneness with all of nature, which lies at the heart of both the Neolithic and the Cretan worship of the Goddess. Increasingly, the work of modern ecologists indicates that this earlier quality of mind, in our time often associated with some types of Eastern spirituality, was far advanced beyond today's environmentally destructive ideology. In fact, it foreshadows new scientific theories that all the living matter of earth, together with the atmosphere, oceans, and soil, forms one complex and interconnected life system. Quite fittingly, the chemist James Lovelock and the microbiologist Lynn Margulis have called this the Gaia hypothesis—Gaia being one of the ancient Greek names of the Goddess.[64]

The Old Society idea of the powers governing the universe as a

giving and nurturing mother is also psychologically more reassuring—
and socially less tension- and anxiety-producing—than the idea of punitive male deities, which still possesses much of our earth. Indeed,
the tenacity with which for millennia of Western history both women
and men have, in the figure of the Christian Virgin Mary, clung to the
worship of a compassionate and merciful mother attests to the human
hunger for such a reassuring image. However, like so many otherwise
puzzling aspects of history, this tenacity only becomes comprehensible
in the context of what we now know about the millennia-long tradition
of Goddess worship in prehistory.

But it is precisely because this new knowledge about the original
direction of our cultural evolution casts such a different light on our
past—and our potential future—that it is so difficult for us to deal with.
And because it represents such a threat to the prevailing system, there
are massive efforts to suppress it.

Within the research that now provides us with the archaeological
findings here reported are many instances of the dynamics of dominator society information suppression at work. A striking example is
how, even though the site's lowest and earliest levels had not yet been
reached, James Mellaart was ordered to halt excavations at the Neolithic
site of Hacilar on grounds that "further work on the site would only
yield repetitive results of no great scientific value."[65] This decision was
made over Mellaart's protests. It was made even though at that time
the outlying parts of the mound, including the surrounding cemeteries
(a standard source of the richest archaeological data for most excavations) had not yet been explored. But without further financial or institutional support, the digging had to be halted. And having since
then been unscientifically ravaged by treasure hunters, the site is now
archaeologically useless.

Undoubtedly other factors contributed to the decision to prema-
turely close down these important archaeological excavations—a decision Mellaart called "one of the most tragic chapters in the history
of archeology."[66] But the question remains to what extent this decision
was driven—albeit unconsciously—by the emerging knowledge that
behind the abundant and diversified artistic activity of Hacilar "there
lay," as Mellaart wrote, "the one great and inspiring force, the old
religion of Anatolia, the cult of the Great Goddess."[67]

As we shall see in the chapters that follow, the efforts of intellectuals
to make reality conform to a dominator worldview go way back into
prehistory. Certainly the main instrument for the dramatic shift in our
cultural evolution was the Blade. But there was another instrument,

one that has in the long run been even more powerful. This is the tool of the scribe and the scholar: the pen or stylus for marking tablets with words. Particularly in our age, when we are trying to create a peaceful society, it is instructive to know that the pen can be as mighty as the sword. For in the end it was this seemingly puny tool that was to literally stand reality on its head.

CHAPTER 6

Reality Stood on Its Head:
Part I

The *Oresteia* is one of our most famous and frequently performed Greek dramas. In this classic, at the trial of Orestes for the murder of his mother, the god Apollo explains that children are not related to their mothers. "The mother is no parent of that which is called her child," he asserts. She is "only nurse of the new planted seed that grows."[1]

"I will show you proof of what I have explained," Apollo goes on. "There can be a father without any mother. There she stands, the living witness, daughter of Olympian Zeus, she who was never fostered in the dark of the womb, yet such a child as no goddess could bring forth."[2]

At this point the goddess Athene (Athena), who according to ancient Greek religion sprang forth full-grown from the head of her father, Zeus, enters and confirms Apollo's statement. Only fathers are related to their children. "There is no mother anywhere who gave me birth," she asserts, adding, "and but for marriage, I am always for the male with all my heart, and strongly on my father's side."[3]

And so, as the chorus—the Eumenides, or Furies, representing the old order—exclaim in horror, "Gods of the younger generation, you have ridden down the laws of the elder time, torn them out of my hands,"[4] Athene casts the deciding vote. Orestes is absolved of any guilt for the murder of his mother.

Mother-Murder Is Not a Crime

Why, one might ask, would anyone try to deny the most powerful and obvious of all human relationships? Why should a brilliant playwright like Aeschylus write a dramatic trilogy around this theme? And why would this trilogy—which was in its time not theater in our sense of the word but ritual drama specifically designed to appeal to the emotions and exact conformity to the prevailing norms—be shown to all the people of Athens, including even women and slaves, on important ceremonial occasions?

In trying to answer the question of what the *Oresteia*'s normative function was, the standard scholarly interpretation has been that it was intended to explain the origins of the Greek Areopagus, or court of homicide. Supposedly in this court, new for its time, justice was to be obtained through the more impersonal legal instruments of the state instead of through clan vengeance.[5] But as the British sociologist Joan Rockwell points out, such an interpretation is nonsensical. It does not even touch upon the central question of why this case, claimed to be the very first ever tried by a Greek court of homicide, is the killing of a mother by her own son. Nor does it address the central question of how, in what is supposedly a "moral lesson" in support of state-administered justice, a son could be acquitted for the premeditated, cold-blooded revenge murder of his mother—and then on the patently preposterous ground that he was not related to her.[6]

To answer the question of what kind of norms the *Oresteia* in fact expresses and affirms, we have to look at the trilogy as a whole. In the first play, *Agamemnon*, the queen Clytemnestra acts to avenge the shedding of her daughter's blood. We learn that on his way to Troy her husband, Agamemnon, tricked her into sending him their daughter Iphigenia, purportedly to marry Achilles, but really to be sacrificed to get the becalmed fleet a fair wind. Upon his return from the Trojan War, while Agamemnon is ritually bathing to cleanse himself of his sins of war, Clytemnestra throws a net around him to entangle him and stabs him to death. She makes it clear that this is done not merely out of personal grief and hatred but in her social role as the head of her clan, responsible for avenging the shedding of kindred blood. In short, she is acting within the norms of a matrilineal society, in which as queen it is her duty to see that justice is done.

In the second play, *The Libation-Bearers*, her son Orestes returns to Argos in disguise. He enters his mother's palace as a guest, kills his mother's new consort Aegisthus and then, after some hesitation, in revenge for his father's death, kills his mother. The third play, the *Eumenides*, presents the trial of Orestes in the temple of Apollo at Delphi. We learn that the Eumenides, as representatives of the old order and in their role as protectors of society, and executors of justice, have been pursuing Orestes. And now a jury of twelve Athenian citizens presided over by the goddess Athene is to decide whether he shall be acquitted or die. But because their vote is evenly divided, Athene casts the deciding vote: Orestes is acquitted on the grounds that he has not shed kindred blood.

The *Oresteia* thus takes us back to a time when there occurred what classical scholars like H. D. F. Kitto and George Thompson call the clash between matriarchal and patriarchal cultures.[7] In our terms, it traces—and justifies—the shift from partnership to dominator norms.

As Rockwell writes, it takes us from "full consent to the justice of Clytemnestra's case in the first play to a point where her daughter is forgotten, her ghost is eclipsed, and her case is non-existent, because women do not have those rights and attributes which she had claimed."[8] For "if a mighty creature like Clytemnestra, with the provocation she has in the murder of her child Iphigenia, has not the right to take revenge, what woman has?"

Through the lesson of what happened to this "uppity" woman, even with such just cause, all women are effectively restrained from even entertaining the idea of rebellious acts. Moreover, Athene's role in this normative drama is, as Rockwell puts it, "a masterful bit of cultural diplomacy; it is very important in an institutional shift that a leading figure of the defeated party is seen to accept the new power."[9]

With Athene, as both the direct descendant of the Goddess and the patron deity of the city of Athens, declaring for male supremacy, the shift to male dominance must be accepted by every Athenian. And so also must the shift from what was once a basically communal or clan-owned system of property (in which descent was traced through women) to a system of private ownership of property *and* women by men. As Rockwell writes: "If the first trial at the new Court of Homicide proves that matricide is not a blasphemous crime because no matrilineal relationship exists, what better argument for sole patrilineal descent?"[10]

In the *Oresteia* every Athenian could see how even the ancient Furies, or Fates, finally gave in. The male-dominant order had been established, the new norms had replaced the old, and their fury was of no avail. Completely defeated, they retire to caves under the Acropolis, as Athene "persuades" them to remain in Athens—having reiterated the remarkable argument that the killing of one's mother is not the shedding of kindred blood and cast the deciding vote. Clearly subservient, they now undertake to invoke their old powers, the powers of the Goddess, and promise in Athene's service to help guard "this city which Zeus all powerful and Ares rule" (Ares, of course, being the god of war).[11]

As the last vestiges of the female power from pre-Olympian times, it is still the Furies who will spin the fates of women and men, who will determine when it is time for mortals to be born and to die. "Like Mother-Kali in Hindu mythology," writes Rockwell, "the woman gives birth and death."[12] But now these last remaining representatives of woman's old powers are driven underground, as lesser and basically marginal figures in a male-dominated pantheon of new gods.

The Dominator and Partnership Mind

The *Oresteia* was designed to influence, and alter, people's view of reality. The striking thing is that this was still necessary almost a thousand years after the Achaeans took control of Athens in the fifth century B.C.E. Even more striking is how the chorus itself, speaking for the Eumenides, should sum up what the *Oresteia* is actually about: "That they could treat me so! I, the mind of the past, to be driven under the ground, out cast, like dirt!"[13]

Although in Aeschylus's time this mind of the past—bearing the fading memories of an earlier time—had not yet been completely destroyed, it was now possible at a great ceremonial occasion to publicly proclaim that the wrongs of men against women, even the killing of a daughter by her own father, should simply be forgotten. So fundamentally had people's minds already been transformed that it could now be said that in truth a mother and child are not related: that matriliny has no basis in reality, that, by contrast, only patriliny does.

Over two thousand years later, some of the giants of Western science, for example, Herbert Spencer in the nineteenth century, were still "explaining" male dominance by asserting that women are no more than incubators for male sperm.[14] In light of the scientific evidence that a child takes an equal number of genes from each parent, this idea that there is no kinship between mother and child is no longer taught us in schools and universities. But even now our most powerful religious leaders, as well as many of our most respected scientists, still tell us women are creatures put on earth by God or nature primarily to provide men with children—preferably sons.

In our time, we continue to identify children through surnames that tell only of their relationship to their father. Moreover, millions of Western families are still normatively socialized in patriliny with Bible reading from pulpits and in homes. And we are not here just talking of all the endless "begats" in the Holy Bible. We are talking about all the biblical passages in which when someone important is identified, it is as the child of his father, and even the people of Israel (as well as all of humanity and the Saviour or Messiah himself) are identified as the children of God the Father.[15]

To us, after thousands of years of relentless indoctrination, this is simply reality, the way things are. But to the mind that was driven out—the mind that worshiped the Goddess as the Supreme Creatrix of all Life and as the Mother not only of humanity but of all animals and plants—reality would have been a far different thing.

To a mind socialized in such a society, in which descent was traced through the mother and women as heads of clans and as priestesses occupied socially important and honored positions, patriliny, and with it the progressive reduction of women to men's private property, would hardly seem "natural." As for a son not being brought to justice for murdering his own mother, this would be totally beyond comprehension to such a mind, as it was to the Eumenides in Aeschylus's play. Likewise inconceivable, and indeed blasphemous, would be the idea that the supreme powers governing the universe should be personified by armed and vengeful deities who not only condone, but actually in the name of righteousness and morality command, that men routinely perform acts of murder, pillage, and rape.

In sum, this old mind was totally unsuitable to function within the new dominator system. For a time it could perhaps be held in check through brute force and threat. But in the long run, nothing short of complete transformation of the way people perceive and process reality would do.

But how could this be done? How can minds be so transformed? It is fascinating that now, as we again stand at the threshold of a massive shift in our cultural evolution, this question of how systems break down in periods of extreme disequilibrium and are replaced by different systems is being studied by scientists.[16] Of particular interest in relation to the question of how one social system can replace another is the work of Humberto Maturana and Francisco Varela in Chile and Vilmos Csanyi and Gyorgy Kampis in Hungary on the self-organization of living systems through what Maturana calls autopoesis and Csanyi terms autogenesis.[17]

Csanyi describes how systems form and maintain themselves through the process he calls replication. Essentially a self-copying process, replication can be observed on the biological level, where to continually replace themselves cells carry what Csanyi calls replicative information in their genetic code or DNA. But this process occurs at all levels: molecular, biological, and social. For every system has its own characteristic replicative information, which forms, expands, and holds systems together.[18]

The replication of ideas, as Csanyi points out, is essential first in forming and then in maintaining social systems. And clearly the particular type of replicative information suitable for a partnership society (the basic idea of equality, for example) is totally unsuitable for a dominator society. The norms—or what is considered normal and right— under these two types of social organization are, as we have seen, poles apart.

So in order to replace a partnership social organization with one based on force-backed domination, fundamental changes in replicative information had to be made. To return to the biological analogy, a completely different replicative code would be required. And this new code would have to be imprinted in the mind of every single man, woman, and child until their ideas of reality had been completely transformed to fit the requirements of a dominator society.

It is impossible in a few pages to even begin to describe a process that went on for millennia and is still going on in our own time: the process whereby the human mind was, sometimes brutally and sometimes subtly, sometimes deliberately and sometimes unwittingly, remolded into the new kind of mind required by this drastic shift in our cultural evolution. It was a process that, as we have seen, entailed enormous physical destruction that continued well into historic times. As we can still read in the Bible, the Hebrews, and later also the Christians and Muslims, razed temples, cut down sacred groves of trees, and smashed pagan idols.[19] It also entailed massive spiritual destruction, again a process that continued well into historic times. Not only through book burning, but through the burning and persecution of heretics, those who did not perceive reality in the prescribed way were killed or converted.

Directly, through personal coercion, and indirectly, through intermittent social shows of force such as public inquisitions and executions, behaviors, attitudes, and perceptions that did not conform to dominator norms were systematically discouraged. This fear conditioning became part of all aspects of daily life, permeating child rearing, laws, schools. And through these and all the other instruments of socialization, the kind of replicative information required to establish and maintain a dominator society was distributed throughout the social system.

For millennia one of the most important of these instruments of socialization was the "spiritual education" carried out by the ancient priesthoods. As an integral part of state power, these priesthoods served, and were members of, the male elites who now everywhere ruled and exploited the people.

The priests who now spread what they said was the divine Word— the Word of God that had magically been communicated to them— were backed up by armies, courts of law, and executioners. But their ultimate backup was not temporal, but spiritual. Their most powerful weapons were the "sacred" stories, rituals, and priestly edicts through which they systematically inculcated in peoples' minds the fear of terrible, remote, and "inscrutable" deities. For people had to be taught to obey the deities—and their earthly representatives—who now arbitrarily exercised powers of life and death in the most cruel, unjust, and capricious ways, to this day still often explained as "the will of God."

Even today people still learn from "sacred" stories what is good or evil, what should be imitated or abhorred, and what should be accepted as divinely ordained, not only by oneself but by all others. Through ceremonies and rituals, people also partake in these stories. As a result, the values there expressed penetrate into the deepest recesses of the mind, where, even in our time, they are guarded as hallowed and immutable truths.

The kind of centralized and homogeneous control exercised over these sacred stories by the priesthoods of the theocratic city-states of antiquity is hard to grasp today when, except where religion, state censorship, or the mass media discourage it, people can read a wide variety of viewpoints. In antiquity, what was available for reading or, in the case of the illiterate masses, for listening was far more limited. And it primarily expressed the officially sanctioned views. Moreover, the replication of any ideas that would undermine the officially sanctioned ideology was almost impossible, for even if the theocratic censorship was somehow evaded, the punishment for such heresy was hideous torture and death.

There were then, as there still are today, folk memories of older myths, rituals, rhymes, and songs. But gradually, with every passing generation, these became more garbled and distorted, as the priests, ode and song writers, poets, and scribes converted them into what they thought would find favor in the eyes of their lords.

Undoubtedly many of these men believed that what they did was also the will of their gods and felt divinely inspired. But whether it was done in the name of gods, bishops, or kings, out of faith, ambition, or fear, this work of constantly fashioning and refashioning normative oral and written literature did not simply follow social change. It was an integral part of the process of norm changing: the process whereby a male-dominated, violent, and hierarchical society gradually began to be seen as not only normal but also right.

The Metamorphosis of Myth

In his book *1984* George Orwell foresaw a time when a "Ministry of Truth" would rewrite all books and refashion all ideas so as to make them fit the requirements of the men in power.[20] But the horrifying thing is that this is not yet to come. It already happened long ago almost everywhere in the ancient world.[21]

In the Middle East, first in Mesopotamia and Canaan, and later in the Hebrew kingdoms of Judaea and Israel, the remaking of sacred stories, along with the rewriting of codes of law, was largely the work of priests. As in Old Europe, this process began with the first andro-cratic invasions and continued for millennia, as Egypt, Sumer, and all the lands of the Fertile Crescent were gradually transformed into male-dominant and warlike societies. And as biblical researchers have now extensively documented, this process of re-mything was still going on as late as 400 B.C.E., when scholars tell us Hebrew priests last rewrote the Hebrew Bible (The Old Testament).[22]

The final reduction of the myths and laws that have so profoundly affected our Western minds into one sacred book—the first half of our Bible—took place about a hundred years after Aeschylus wrote the *Oresteia* in Greece. At this time in Palestine the biblical mythology on which Judaism, Christianity, and Islam are still based was again sifted, edited, and added to by a group of Hebrew priests identified by biblical scholars as P or the Priestly school. This label was to distinguish them from earlier re-mythers, such as E or the Elohim school, who wrote in the northern kingdom of Israel, and J or the Jahweh school of the southern Kingdom of Judaea. These E and J editorial teams had earlier reworked Babylonian and Canaanite myths, as well as Hebraic history, to suit their purposes. Now the P team came in to work over these heterogeneous ancient texts and try to produce a new holy package. Their aim, to quote the biblical scholars who annotated the famous Dartmouth Bible, was "to translate into reality the blueprint for a theo-cratic state."[23]

We are also told by these same religious scholars that, whether or not this politically motivated final remything entailed a conspiracy of thoughts, it certainly involved a conspiracy of deeds. "They merged the J and E material," write the Dartmouth Bible annotators about the P or Priestly school, "introducing much known as the P strand." They continue: "The quantity and nature of this late contribution by the Priestly authors surprise those unfamiliar with their work. It is thought to include nearly half of the Pentateuch, for many scholars ascribe to P eleven chapters out of the fifty in Genesis, nineteen of the forty in Exodus, twenty-eight out of the thirty-six in Numbers, and the whole of Leviticus."[24]

In addition, much that had formerly been considered holy, like some of the so-called Apocrypha, was dropped. Moreover, as we are also told in the Dartmouth Bible, here "sanction is given to the religious practices of the time by throwing their origin back into the remote past, or by ascribing divine origin to various ordinances."[25] In sum, in the words of the Dartmouth Bible, this final remything of what has come down to us as the Old Testament was "a patching process."[26]

This explains why, despite attempts "to give an impression of unity,"[27] there are so many contradictions and internal inconsistencies in the Bible. One well-known example is the two different stories of how God created human beings found in chapter 1 of Genesis. The first tells that woman and man were simultaneous divine creations. The second, more elaborate one tells that Eve was created as an afterthought out of Adam's rib.

Many of these inconsistencies are obvious clues to the still ongoing conflict between the old reality, which lingered in the people's culture, and the newer realities the priestly ruling class was trying to impose. Sometimes the clash between old and new norms is obvious, as in the equalitarian versus the male-supremacist tale of the first human pair. But more often the conflict between the old and new is less obvious.

A striking case in point is the biblical treatment of the serpent. Indeed, the part the serpent plays in humanity's dramatic exit from the Garden of Eden only begins to make sense in the context of the earlier reality, a reality in which the serpent was one of the main symbols of the Goddess.

In archaeological excavations all through the Neolithic, the serpent is one of the most frequent motifs. "The snake and its abstract derivative, the spiral, are the dominant motifs of the art of Old Europe," writes Gimbutas.[28] She also points out that the association of the serpent and the Goddess survived well into historic times, not only in its original form, as in Crete, but through a variety of later Greek and Roman myths, such as those of Athene, Hera, Demeter, Atargatis, and

Dea Syria.[29] In the Middle East and much of the Orient, it is the same. In Mesopotamia, a Goddess excavated from a twenty-fourth-century B.C.E. site has a serpent coiled around her throat. So does an almost identical figure from 100 B.C.E. India.[30] In ancient Egyptian mythology the cobra Goddess Ua Zit is the original Creatrix of the world. The Canaanite Goddess Ashtoreth, or Astarte, is depicted with the serpent. In a 2500 B.C.E. Sumerian bas relief called The Goddess of the Tree of Life we find two serpents right next to two images of the Goddess.[31]

Clearly the serpent was too important, too sacred, and too ubiquitous a symbol of the power of the Goddess to be ignored. If the old mind was to be refashioned to fit the new system's requirements, the serpent would either have to be appropriated as one of the emblems of the new ruling classes or, alternately, defeated, distorted, and discredited.

Thus, in Greek mythology, at the side of Olympian Zeus the serpent becomes a symbol of the new power.[32] Similarly, there is a serpent on the shield of Athene, the now metamorphosed deity of not only wisdom but also war. A live serpent was even kept in the Erechtheum, a building next to Athene's temple on the Acropolis.[33]

This appropriation of the serpent by Greece's new Indo-European overlords served very practical political purposes. It helped to legitimize the power of the new rulers. Through the disorienting effects of finding a powerful symbol that once belonged to the Goddess in alien hands, it also served as a constant reminder of the defeat of the Goddess by the conqueror's gods of violence and war.

Further symbolizing the defeat of the old order are the many killings of serpents we read about in Greek legend. Zeus slays the serpent Syphon; Apollo kills the serpent Python; and Hercules kills the serpent Ladon, guardian of the sacred fruit tree of the Goddess Hera, said to have been given her by the Goddess Gaia at the time of her marriage to Zeus.

Similarly, in the Fertile Crescent we find the myth of Baal (who is now both the storm god and the brother-consort of the Goddess) subduing the serpent Lotan or Lowtan (significantly, Lat in the Canaanite language meant Goddess). And from Anatolia, we have the story of how the Indo-European Hittite god slays the dragon Illuyankas.[34]

In Hebrew myth, as we can still read in Job 41:1 and in Psalm 74, Jehovah kills the serpent Leviathan, now represented as a terrible sea monster with many heads. But at the same time we read in the Dartmouth Bible that the most sacred symbol of Hebrew religion, the ark of the covenant, probably did *not* originally contain the Ten Commandments. In this ark, which to this day holds the central place in Jewish rites, there was a serpent made of bronze.[35]

This was the brazen serpent we are told of in 2 Kings 18, which as Joseph Campbell writes, was "worshipped in the very temple of Jerusalem along with an image of his spouse, the mighty goddess, who was known there as the Asherah."[36] As we also read in the Bible, it was not until circa 700 B.C.E., during the great religious persecutions of King Hezekiah, that this brazen serpent, said to have been made in the desert by Moses himself to prove Jehovah's power, was finally taken out of the Temple and destroyed.[37]

But the most astonishing evidence of the lingering power of the serpent comes to us from the story of Eve's and Adam's fall from paradise.[38] For it is the serpent who counsels woman to disobey Jehovah and to herself eat from the tree of knowledge, the counsel that to this day is still said to doom humanity to eternal punishment.

There have been many attempts by theologians to interpret the fall from paradise story in ways that do not "explain" barbarity, cruelty, and insensitivity as the inevitable result of "original sin." Indeed, the reinterpretation of this most famous of all religious myths in new and more prohuman symbolism is integral to the ideological transformation that must accompany the social, economic, and technological shift from a dominator to a partnership system. But it is also essential that we clearly understand the social and ideological meaning of this important story in terms of its historical context.

In fact, it is only from this historical perspective that the story of Eve taking counsel from a serpent makes any sense. The fact that the serpent, an ancient prophetic or oracular symbol of the Goddess, advises Eve, the prototypical woman, to disobey a male god's commands is surely not just an accident. Nor is it an accident that Eve in fact follows the advice of the serpent: that, in disregard of Jehovah's commands, she eats from the sacred tree of knowledge. Like the tree of life, the tree of knowledge was also a symbol associated with the Goddess in earlier mythology. Moreover, under the old mythical and social reality (as was still the case with the Pythoness of Greece and later the Sibyl of Rome) a woman as priestess was the vehicle for divine wisdom and revelation.

From the perspective of that earlier reality, the orders of this powerful upstart God Jehovah that Eve may not eat from a sacred tree (either of knowledge or divine wisdom or of life) would have been not only unnatural but sacrilegious. Groves of sacred trees were an integral part of the old religion. So were rites designed to induce in worshipers a consciousness receptive to the revelation of divine or mystical truths—rites in which women officiated as priestesses of the Goddess.

So in terms of the old reality, Jehovah had no right to give such orders. But having been given them, neither Eve nor the serpent, as representatives of the Goddess, could be expected to obey.

But while this part of the story of the Fall only makes sense in terms of the old reality, the rest makes sense only in terms of the power politics of imposing a dominator society. For like the later transformation of the horned bull (another ancient symbol associated with the worship of the Goddess) into the horned and hoofed devil of Christian iconography, the transformation of the ancient symbol of oracular wisdom into a symbol of satanic evil and the blaming of woman for all the misfortunes of humanity were political expedients. They were deliberate reversals of reality as it had formerly been perceived.

Directed to the original audience for the Bible—the people of Canaan, who would still have remembered the terrible punishments inflicted on their ancestors by the men who brought with them the new gods of war and thunder—the horrible consequences of Eve's disobedience of Jehovah's orders were more than just an allegory about humanity's "sinfulness." They were a clear warning to avoid the still persistent worship of the Goddess.

The "sin" of Eve when she defied Jehovah and herself dared to go to the source of knowledge was in essence her refusal to give up that worship. And because she—the first and symbolic woman—clung to the old faith more tenaciously than did Adam, who only followed her lead, her punishment was to be more dreadful. Henceforth, she would have to submit in all things. Not only her sorrow, but her conception— the number of children she must bear—would be greatly multiplied.[39] And for all eternity she was now to be ruled by this vengeful God and his earthly representative, man.

Beyond this, the vilification of the serpent and the association of woman with evil were a means of discrediting the Goddess. And indeed, the most revealing example of how the Bible served to establish and maintain a reality of male dominance, hierarchism, and war is not how it dealt with the serpent. Even more revealing—and, as we will see in the chapter that follows, unique—is how the men who wrote the Bible dealt with the Goddess herself.[40]

CHAPTER 7

Reality Stood on Its Head:
Part II

At first the invaders were simply marauding bands that killed and plundered. In Old Europe, for example, the abrupt disappearance of established cultures coincides with the first appearance of Kurgan chieftain tombs.[1] And in the Bible we read how whole cities were routinely burnt to the ground and how works of art—including the conquered people's most sacred images, the "heathen idols" biblical scholars tell us about—were melted down into gold for easier transport.[2]

But after a while, the new overlords themselves began to change. They—and their sons and grandsons, and in turn, *their* sons and grandsons—adopted some of the more advanced technologies, values, and ways of life of the conquered populations. They settled and often took local women for wives. Like the Mycenaean overlords in Crete and King Solomon in Canaan, they became more interested in the "finer" things in life. They built palaces for themselves and commissioned works of art.

And so gradually, after each succeeding wave of invasions, the momentum toward greater technological and cultural refinement and complexity reasserted itself. Each time, after some period of cultural regression, the interrupted course of civilization resumed. But civilization now took a very different turn. For if the men on top were to maintain their positions of dominance, there was one aspect of the earlier culture that could not be absorbed. This aspect or, more properly, complex of aspects was the sexually and socially equalitarian and peaceful core of the earlier partnership model of society.

The Rerouting of Civilization

The continuation of two systems—a dominator one superimposed on the earlier partnership one—entailed too great a risk that the older system, with all its appeal to people hungering for peace and freedom from oppression, might regain its strength. The older socioeconomic system, in which the heads of the matrilineal clans held the land as trustees for the people, was thus a constant threat.

To consolidate the power of the new ruling elites, these women would have to be stripped of their decision-making powers. At the same time, priestesses would have to be stripped of spiritual authority. And patriliny would have to replace matriliny even among the conquered peoples—as it in fact did, in Old Europe, in Anatolia, in Mesopotamia, and in Canaan, where women were now increasingly viewed as male-controlled technologies of production and reproduction rather than as independent, leading members of the community.

But not only were women removed from their former positions of responsibility and power. Just as critically, as new technological advances were made, these too were used to consolidate and maintain a socioeconomic system based on ranking.

As is characteristic of dominator societies, technologies of destruction were now given highest priority. Not only were the strongest and most brutal men highly honored and rewarded for their technical prowess in conquering and pillaging; material resources were also now increasingly channeled into ever more sophisticated and lethal weaponry. Precious stones, pearls, emeralds, and rubies were embedded in the hilts of shields and swords. And though the chains with which conquerors dragged their prisoners behind them were still made of base metals, even the chariots of these more cultivated warlords, kings, and emperors were fashioned of silver and gold.

As technological evolution picked up again, following the standstill or regression of invasion times, the quantity of goods and other material accumulations increased. But their distribution changed. Crete had stressed public works and a good standard of living for all. Now, as better technologies increased the production of material goods, the bulk of this new wealth was appropriated by the men on top with only the leftovers for their subjects.

Social evolution, too, resumed its upward thrust, and political, economic, and religious institutions continued to become more complex. But as new specializations and administrative functions were required by new technologies, these also were taken over by the strongman conquerors and their descendants.

In the typical pattern for this takeover, these men first attained positions of dominance by destroying and appropriating the wealth of conquered territories rather than by creating new wealth. Then, as greater technological and social complexity created the need for new roles in the production and administration of wealth, these were also appropriated. The most advantageous and lucrative roles were retained by the men in power; the rest were distributed to those among their subjects who best served and obeyed them. These included, for example, the new lucrative positions of tribute collector (and later tax-collector) as well as other bureaucratic positions that gave their holders not only power and prestige but also wealth.[3]

The prestigious and remunerative new roles would certainly *not* be given to the heads of the matrilineal clans or the priestesses who still clung to the old ways. Instead, as we see in the records of Sumerian cities like Elam, all the new social roles and specializations of any power or status—and increasingly also the old ones—were systematically transferred from women to men.[4]

For now force and the threat of force determined who controlled the channels of economic distribution. Ranking was the established principle of social organization. Beginning with the ranking of the physically stronger male half of humanity over the female half, all human relations would conform to this mold.

Still, force could not be constantly used to exact obedience. It had to be established that the old powers that ruled the universe—as symbolized by the life-giving Chalice—had been replaced by newer and more powerful deities in whose hands the Blade was now supreme. And to this end one thing above all had to be accomplished: not only her earthly representative—woman—but the Goddess herself had to be pulled down from her exalted place.

In some Middle Eastern myths this is accomplished by a story of how the Goddess is slain. In others she is subdued and humiliated by being raped. For instance, the first mention of the powerful Sumerian god Enlil in Middle Eastern mythology is associated with the rape of the Goddess Ninlil. Such tales served a very important social purpose. They both symbolized and justified the imposition of male dominance.

Another common device was to reduce the Goddess to the subordinate status of consort (wife) of a more powerful male god. Still another was to transform her into a martial deity. For example, in Canaan we find the bloodthirsty Ishtar, both revered and feared as a goddess of war. Similarly, in Anatolia the Goddess was also transformed into a martial deity, a feature which, as E. O. James notes, is entirely absent in earlier texts.[5]

At the same time, many of the functions formerly associated with female deities were reassigned to gods. For example, as the cultural anthropologist Ruby Rohrlich-Leavitt points out, "When the patron of the scribes changed from a goddess to a god, only male scribes were employed in the temples and palaces, and history began to be written from an androcentric perspective."[6]

But though Canaan, like Mesopotamia, had already for some time been moving toward a dominator society, there is no question that the invasions of the thirteen Hebrew tribes not only accelerated, but also radicalized, this process of social and ideological transformation. For only in the Bible is the Goddess as a divine power entirely absent.

The Absence of the Goddess

This absolute denial that the feminine—and thus woman—partakes of divinity is remarkable in light of the fact that so much of Hebrew mythology was drawn from earlier Mesopotamian and Canaanite myths. It is even more remarkable in light of the archaeological evidence showing that long after the Hebrew invasions the people of Canaan, including the Hebrews themselves, continued to worship the Goddess.

As the biblical scholar Raphael Patai writes in his book *The Hebrew Goddess*, archaeological finds leave "no doubt that to the very end of the Hebrew monarchy the worship of the old Canaanite gods was an integral part of the religion of the Hebrews." Moreover, "the worship of the goddess played a much more important role in this popular religion than that of the gods."[7] For example, in the mound of Tell Beit Mirsim (the biblical town of Devir to the southwest of modern Hebron), the most common religious objects found in the later Bronze levels (twenty-first to thirteenth centuries B.C.E.) were the so-called Astarte figurines or plaques. But even after the town was rebuilt following its destruction during the Hebrew invasion of circa 1300–1200 B.C.E., as Patai notes, "The archeological evidence leaves no doubt that these figurines were very popular among the Hebrews."[8]

There are, of course, some allusions to this in the Bible itself. The Prophets Ezra, Hosea, Nehemiah, and Jeremiah constantly rail against the "abomination" of worshiping other gods. They are particularly outraged at those who still worship "the Queen of Heaven."[9] And their greatest wrath is against the "unfaithfulness of the daughters of Jerusalem," who were understandably "backsliding" to beliefs in which all temporal and spiritual authority was not monopolized by men. But other than such occasional, and always pejorative, passages, there is no hint that there ever was—or could be—a deity that is not male.

Be it as the god of thunder, of the mountain, or of war, or later on as the more civilized God of the prophets, there is here only one God: the "jealous" and inscrutable Jehovah, who in later Christian mythology sends his only divine Son, Jesus Christ, to die and thereby atone for his human children's "sins." And although the Hebrew word *Elohim* has both feminine and masculine roots (incidently explaining how in the first creation story in Genesis both woman and man could be created in Elohim's image), all the other appellations of the deity, such as King, Lord, Father, and Shepherd, are specifically male.[10]

If we read the Bible as normative social literature, the absence of the Goddess is the single most important statement about the kind of social order that the men who over many centuries wrote and rewrote this religious document strove to establish and uphold. For symbolically the absence of the Goddess from the officially sanctioned Holy Scriptures was the absence of a divine power to protect women and avenge the wrongs inflicted upon them by men.

This is not to say that the Bible does not contain important ethical precepts and mystical truths, or that Judaism as it later evolved did not also make positive contributions to Western history. Indeed, even though it is increasingly apparent that they are rooted in older wisdoms, much in Western civilization that is humane and just was derived from the teachings of the Hebrew prophets. For example, many of the teachings of Isaiah, from which many of the later teachings of Jesus derived, are designed for a partnership rather than a dominator society. Nonetheless, interlaced with what is humane and uplifting, much of what we find in the Judeo-Christian Bible is a network of myths and laws designed to impose, maintain, and perpetuate a dominator system of social and economic organization.[11]

Like the Kurgans, who several millennia earlier overran Old Europe, the Hebrew tribes that swept into Canaan from the deserts of the south were peripheral invaders who brought with them their god of war: the fierce and jealous Yahweh, or Jehovah. They were more technologically and culturally advanced than the Kurgans, but like the Indo-Europeans, they too were dominated by extremely violent and warlike men. In passage after passage of the Old Testament we read how Jehovah gives orders to destroy, plunder, and kill—and how in fact these orders are faithfully carried out.[12]

Hebrew tribal society, like that of Kurgans and other Indo-Europeans, was also extremely hierarchic, ruled from the top by the tribe of Moses, the Levites. Superimposed on them was an even smaller elite. This was the family of Konath or Cohen, the hereditary priests descending from Aaron, who were the ultimate authorities. As we read in the Old Testament, the men of this clan claimed their powers directly from Jehovah. Moreover, what biblical scholars tell us is that it was this priestly elite that most likely carried out a good part of the job of rewriting myth and history to solidify their dominant position.[13]

Finally—completing and buttressing the dominator society configuration of violence, authoritarianism, and male dominance—is the Old Testament's explicit proclamation that it is God's will that woman be ruled by man. For like that of the Kurgans and the other Indo-European invaders that wreaked such havoc in Europe and Asia Minor, ancient Hebrew tribal society was a rigidly male-dominated system.

Once again, it is imperative to stress that by no stretch of the imagination is this meant to imply that the religion of the ancient Hebrews—much less Judaism—is to blame for the imposition of a dominator ideology. The shift from a partnership to a dominator reality began long before the Hebrew invasions of Canaan and was going on simultaneously in many parts of the ancient world. Moreover, Judaism goes far beyond the Old Testament in its conceptions of deity and morality, and in the mystical tradition of the Shekhina it actually retained many of the elements of the old worship of the Goddess.

As we have seen, the worship of the Goddess was in fact widespread in the Hebrew peoples' religion well into monarchic times. There were also occasional women, such as the prophetess and judge Deborah, who still rose to positions of leadership. But, by and large, ancient Hebrew society was run from the top by a small elite of men. Most critically, as we can still read in the Old Testament, the laws fashioned by this male ruling caste defined women, not as free and independent human beings, but as the private property of men. First they were to belong to their fathers. Later on, they were to be owned by their husbands or their masters, as were any children they bore.

We know from the Bible that girl children and women of conquered city-states who, as our King James Bible puts it, had not "known a man by lying with him" were regularly enslaved in accordance with Jehovah's commands.[14] We also read in the Old Testament of indentured

servants, what the King James Bible calls menservants and maidservants, and how the law provided that a man could sell his daughter
as a maidservant. Most tellingly, when a manservant was set free, according to biblical law his wife and her children remained behind—
the master's property.[15]

But it was not only that maidservants, concubines, and their offspring were male property. The well-known story of Abraham setting
out to sacrifice his and Sarah's son Isaac to Jehovah dramatically illustrates that even the children of lawful wives were under men's absolute
control. And, as the famous story of how Jacob purchased his wife
Leah by working seven years for her father illustrates, essentially so
were all women.

Sex and Economics

Perhaps nowhere is this dehumanized view of women so clear as
from a careful reading of the mass of biblical prescriptions and proscriptions we have all been taught are intended to protect women's
virtue. For example, in Deuteronomy 22:28–29 we read, "If a man find
a damsel that is a virgin, which is not betrothed, and lay hold on her,
and lie with her and they be found; then the man that lay with her
shall give unto the damsel's father fifty shekels of silver, and she shall
be his wife." The impression we have been given is that this kind of
law represented a great advancement, a moral and humane step forward in the civilization of immoral and sinful heathens. But if we look
at this law objectively, in the social and economic context in which it
was enacted, it is evident that it did not stem from any moral or humane considerations. Rather, it was designed to protect men's property
rights in "their" wives and daughters.

What this law says is that since an unmarried girl who is not a virgin
is no longer an economically valuable asset, her father must be com-
pensated. As for the legal requirement that the man who caused this
economic problem marry the girl, in a society where husbands had
practically unlimited power over their wives, such a forced marriage
can hardly be said to stem from any concern for the girl's welfare. This
punishment too is concerned with male economics: since the girl is
now a worthless commodity with no further market value, it would
not be "fair" to continue to saddle her father with her. She has to be
acquired by the man who caused her to lose her value.

The real purpose of this whole system of "moral" sexual customs
and laws is even more brutally demonstrated in Deuteronomy 22:13–

21. These verses deal with the case of a man who alleges that since he has discovered his bride is not a virgin he "hateth her" and wishes to get rid of her. The legal remedies provided in the Bible to deal with this kind of situation are as follows: If the wife's parents can produce "the tokens of the damsel's virginity" and "spread the cloth before the elders of the city," the husband has to pay the bride's father one hundred silver shekels. And he may not send his wife back to her parents as long as she lives. But if the bride's virginity is not satisfactorily established, the husband can indeed get rid of her. For the law required that "they shall bring out the damsel to the door of her father's house, and the men of her city shall stone her with stones that she die."

We are informed in the Bible that there is a good reason for the killing of a woman who was not a virgin when she marries. This is that "she has wrought folly in Israel to play the whore in her father's house." Translated into contemporary language, she is to be killed as punishment for bringing dishonor, not only to her father, but to her larger family, the twelve tribes of Israel. Only what does this dishonor consist of? What injury or damage did the loss of the girl's virginity actually cause her people and her father?

The answer is that a woman who behaves as a sexually and economically free person *is* a threat to the entire social and economic fabric of a rigidly male-dominated society. Such behavior cannot be countenanced lest the entire social and economic system fall apart. Hence the "necessity" for the strongest social and religious condemnation and the most extreme punishment.

On a very practical level, these laws regulating women's virginity were designed to protect what were essentially economic transactions between men. By requiring compensation to the father if the accusation against the woman was proven false, the law provided a punishment for falsely slandering the man's reputation as an honest merchant. It also offered the father a further protection. If the accusation was untrue, the merchandise in question (his daughter) could now never be returned. On the other hand, by having the men of the city stone his daughter to death if the accusation *was* true, the law also protected the father. Since the dishonored bride could not be resold, provision was made for the destruction of this now economically worthless asset. Similarly, biblical adultery laws, requiring that both the adulterer and adulteress be killed, provided for the punishment of a thief (the man who has "stolen" another man's property) and the destruction of a damaged asset (the wife who has brought "dishonor" to her husband).

But the men who made the rules that would maintain this socio-economic order did not talk in such crass economic terms. Instead, they said their edicts were not only moral, righteous, and honorable but the word of God. And to this day, having been brought up to think of our sacred Scriptures as the product of divine, or at least moral, wisdom, it is hard for us to objectively look at the Bible and see the full significance of a religion in which the supreme, and only, deity is male.

We have been taught that the Judeo-Christian tradition is the greatest moral advance of our species. The Bible is indeed primarily concerned with what is right and wrong. But what is right and wrong in a dominator society is not the same as what is right and wrong in a partnership society. There are, as already noted, many teachings in both Judaism and Christianity suitable for a partnership system of human relations. But to the extent that it reflects a dominator society, biblical morality is at best stunted. At worst, it is a pseudomorality in which the will of God is a device for covering up cruelty and barbarity.

In Numbers 31, for example, we read of what happened after the fall of Midian. Having slain all the adult males, the ancient Hebrew invaders "took all the women of Midian captives, and their little ones." And now they were told by Moses that this was the command of the Lord: "Kill every male among the little ones and every woman who hath known man by lying with him, but all the women children that have not known a man by lying with him, keep alive for yourselves."[16]

As we often read in the Bible, God's command was a punishment. A plague that broke out after the victory was, according to Moses, the fault of these captured women. But even this would not account for why God would command that "all the women children that have not known a man" were to be kept "alive for yourselves." What *would* account for it is the recognition by the men of the ruling castes that though the men they commanded would be willing to kill the older women and boys, they would be very reluctant to destroy their booty of virgin women-children. For these could be sold for concubines, slaves, and even wives.

Dominator Morality

So effectively has the imposition of a dominator morality been that even today men and women who think of themselves as good, moral people are able to read passages like this without questioning how a just and righteous God could order such horrible and inhuman acts. Nor do they seem to question the morality of some of the Muslim men who, even in our own time, for any real or imagined sexual infraction, consider it their duty to "protect women's virtue" by threatening to kill—even killing—their own daughters, sisters, wives, and grand-daughters. Neither do they question why precepts that, in their own eyes as well as in the eyes of men generally, strip the female half of humanity of any value unless they are sexually "pure" should still be respectfully termed "morality."

For once we ask these questions, ours is no longer the kind of mind needed for a dominator society, in which our moral development can go only so far and no farther. And so, through the processes of systems replication now being uncoverd by scientists like Vilmos Csanyi, millions of people still today seem incapable of perceiving what our sacred literature really says, and how it functions to maintain the boundaries that keep us imprisoned in a dominator system.

Perhaps the most striking example of this systems-induced blindness concerns the biblical treatment of rape. In the Book of Judges, chapter 19, the priests who wrote the Bible tell us of a father who offers his virgin daughter to a drunken mob. He has a male guest in his house, a man from the high-caste tribe of Levites. A bunch of rowdies from the tribe of Benjamin demand to see him outside, apparently with the intention of beating him up. "Behold," the father says to them, "here is my daughter, a maiden, and his [the guest's] concubine; them I will bring out now, and humble ye them, and do with them what seemeth good unto you, but unto this man do not so vile a thing."[17]

We are told this casually, as a matter of little importance. Then, as the story unfolds, we are further told how "the man took his concubine, and brought her forth unto them, and they knew her, and abused her all night until the morning"; how she crawled back to the threshold of the house where "her lord" was sleeping; how when he woke up "and opened the door of the house, and went out to go his way" he stumbled on her and commanded, "Up, and let us be going"; and how finally, finding that she was dead, he loaded her body on his ass, and went home.[18]

Nowhere in the telling of this brutal story of the betrayal of a daughter's and a mistress's trust and the gang rape and killing of a helpless woman is there even a hint of compassion, much less moral indignation or outrage. But more significant—and mind-boggling—is that the father's offer to sacrifice what in that day was his own daughter's most precious attribute, her virginity, and possibly also her life violated no law. Even more mind-boggling is that the actions that predictably led to the gang rape, torture, and ultimately murder of a woman who was essentially the Levite's wife likewise violated no law—and this in a book full of seemingly endless prescriptions and proscriptions about what is morally and legally right and wrong.

In short, so stunted is the morality of this sacred text ostensibly setting forth divine law that here we may read that one half of humanity could legally be handed over by their own fathers and husbands to be raped, beaten, tortured, or killed without any fear of punishment—or even moral disapproval.

Even more brutal is the message of a story that to this day is regularly read as a moral parable to congregations and classes of Sunday school children all over the Western world: the famous story of Lot, who alone was spared by God when the sinful and immoral cities of Sodom and Gomorrah were destroyed. Here once again we read in Genesis 19:8 that, with the same matter-of-fact callousness, in what was apparently a widespread and socially accepted custom, Lot offers his two virgin daughters (probably still children, since girls were then married off so early) to a mob threatening two male guests in his house. Once again there is no hint of any violation of law or any expression of righteous indignation that a father should so unnaturally treat his own daughters. Quite the contrary, since Lot's two guests turn out to have been angels sent by God, when the Lord "rained upon Sodom and Gomorrah brimstone and fire" for their "perversions," for *his* perversion Lot is actually rewarded! Only he and his family are spared.[19]

From the perspective of cultural transformation theory, what may we learn from these examples of biblical morality and of the system it was designed to maintain? Clearly the morality enforcing women's sexual slavery to men was imposed to meet the economic requirements of a rigidly male-dominant system that property be transmitted from father to son and that the benefits from women's and children's labor accrue to the male. It was also imposed to meet the political and ideological requirement that the social realities of the old order in which women were sexually, economically, and politically free agents, and in which the Goddess was the supreme deity, be fundamentally reversed. For only through such a reversal could a power structure based on rigid rankings be maintained.

As we have seen, it was not coincidental that everywhere in the ancient world the imposition of male dominance was part of the shift from a peaceful and equalitarian way of organizing human society to a hierarchic and violent order ruled by brutal and greedy men. Nor, looked at from a systems perspective, is it coincidental that in the Old Testament women were excluded from their former role as priestesses, so that the religious laws that now governed society were made only by men. Also not coincidence is that the trees of knowledge and of life, once associated with the worship of the Goddess, are here presented as the private property of a supreme male deity—symbolizing, and legitimizing, the absolute life-and-death power over society of the ruling castes of men, as well as of all men over women.

Knowlege Is Bad, Birth Is Dirty, Death Is Holy

As we have seen in the Genesis account of how Adam and Eve are eternally punished for defying Jehovah's orders to stay away from the tree of knowledge, any rebellion against the authority of the ruling male priesthood—and by Jehovah's direct command, men in general— was made a heinous sin. Both authoritarianism and male dominance were here solidly justified by the same dictum that modern totalitarians and would-be totalitarians, be they of the theistic right or the atheistic left, still preach to their followers: Don't think, accept what *is*, accept what *authority* says is true. Above all, do *not* use your own intelligence, your own powers of mind, to question us or to seek independent knowledge. For if you do, your punishment will be horrible indeed.

But at the same time that disobeying authority and daring to seek independent knowledge of what is good and evil are presented as the most abhorrent of crimes, killing and enslaving one's fellow human beings and destroying and appropriating their property is, in our Bible, frequently condoned. Killing in war is in fact divinely sanctioned, as is plundering for booty, raping women and children, and razing entire cities. The death penalty for all kinds of nonviolent offenses, including sexual ones, is also presented as an instrument of divinely ordained justice. And even the premeditated murder of one brother by another is not as serious an offense as disobeying authority by eating from the tree of knowledge. For it is not Cain's killing of his own brother Abel that condemns humanity to live forever in sorrow; it is, rather, Eve's unauthorized or independent "taste" of what is evil or good.

At the same time that shedding blood by killing and injuring other human beings—in wars, in brutal punishments, and in the exercise of the male's practically absolute authority over women and children— becomes the norm, the act of giving life now becomes tainted and unclean. In the Old Testament, squeezed in between purifications concerning leprosy and clean and unclean meats, we find those concerning childbirth. Here in Leviticus 12, we read that a woman who has given birth to a child must be ritually purified lest her "uncleanness" contaminate others. This not only entails her isolation, but also payments to priests and certain ritual acts. Only after making a "sin offering unto the door of the tabernacle of the congregation unto the priest; who shall offer it before the Lord and make an atonement for her" can she once again be certified "clean."[20]

And so, first in Mesopotamia and Canaan and later in the theocracies of Judaea and Israel, warfare, authoritarian rule, and the subjugation of women become integral parts of the new dominator morality and society. Through skillful re-mything, knowledge had been made sinful. Even birth had been made dirty. In short, the rerouting of our cultural evolution was so successful that reality had been stood completely on its head.

Still, when we look back into history, even history as recorded by historians, philosophers, and priests in the service of their powerful overlords, we find the old mind—the early mind of humanity on a totally different evolutionary course—struggling to reassert itself.

The Great Goddess, whose worship was once the ideological core of a more peaceful and equalitarian society, has not completely vanished. Though she is no longer the supreme principle governing the world, she is still a force to be reckoned with—a force that even in the European Middle Ages is worshiped as the Mother of God. Despite centuries of prophetic prohibitions and priestly prohibitions, her worship has not been wholly stamped out. Like Horus and Osiris, like Helios and Dionysus, and, long before them, the young god of Catal Huyuk, and like the young goddess Persephone, or Kore, in the ancient Eleusinian Mysteries, Jesus too is still the child of a divine Mother. He is in fact still the child of the Goddess and, like her earlier divine children, symbolizes the regeneration of nature by his resurrection every spring at Easter.

Just as the son of the Goddess was once also her consort, in Christian mythology "Christ, too, is the bridegroom of Mary—Mother Church, who is and remains his mother."[21] The baptismal font, or chalice, so central to Christian rites, is still the ancient feminine symbol of the vessel or container of life, with baptism, as the Jungian historian of myth Erich Neumann writes, signifying "the return to the mysterious uterus of the Great Mother and its water of life."[22]

Even the birthday chosen for Jesus (his own is historically unknown) is now known to be the usurpation of festivals once associated with the worship of the Goddess. The time for Christmas, or Christ's mass, was chosen because this was the time of year when the ancients traditionally celebrated the winter solstice—the day the Goddess gives birth to the sun, usually falling between December 21 and 24. Also, this was the period from December 21 to January 6 (chosen for Epiphany) when a number of popular birth and renewal festivals were still celebrated in Roman times.[23]

But with all these similarities, there are fundamental differences. In the official Christian pantheon the only woman is now also the only mortal figure. She is still worshiped as the merciful and compassionate Mother. And in some of the iconography, as, for example, in the *Vierges Ouvrantes*, she still contains within her body the ultimate miracle and mystery of life.[24] But she is now clearly a minor figure. Moreover, the central mythical image of this male-dominant religion is no longer the birth of the young god. It is his crucifixion and death.

His mother only gives birth to Christ; it is his divine Father who sends him to earth: a sacrificial scapegoat to atone for human evil and sin. As with the humans he is sent to "save," his brief stay in this "vale of tears" is not what matters. It is his death and his promise of a better life after death that counts—but only for those who faithfully obey the Father's commands. For the rest, there is not even hope in death—only eternal torture and damnation.

No longer is the emphasis of religious imagery on the life-giving, life-sustaining, and life-regenerating powers of the Goddess. Gone are the flowers and birds, the animals and trees, except as background props. There is still the memory of the Goddess cradling the divine child in her arms: the Madonna and Child. But now the mind of man—and of woman—is both possessed and consumed by an overriding theme that permeates all Christian art. We see it in canvas after canvas of Christian saints tormenting their bodies with fiendish tortures, in painting after painting of Christian martyrs being slaughtered in all sorts of cruel and ingenious ways, in Dürer's gruesome visions of the Christian hell, in Michelangelo's *The Last Judgment*, in Salome endlessly dancing with John the Baptist's severed head.

Now, perhaps nowhere as poignantly as in the omnipresent theme of Christ dying on the cross, the central image of art is no longer the celebration of nature and of life but the exaltation of pain, suffering, and death.[25] For in this new reality that is now said to be the sole creation of a male God, the life-giving and nurturing Chalice as the supreme power in the universe has been displaced by the power to dominate and destroy: the lethal power of the Blade. And it is this reality that to our day afflicts all humanity—both women and men.

CHAPTER 8

The Other Half of History: Part I

Like travelers through a time warp, we have, through archaeological discoveries, journeyed into a different reality. On the other side we found not the brutal stereotypes of an eternally depraved "human nature" but amazing vistas of possibilities for a better life. We saw how in the early days of civilization our cultural evolution was truncated and then completely turned around. We saw how when our social and technological evolution resumed it was in a different direction. But we also saw how the old roots of civilization were never eradicated.

The old love for life and nature and the old ways of sharing rather than taking away, of caring for rather than oppressing, and the view of power as responsibility rather than domination did not die out. But, like women and qualities associated with femininity, they were relegated to a secondary place.

Neither did the human yearning for beauty, truth, justice, and peace disappear. Rather, it was submerged and suppressed by the new social order. The old yearning would still occasionally struggle for expression. But increasingly it would be without any clear sense that the underlying problem was a way of structuring human relations (beginning with the relation between the two halves of humanity) into rigid, force-based rankings.

So successful had the transformation of reality been that this seemingly self-evident fact—that the way a society structures the most fundamental of human relations profoundly affects all aspects of living and thinking—was in time almost totally obscured. As a result, even our complex modern languages, with technical terms for everything one can and cannot imagine, have no gender-specific words to describe the profound difference between what we have until now called a dominator and a partnership society.

At best, we have words like *matriarchy* to describe the opposite of patriarchy. But these words only reinforce the prevailing view of reality (and "human nature") by describing two sides of the same coin. Moreover, by bringing to mind emotion-laden and conflicting images of tyrannical fathers and wise old men, patriarchy does not even accurately describe our present system.

Partnership and *dominator* are useful terms to describe the two contrasting principles of organization we have been examining. But though they capture an essential difference, they do not specifically convey one critical point: there are two contrasting ways of structuring the relations between the female and male halves of humanity that profoundly affect the totality of a social system.

We are now at the point where for both clarity and economy of communication we need more precise terms than those offered by our conventional vocabulary in order to continue probing how these two alternatives affect our cultural, social, and technological evolution. We are also about to take a close look at the civilization of ancient Greece, which was noted for the first precise expression of scientific thinking. The two new terms I propose, and will in certain contexts be using as alternatives to dominator and partnership, draw from this precedent.

For a more precise term than *patriarchy* to describe a social system ruled through force or the threat of force by men, I propose the term *androcracy*. Already in some use, this term derives from the Greek root words *andros*, or "man," and *kratos* (as in *democratic*), or "ruled."

To describe the real alternative to a system based on the ranking of half of humanity over the other, I propose the new term *gylany*.[1] *Gy* derives from the Greek root word *gyne*, or "woman." *An* derives from *andros*, or "man." The letter *l* between the two has a double meaning. In English, it stands for the *linking* of both halves of humanity, rather than, as in androcracy, their ranking. In Greek, it derives from the verb *lyein* or *lyo*, which in turn has a double meaning: to solve or resolve (as in ana*l*ysis) and to dissolve or set free (as in cata*l*ysis). In this sense, the letter *l* stands for the resolution of our problems through the freeing of both halves of humanity from the stultifying and distorting rigidity of roles imposed by the domination hierarchies inherent in androcratic systems.

This leads to a critical distinction between two very different kinds of hierarchies that is not made in conventional usage. As used here, the term *hierarchy* refers to systems of human rankings based on force or the threat of force. These *domination hierarchies* are very different from a second type of hierarchy, which I propose be called *actualization hierarchies*. These are the familiar hierarchies of systems within systems, for examples, of molecules, cells, and organs of the body: a progression toward a higher, more evolved, and more complex level of function. By contrast, as we may see all around us, domination hierarchies characteristically inhibit the actualization of higher functions, not only in the overall social system, but also in the individual human. This is a major reason that a gylanic model of social organization opens up far greater evolutionary possibilities for our future than an androcratic one.

Our Hidden Heritage

It seems particularly fitting to use terms of Greek derivation to describe how these two contrasting social models have affected our cultural evolution. For the conflict between gylany and androcracy as two very different ways of living on this earth—and the advancement of our evolution through gylanic influences—is dramatically illustrated if we take a fresh look at ancient Greece from the new perspective offered by cultural transformation theory.

Most courses on Western civilization start with readings from Homer, selections from Greek philosophers like Pythagoras, Socrates, Plato, and Aristotle, and works by modern classical historians extolling the glories of Pericles' Golden Age of Greece. We are taught that European history begins with the earliest known records of Indo-European or Aryan culture (Homer and Hesiod) and that we owe many of our modern ideas about justice and democracy to the remarkable civilization of classical Greece.

Occasionally, browsing through supplementary readings, we may find out that Pythagoras was taught ethics by a certain Themistoclea, a priestess of Delphi, or that Diotema, a priestess of Mantinea, taught Socrates.[2] We might even stumble across the seemingly curious information that leaders from all over the Greek world traveled to Delphi, where a priestess called the Pythoness advised them on the most important social and political questions of their time. But for the most part, women are hardly mentioned in what we read. Nor is there usually any mention of Crete.

In fact, we are left with the impression that there was no earlier European civilization; that until the arrival of its Indo-European conquerors Europe was inhabited by savage peoples with no significant culture of any kind. We are also led to believe that when the first flowering of European civilization occurred in Greece, by and large women had no civil or political rights, and certainly no positions of power.

Yet in Homer's *Odyssey* some of the most powerful figures are female. When the action opens, Odysseus is being detained by the nymph Calypso, who rules the island of Ogygia. When, after the intervention of the Goddess Athene, Odysseus finally gets to leave Ogygia there is a storm, and he is saved from drowning by a veil that the Goddess Ino gives him. This buoys him up until he is washed ashore to the land of the Phaecians, where he is found by the princess Nausicaa.

In the magnificent Phaecian court, considered by many scholars an accurate portrait of Mycenaean royal houses, Nausicaa's mother, Queen Arete, is honored by the king "as no other woman is honored" and worshiped by "all the folk, who look upon her as a goddess . . . when she goes about the town."[3] After Odysseus leaves Phaecia, he is again confronted by a formidable contingent of female figures: the terrible gorgons Scylla and Charybdis, the seductive Sirens, and the powerful queen-sorceress Circe.

Even upon his return home we find that Penelope, his wife, is a strong and determined woman. Significantly, she is resisting a mass of suitors who would marry her to gain control over Ithaca—strongly suggesting that even after the Achaean invasions of Greece, matrilineal succession was still the norm, as well as the prerequisite to any claim of rulership.[4]

We have already seen that Hesiod's references to a "golden race" who lived "in peaceful ease" and to whom "the fruitful earth poured forth her fruits" are memories of the more peaceful and equalitarian farming peoples of the Neolithic who were even by this time remembered only in legend. The fact that in Hesiod's mythology a male figure named Chaos is credited with the creation of the world further confirms what we now know from the archaeological record: Indo-European rule was imposed through the chaos of massive physical destruction and cultural disruption.

Like Homer's, Hesiod's work is full of remnants of an earlier, more gylanic society and mythology. For example, it is still "wide-bosomed Earth" who, like the Goddess of old, gives birth to Heaven and "the lofty hills, the happy haunts of goddess nymphs." And it is still, as in the older religion, a female power who "without sweet union of love"— in other words, alone—bears the sea.[5]

Hesiod's world is already male dominated, warlike, and hierarchic.

But it is still a world in which the old partnership or, more specifically, gylanic values are not completely forgotten. For Hesiod war is not inherent in human nature—or, as the later Greek philosopher Heraclitus was to assert, "the father of all" and "king of all."[6] Hesiod explicitly writes that war and the war god Ares were brought to Greece by a "lesser race of men," the Achaeans who invaded Greece with bronze weapons, and who were eventually followed by the men most despised by Hesiod, the Dorians, who laid waste to Greece with their weapons of iron.

One could say that if Freud and Jung were right, and there is such a thing as a genetically transmitted race memory, it might be what prompted Hesiod to write about a better and lost past. But a far more likely explanation is simply that Hesiod was still under the influence of stories handed down from generation to generation about the way things once were.

It is revealing that Hesiod explicitly states: "Not from me, but from my mother, comes the tale of how earth and sky were once one form."[7] This not only suggests that his work is indeed based on stories handed down from generation to generation; it indicates that his mother, a woman, still found some solace in her now male-dominated world through the fading memories of an earlier and less oppressive time.

Hesiod wrote toward the end of what historians call the Greek Dark Age. This period ended with the emergence of classical Greece a half millennium after the Dorian invasions plunged Europe into chaos. But clearly, as Nicolas Platon, Jacquetta Hawkes, J. V. Luce, and others have pointed out, Greek civilization did not spring up full-grown out of the ashes of the Dorian devastation of Europe—as Athene supposedly did out of the head of Zeus. Nor would these barbarian invaders have brought with them the seeds of this civilization. Neither is it likely, as is sometimes asserted, that Greek civilization was mainly the result of "cultural diffusion," of "borrowings" from older and more advanced Middle Eastern cultures through trade and other contacts.

What is much more likely and more congruent with the archaeological data is something else: the earlier Achaean invaders who ruled in Mycenaean times, as well as the Dorian overlords who displaced them, were able to move forward only after they had absorbed much of the material and spiritual culture of the peoples they conquered.

Luce has tried to reconstruct this process. "Like a fire-ravaged olive tree, Minoan culture went dormant for a time," he writes, "and then sent up fresh shoots in the shades of the Mycenaean citadels. . . . Minoan princesses, the 'daughters of Atlas,' married into the houses of

Mycenaean war-lords. Minoan architects designed the mainland palaces, and Minoan painters adorned them with frescoes. Greek first became a written language in the hands of Minoan scribes."[8]

Then, after the next barbarian onslaught, albeit in still more altered form, these same Minoan shoots came up once again. "It is probably no accident," Luce writes, "that Dorian Crete in the Archaic period was noted for the excellence of its laws and institutions. The stock that had been tended so lovingly through the long peaceful centuries was not to be easily eradicated. Grafts from the same stock were transplanted to Greece itself, and took root and flourished there too."[9]

So even after the Dorian devastation, as Luce writes, "not everything was lost."[10] Certainly much is forgotten, as now even the memory of Minoan civilization begins to fade into legend. And much is changed, as the Great Goddess—in such forms as Hera, Athene, and Aphrodite—is now subordinate to Zeus in the official Greek pantheon. Nonetheless, there are still important elements of Greek civilization that better fit a partnership than a dominator society. Or, to use more specific terms, they are more *gylanic* than *androcratic*.

The Cyclic Unity of Nature and the Harmony of the Spheres

One of the first manifestations of Greek civilization was the emergence of the so-called pre-Socratic philosophers and scientists. It has been pointed out that their worldview (which foreshadowed ideas many people still today consider shocking and controversial) was the first known secular, scientific approach to reality.[11] For here, for the first time in recorded history, knowledge is no longer described as a function of divine revelation through sacred myths and religious rites but of empirically provable and disprovable facts. For example, in Homer the rainbow is still identified with the Goddess Iris. In Anaximenes, it is produced by the rays of the sun falling on dense, moist air.[12]

In this respect, the ideas of pre-Socratic philosophers like Xenophanes, Thales, Diogenes, and Pythagoras certainly represented a sharp break from the earlier religious worldview. But the extraordinary thing is that in many ways the fundamental assumptions of these men are more congruent with the earlier, more gylanic worldview than with the later androcratic one.

For example, Xenophanes is said to be the first source of what the philosophical historian Edward Hussey calls the "radical monotheism so foreign to the traditional Greek religion."[13] Hussey points out that

Xenophanes' idea that the universe is ruled by one all-encompassing and infinite intelligence is in sharp contrast with the worldview expressed in the official Olympian pantheon. Here an unpredictable and often armed multiplicity of deities—remarkably like the myriad petty chieftains and kings who came in and overrran the ancient world—exercise arbitrary and capricious power over both the rhythms of nature and the lives of their human "subjects."[14] But in light of what we now know about prehistory, it could just as easily be said that it was actually this dominator or androcratic view of the universe that was "new and revolutionary," and not, as Hussey writes, the worldview underlying the political and social developments of sixth century Greece.[15]

It could also be said that it was not coincidental that as civilization began to reemerge after the Dorian onslaught, the older vision of a coherent and cyclical world order—earlier symbolized by the Great Goddess, the Mother and Giver of All—should reemerge, albeit in different form. Neither is it coincidental that this happened where it did: in cities that were part of the Anatolia where once Catal Huyuk flowered, and in islands near the once glorious civilization of Minoan Crete, where in her various aspects of Mother, Maid, and Creatrix or Ancestress the Goddess remained supreme until the Dorian takeover.[16]

Earlier we noted how Goddess worship was both polytheistic and monotheistic. The Goddess was worshiped in many forms, but these various deities had certain commonalities—notably that the Goddess as the Mother and Giver of All was everywhere seen as the source of all nature and life.[17] So in this respect the pre-Socratic idea of an orderly and coherent world order is far closer to the older vision of the Goddess as a supreme all-giving and all-encompassing superhuman power than to the view symbolized by the later Olympian pantheon, from which a group of quarrelsome, competitive, and generally unpredictable deities ruled the world.

The Pythagorean idea of the cosmos as a vast musical harmony (the famous "harmony of the spheres") also seems more congruent with the old religious cosmology than with the strife-torn Olympian pantheon. In the cosmology of the pre-Socratics, instead of the Goddess we now find more impersonal forces, with occasional references to an all-encompassing and presumably male divinity. But their world is still a far cry from the chaotic and purely random universe envisioned by some androcratic thinkers.

One of the principles governing the pre-Socratic view of the universe is that the world order behaves with observable regularity, "the principal changes repeating themselves in daily and yearly cycles."[18]

This view is strikingly reminiscent of what we may call the Old Religion, in which the cycles of nature—and of woman—are recurrent themes. Thales, who according to Aristotle was the pioneer of "natural" philosophy, is reported by Aristotle to have held that water was the origin of all things. This view is again strikingly reminiscent of the earlier idea that the Goddess, and with her the earth, originally emerged from the primeval waters.[19]

Similarly, the dialectical concept of the balancing of opposites as an essential principle of both change and stability was already being expressed in the sixth and fifth centuries B.C.E. by such philosophers as Anaximander, Zeno, and Empedocles.[20] But what can now be seen is that it seems to have been foreshadowed still earlier in the cosmological imagery of the Goddess-worshiping era.

In the decorated pottery of European Cucuteni culture from the mid-fourth millennium B.C.E., tension between pairs as well as opposites is a frequent theme.[21] The dynamism of nature and its periodic rejuvenation through the seeming opposites of death and birth was central to old religious mythology; the Goddess incarnated both the unity and the duality of life and death. The contrasting principles of motherhood and virginity were likewise fused in the Goddess.[22] Often femininity and masculinity were fused as well, both in the Goddess's earlier androgynous images and in the later ritual of the Sacred Marriage. In fact, the birth and death of all humanity, as well as all of nature, were in old religious mythology manifestations of the juxtaposition and essential unity of the creative and destructive powers of the Goddess. This all-encompassing transformative character of the earlier deity is summarized by Erich Neumann in the phrase "goddess of opposites."[23]

Because there are similarities with the ideas of Egyptian, Mesopotamian, and other Middle Eastern cultures, some scholars have tried to explain the pre-Socratic ideas as "borrowings" from these older, more advanced, and by then already predominantly dominator/androcratic civilizations. Cultural diffusion was, no doubt, a factor in the development of the pre-Socratic worldview. But the more important factor—until now, suppressed or overlooked—seems to be the influence of local tradition and legend.

Specifically, local developments seem to have led to a gradual "softening" of the protoandrocratic system. During a period of relative peace among the various Greek city-states and freedom from foreign invasions, there was not only a resurgence of arts and crafts, but also a movement toward replacing strongman kings and chieftains with oligarchic democracies (elected governments composed of aristrocratic or propertied men).

Not surprisingly then, as Hussey points out, the ideas of Greek philosophers reflected and also spurred on "the spread of political equality" as well as the re-emergence of law as "something determinate, impartial, and unchanging."[24] Certainly the Pythagorean idea of "geometric equality"[25] among both the elements of the cosmos and human beings is not congruent with the strongman rule of the new order, although in actual fact Pythagorean settlements seem to have been ruled by oligarchies along the lines of Plato's later notion of philosopher-kings.[26]

In this connection it is surely significant that we know from Aristoxenus that Pythagoras received most of his ethical lore from a woman, Themistoclea, who was a priestess at Delphi. It is also said that Pythagoras introduced ancient mysticism into Greek philosophy and even that Pythagoras was a feminist.[27] In his reform of the Orphic mystery religion Pythagoras also seems to have stressed the worship of the feminine principle.[28] And Diogenes tells us that women studied in the Pythagorean school along with men, as they did later in Plato's Academy.[29]

It is also significant that much of Platonic philosophy, as the classical historian Jane Harrison notes, is based on Pythagorean influences, as well as Orphic symbols, which preserve elements of preandrocratic religion and morality.[30] The Platonic conceptions of an orderly and harmonious ideal universe lying beyond the "dark cave" of human perception seems to come out of that same tradition. And Plato's advocacy of educational equality for women in his ideal state in the *Republic* is certainly *not* an idea congruent with androcratic thinking, in which above all else women must be suppressed.[31]

Ancient Greece

As we look back at ancient Greece, it seems clear that much of what was finest in this remarkable civilization—the great love of art, the intense interest in the processes of nature, the rich and varied feminine as well as masculine mythical symbology, as well as the brief, and limited, attempt to establish the more equalitarian form of political organization the Greeks called democracy—can be traced back to the earlier era. At the same time it is not hard now to find the source of what was less culturally advanced about the Greeks. The fact that Greek democracy excluded most of the population (giving no participation to women and slaves) was a function of the androcratic superstructure imposed upon the earlier more peaceful and more equalitarian order. And so was the Greek ruling class's preoccupation with war, their idealization of the so-called manly virtues of heroism and armed conquest, and the massive deterioration of the status of women.

We clearly see both the conflict and the interplay between the androcratic and gylanic elements of classical Greece in Athene. Reflecting the norms of the older partnership direction of cultural evolution, she is still the Goddess of wisdom, with her ancient emblem of the serpent. But at the same time, reflecting the new dominator norms, she is the new goddess of war, complete with helmet and spear, her chalice now a shield. We also see these two elements in Plato's *Republic*, with its paradoxically hierarchical and humanistic-equalitarian state.

On the one hand, Plato advocates a three-class society upheld by what he ironically called "a noble lie": the story that the ruling class or "guardians" are made of gold, the warriors of silver, and the rest (workers and peasants) of base metals. On the other hand, for the guardians this is to be an equalitarian, indeed austerely communistic, system, and their exercise of power is to be governed by equitable principles more congruent with those symbolized by the Chalice than by the Blade. And, although Plato can by no stretch of the imagination be termed a feminist, in sharp contrast to Athenian practice, he advocates in the *Republic* that the women in the ruling class be given the same education as men.

Most vividly, we see the juxtaposition of gylany and androcracy in Greek art. The old love for life and nature is expressed in exquisite renderings of both female and male bodies. But strife and armed conflict are also frequent themes.

We see further evidence of two conflicting cultures in Greek religion. Attesting to the earlier roots of Greek religion in a worldview in which women and "feminine" values are not suppressed, is the fact that in the Olympian pantheon and, even more, in local shrines female deities are still worshiped. Officially Zeus is the supreme deity. But goddesses are still powerful, sometimes more powerful than gods. We also clearly see the same cultural roots in the great Eleusinian Mysteries, celebrated each year at Eleusis, a few miles from Athens. Here the Goddess, in her twin forms of Demeter and Kore, still revealed the highest mystical truths to religious initiates. And still today we can see preserved for us on a Boeotian gold seal and a vase painting from Thebes how in these rites the ancient Feminine Vessel, the Chalice, or sacred font, was the central image.[32]

We also see the gylanic and androcratic elements of Greek society in the paradoxical situation of Athenian women, which despite great legal and social restrictions, was at least for some women significantly better than that of women in the theocracies of the Middle East. In fact, precisely because women may here have been less suppressed, there are indications there may even have been in Athens something akin to a "women's movement."

It is true that, like slaves of both sexes, all women were excluded from the celebrated Athenian democracy. Indeed, the story preserved by Augustine of how the women of Athens lost the right to vote at the same time that there was a shift from matriliny to patriliny indicates that the imposition of androcracy marked the end of true democracy.[33] Moreover, by classical times, most upper-class women had to live in the unhealthy and stultifying confinement of the gynecaeum, or women's quarters. But there is also evidence that in this same Athens— where among the Greek city-states, as the cultural historian Jacquetta Hawkes writes, women's "position was worst (or only most grumbled at?)"—some women played important roles in intellectual and public life.[34] For example, Aspasia, the companion of Pericles, worked both as a scholar and as a statesperson, supporting the education of Athenian housewives and in general helping to create the remarkable civic culture historians call "Pericles' Golden Age."[35]

Although the much celebrated Athenian education was generally limited to men, as we noted earlier, there were women who studied in Plato's Academy. This is particularly revealing of the strong partnership/gylanic strain in Greek culture if we consider that in the United States women did not gain access to higher education until the nineteenth and early twentieth centuries.

Just as revealing is that there were, in various periods of Greek history, women whose works were still to be found in the "pagan" libraries that were later destroyed by Christian and Muslim zealots. For example, a Greek woman said to have studied in the Pythagorean school, the philosopher Arignote, edited a book called *Sacred Discourse* and was the author of *Rites of Dionysus* and other works.[36] There is some speculation that the *Odyssey* may have been written by a woman. There is even evidence that women headed philosophical schools of their own. One of these was the school of Arete of Cyrene, whose major interest was natural science and ethics and whose primary concern was a "world in which there would be neither masters nor slaves."[37] Telesila of Argos was known for political songs and hymns. Corinna of Boeotia, Pindar's teacher, according to the women's histo-

rian Elise Boulding, "won five times over him in poetic competition."
And Erinna was called by the ancients the equal of Homer.

From the few fragments of her work that survived, we know that
the Greek poet Sappha or Sappho of Lesbos (who also ran a school for
women) wrote beautiful poetry, extolling love rather than, as in so
much of Greek poetry, war. "Some say cavalry and others claim in-
fantry or a fleet of long oars is the supreme sight on the black earth,"
she wrote. "I say it is the one you love."[38]

For some Greek women, the profession of *hetaera* offered a more
independent and relatively respected alternative to the subordinate role
of wife. Although *hetaerae* have been erroneously equated with pros-
titutes, this was not the view of ancient Greeks. *Hetaerae* were more
like the courtesans who in seventeenth- and eighteenth-century Europe
often wielded significant political power. They were skilled entertainers
and hostesses, with varying degrees of education and cultural interest.
But what is most interesting are the records of *hetaerae* who were scholars and even leading public figures. "The hetaerae from the city-states
of Ionia and Aetolia were considered the most brilliant," writes Boulding. "Two of Plato's best known pupils were Lashenia of Mantua and
Axiothea."[39] Aspasia, who contributed so much to Athenian culture, is
believed to have been a *hetaera*.

Perhaps most significant is the evidence for something in ancient
Greece that bespeaks a movement to return to a social organization in
which the two halves of humanity are no longer ranked—something
perhaps akin to a women's liberation movement. This is bitingly
recorded in misogynistic satires by men like Aristophanes and Cratinus
about women who meet in groups and talk in unseemly ways indicating their "wanting to be like men."[40] It is indeed likely that women
who met regularly and frequently at religious celebrations and gath-
erings for women only, where they honored a female deity, would
have retained a strong sense of female identity. Thus, well into classical
times many Greek women had a source of empowerment, something
women have lacked in most Western cultures, in which the Goddess
was eventually driven underground or completely expunged.

Of equal interest are the indications of antiwar activism by women
in ancient Greece. What may have been an organized movement for
peace, much in tune with the peace movement in our own time, is
recorded most tellingly for us in surviving Greek plays like Aristophanes' famous *Lysistrata*, in which the women threaten to withhold
their sexual favors until the men cease their wars. That this theme was
developed into an entire play by this extremely popular comic play-

wright is an indication both of the probable strength of the movement and of a strategy still typical of male-dominant societies in our time: maintaining male control over women through the use of ridicule and trivialization.

This device of trivializing—indeed, the even more common device of simply not including data about women—has been characteristic of most Greek histories. Here, as in our histories of everywhere else, anything associated with women is, ipso facto, secondary—or more often, simply not counted at all. Conventional historians have, accordingly, consistently ignored the activities of women working for a just and humane society. But in fact after fact now being uncovered, our lost history shows these activities of women to be extremely significant. For, as we will later examine in more detail, they show that in Greece, and elsewhere, given even half a chance, women actively worked to make "feminine" values such as peace and creativity operational social priorities.

Like the absence of gender-specific terms such as *gylany* and *androcracy* from the vocabulary of historians, the systematic omission of women from accounts of our past serves to maintain a system founded on male-female ranking. It reinforces the central tenet of male dominance: women are not as important as men. By omitting any hint that "women's issues" are central to our social and ideological organization, it also effectively serves to conceal the social alternatives described by gylany and androcracy.

If, however, we look at history from a gender-holistic perspective, we can begin to see the hidden conflict between gylany and androcracy as two ways of living on this earth. Then the relatively greater freedom of some Greek women, as compared to women in the theocracies of the Middle East, can be seen as an important social indicator. It can, for example, be seen as both a cause and an effect of the persistence, and resurgence, in Greece of the more humanistic view of political power as responsibility for, rather than control over, that was characteristic of the preandrocratic era.

Many of our Western ideas about social justice—the ideas of liberty and democracy, for example—derive from Greek philosophers such as Socrates and Pythagoras. The conclusion that such concepts flowered from earlier gylanic roots is strengthened by the fact that both these men were taught by women. It is also revealing that both Themistoclea, who taught Pythagoras, and Diotema, who taught Socrates, were priestesses: repositories and transmitters of earlier religious and moral traditions.

But while we can see in ancient Greece many signs of gylanic re-surgence, we can also see the fierce androcratic resistance to this evolutionary thrust. The official Greek religion was in key respects a dominator religion: Zeus establishes and maintains his supremacy through acts of cruelty and barbarism, including his many rapes of both goddesses and mortal women. We have already noted how great ritual dramas of classical times like the *Oresteia* were designed to maintain and reinforce androcratic norms of male dominance and male violence. This reflected the policy of the ruling Greek elites. For no matter how "civilized" these men became, if they were to maintain their dominant positions they could not afford to countenance any fundamental change in the three-way configuration of male dominance, authoritarianism, and institutionalized social violence that characterizes androcratic systems.

Androcratic Right and Wrong

Humanism could be countenanced, and even at times admired, by the men who ruled ancient Greece. But it could be allowed to go only so far and no further. In this regard, that odd and most troubling of personal events in classical Greece, the sentencing to death of the seemingly harmless old philosopher Socrates, has much to reveal. For what were the "radical" notions for which even a great philosopher like Socrates had to be condemned to death for "corrupting" Athenian youth? Significantly, they were ideas that included gylanic heresies such as equal education for women and a view of justice that frontally attacked the androcratic tenet that might makes right.

Socrates' challenge to a system of force-based rankings is powerfully expressed in Plato's *Republic*. There we find his ideas about educational equality for women, ideas still found shocking by so supposedly enlightened an eighteenth-century philosopher as Jean Jacques Rousseau. In this classic of Western philosophy, we also find Socrates' dialogue with the Sophist philosopher Glaucon. And the position articulated by Glaucon, and sharply questioned by Socrates, is that for men of the ruling class justice and law are merely matters of expedience.

The Sophists too were sometimes accused of undermining conventional morality because some of them openly rejected the Greek gods. But in this dialogue Plato shows that their philosophical teachings actually expressed the conventional morality of their time without any veneer of pretense or dissemblement.[41]

The worldview the Sophists bluntly articulated was simply that of the men who ruled Greece—as it is of the men who rule much of the world today. For the Sophists went beyond moral pronouncements to the political and social realities of androcratic life in which, then as now, men prove they are right by their armed might.

In the *Republic* Glaucon tells Socrates that laws are no more than the invention of the weak, who are cunning enough to see it is in their best interest to restrain the strong. As for justice, it is merely a "compromise" between "what is best of all—doing wrong and getting away with it—and what is worst—being wronged and not being able to get revenge."[42]

It is particularly revealing that this same view of the world—and of justice—is expressed in the writings of the celebrated Greek historian-general Thucydides, who chronicled the Peloponnesian War of 431 to 403 B.C.E. In Thucydides' account of a dialogue between the Athenian emissaries and the representatives of Melos, a small city-state in the Cyclades the Athenians wanted to annex, the Athenians bluntly tell the Melians they are not interested in right or wrong; their interest is only in what is expedient. For "the question of justice arises only between parties equal in strength while the strong do what they can and the weak suffer what they must."[43]

This morality of expedience, as John Mansley Robinson points out in his analysis of Greek philosophy, is founded in part on the premise that human beings are "ruthless, grasping, self-centered animals."[44] This is in turn founded on another premise: that human rankings based on force are "natural" and therefore right. According to this view, as Aristotle put it in his *Politics*, there are in nature elements meant to rule and elements meant to be ruled. In other words, the principle that *ought* to govern social organization is ranking rather than linking. And as Aristotle explicitly stated, articulating the foundations of androcratic philosophy and life, just as slaves are naturally meant to be ruled by free men, women are meant to be ruled by men. Anything else violated the observable, and therefore "natural," order.[45]

As we have seen, these same philosophical premises have also been integral to the other major tradition that has shaped Western civilization: our Judeo-Christian heritage. Here they are expressed in such Christian ideas as original sin and a religious mythology in which the ranking of God above man and man above woman, children, and nature is presented as divinely ordained.[46]

In fact, if we study Christian history we learn that the conventional word for expressing the idea of ranking, *hierarchy*, referred originally to the government of the Church. It derives from the Greek *hieros* (sacred) and *arkhia* (rule) and describes the rank orderings or levels of power through which the men who headed the Church exerted authority over their priests and over the people of Christian Europe.[47]

But there is another, very different, side to our Judeo-Christian heritage that has been the basis for an often forlorn but still persistent hope that the spiritual evolution of humanity may still one day break free from a system that has kept us mired in barbarity and oppression. This, as we shall see in the chapter that follows, is the side that two thousand years ago might have brought about a second, or gylanic, transformation in Western norms.

CHAPTER 9

The Other Half of History: Part II

Almost two thousand years ago on the shores of Lake Galilee a gentle and compassionate young Jew called Jesus denounced the ruling classes of his time—not just the rich and powerful but even the religious authorities—for exploiting and oppressing the people of Palestine. He preached universal love and taught that the meek, humble, and weak would some day inherit the earth. Beyond this, in both his words and actions he often rejected the subservient and separate position that his culture assigned women. Freely associating with women, which was itself a form of heresy in his time, Jesus proclaimed the spiritual equality of all.

Not surprisingly, according to the Bible, the authorities of his time considered Jesus a dangerous revolutionary whose radical ideas had to be silenced at all cost. How truly radical these ideas were from the perspective of an androcratic system in which the ranking of men over women is the model for all human rankings is succinctly expressed in Galatians 3:28. For here we read that for those who follow the gospel of Jesus, "there is neither Jew nor Greek, there is neither bond nor free, there is neither male nor female: for you are all one in Christ Jesus."

Some Christian theologians, such as Leonard Swidler, have asserted that Jesus was a feminist, because even from the official or "sacred" texts it is clear that he rejected the rigid segregation and subordination of women of his time.[1] But feminism has as its primary aim the liberation of women. So to call Jesus a feminist would not be historically accurate. It would seem more accurate to say that Jesus' teachings embody a gylanic view of human relations.

This view was not new and was, as we have noted, also contained in those portions of the Old Testament congruent with a partnership society. But it was obviously most forcefully—indeed, in the eyes of the religious elites of his time, heretically—articulated by this young carpenter from Galilee. For although the liberation of women was not his central focus, if we look at what Jesus preached from the new perspective of cultural transformation theory, we see a startling, and unifying, theme: a vision of the liberation of *all* humanity through the replacement of androcratic with gylanic values.

Jesus and Gylany

The writings in the New Testament attributed to disciples who had ostensibly known Jesus, the Gospels of Matthew, Mark, Luke, and John, are generally considered the best source on the "real" Jesus. Although they too were written years after Jesus died, and were undoubtedly heavily edited, they are probably still a more accurate reflection of Jesus' teachings than other portions, such as Acts or Corinthians.

Here we find that the cornerstone of dominator ideology, the masculine-superior/feminine-inferior species model is, but for a few exceptions, conspicuous by its absence. Instead, permeating these writings is Jesus' message of spiritual equality.

Even more striking—and all-pervasive—are Jesus' teachings that we must elevate "feminine virtues" from a secondary or supportive to a primary and central position. We must not be violent but instead turn the other cheek; we must do unto others as we would have them do unto us; we must love our neighbors and even our enemies. Instead of the "masculine virtues" of toughness, aggressiveness, and dominance, what we must value above all else are mutual responsibility, compassion, gentleness, and love.

When we look closely, not only at what Jesus taught but at how he went about disseminating his message, time and time again we find that what he was preaching was the gospel of a partnership society. He rejected the dogma that high-ranking men—in Jesus' day, priests, nobles, rich men, and kings—are the favorites of God. He mingled freely with women, thus openly rejecting the male-supremacist norms of his time. And in sharp contrast to the views of later Christian sages, who actually debated whether woman has an immortal soul, Jesus did *not* preach the ultimate dominator message: that women are spiritually inferior to men.

Whether Jesus ever actually existed has long been debated. The argument (very well documented) is that there is absolutely no corroborating evidence of his existence in documents other than highly suspect Christian sources. Analysts also note that practically all the events of Jesus' life, as well as many of his teachings, appear in the lives and utterances of mythical figures of other religions. This would indicate that Jesus was manufactured from borrowings from elsewhere to serve the purposes of early church leaders. Curiously, perhaps the most compelling argument for the historicity of Jesus is his feminist and gylanic thought and actions. For, as we have seen, the overriding requirement of the system has been the manufacture of gods and heroes that support rather than reject androcratic values.

It is thus hard to see why a figure would have been invented who, as we read in John 4:7–27, violated the androcratic customs of his time by talking openly with women. Or whose disciples "marveled" that he should talk at all with women, and then at such great length. Or who would not condone the customary stoning to death of women who, in the opinion of their male overlords, were guilty of the heinous sin of having sexual relations with a man who was not their master.

In Luke 10:38–42, we read how Jesus openly included women among his companions—and even encouraged them to transcend their servile roles and participate actively in public life. He praises the activist Mary over her domestic sister Martha. And in every one of the official Gospels we read about Mary Magdalene and how he treated her—presumably a prostitute—with respect and caring.

Even more astonishing, we learn from the Gospels that it is to Mary Magdalene that the risen Christ first appears. Weeping in his empty sepulcher after his death, it is Mary Magdalene who guards his grave. There she has a vision in which Jesus appears to her *before* he appears in visions to any of his much-publicized twelve male disciples. And it is Mary Magdalene whom the risen Jesus asks to tell the others that he is about to ascend.[2]

It is not surprising that in his time the teachings of Jesus had—as they still have—great appeal to women. Although Christian historians rarely refer to this, even in the official scriptures or New Testament, we find women who are Christian leaders. For example, in Acts 9:36 we read of a *disciple* of Jesus called Tabitha or Dorcas, conspicious for her absence from the well-known, official count of twelve. In Romans 16:7 we find Paul respectfully greeting a woman apostle named Junia, whom he describes as senior to himself in the movement. "Greet Mary, who bestowed labor on us," we read. "Salute Andronicus and Junia, my kin and my fellow prisoners, who are of note among the apostles, who also were in Christ *before me*" (emphasis added).

Some scholars believe that the New Testament epistle Hebrews may actually have been written by a woman named Priscilla. The wife of Aquila, she is described in the New Testament as working with Paul, with her name usually mentioned before that of her husband.[3] And as the historical theologian Constance Parvey points out, in Acts 2:17 we find the explicit designation of women as *prophets*. Here we read, "I will pour out my Spirit upon all flesh, and your sons and *your daughters* shall prophesy" (emphases added).

So, clearly, despite the very strong social pressures of that time for rigid male dominance, women took leading roles in the first Christian communities. As the theologian Elisabeth Schussler Fiorenza points out, this is further confirmed by the fact that so many meetings of early Christians mentioned in the New Testament were in women's houses. In Colossians 4:15, for example, we read of the church in the house of Nympha. In 1 Corinthians 1:11 we read of the church in the household of Chloe. In Acts 15:14, 15 and 40 we read that the church in Philippi began with the conversion of the businesswoman Lydia. And so on and on.[4]

As already noted, in this same New Testament we keep reading about Mary Magdalene. She is discredited as a prostitute—a woman who has violated that most fundamental androcratic law that she should be the sexual chattel of her husband or master. However, she is clearly an important member of the early Christian movement. In fact, as we shall see, there is compelling evidence that Mary Magdalene was a leader of the early Christian movement after Jesus died. Indeed, she is portrayed in one suppressed document as sharply resisting the reimposition within some Christian sects themselves of the kinds of rankings Jesus challenged—evidence that would obviously *not* be included in the scriptures the leaders of these sects were to put together as the New Testament.

To the androcratic mind the idea that Jesus was involved in a gylanic counterrevolution is inconceivable. To paraphrase the parable, it would seem easier for a camel to pass through the eye of a needle than for such a notion to enter the minds of fundamentalists whose cars today bear bumper stickers exhorting others to "get right with Jesus." To begin with, why would Jesus have concerned himself with the elevation of women and feminine values from their subservient place? To them it would seem obvious that, being who he was, Jesus would have been consumed by far more important concerns—which, by conventional definition, rules out anything that could be called women's issues.

It is, in fact, remarkable that Jesus taught what he did. For Jesus was himself an androcratic product, a Jew born into a time when Judaism was still rigidly male dominant. This was a time when, as we read in John 8:3–11, women were still regularly stoned to death for adultery, in other words, for violating their husband's or master's sexual property rights. It is in this instance most revealing that Jesus not only prevented such a stoning but in so doing defied the scribes and Pharisees who deliberately set up this situation to trap him into revealing himself as a dangerous rebel.

There is, however, a way in which Jesus' gylanic teachings are not so remarkable. Jesus has long been recognized as one of the greatest spiritual figures of all time. By any criterion of excellence, the figure portrayed in the Bible displays an exceptionally high level of sensitivity and intelligence as well as the courage to stand up to established authority and, even at the risk of his life, speak out against cruelty, oppression, and greed. So it is not surprising that Jesus should have been aware that the "masculine" values of dominance, inequality, and conquest he could see all around him debasing and distorting human life must be replaced by a softer, more "feminine" set of values based on compassion, responsibility, and love.

Jesus' recognition that our spiritual evolution has been stunted by a way of structuring human relations based on violence-backed rankings could have led to a fundamental social transformation. It could have freed us from the androcratic system. But as in other times of gylanic resurgence, the system's resistance was too strong. And in the end the church fathers left us a New Testament in which this perception is often smothered by the superimposition of the completely contradictory dogmas required to justify the Church's later androcratic structure and goals.

The Suppressed Scriptures

The reality of old masterpieces has often been revealed by art restorers, who must scrape away layer upon layer of distorting overpainting, grime, and old shellac. In the same way, the gylanic Jesus is now being revealed by the new scholarship of theologians and religious historians probing beneath and beyond the New Testament.

To gain a better understanding of the real nature of early Christianity, we have to go outside the official scriptures contained in the New Testament to other ancient Christian documents, some of which have only recently been found. Of these, the most important—and revealing—are the fifty-two Gnostic gospels unearthed in 1945 in Nag Hammadi, an outlying province of Upper Egypt.[5]

Elaine Pagels, a professor of religious studies at Princeton, writes in her book *The Gnostic Gospels*, that "those who wrote and circulated these texts did not regard *themselves* as 'heretics.' "[6] Nonetheless, much of what has been previously known about such "heretic" scriptures came from the men who attacked them—which would hardly be calculated to give us an objective view.

In fact, the men who starting about 200 C.E. took control of what later was called the "orthodox," or only true, church ordered all copies of such texts destroyed. But, as Pagels writes, "Someone, possibly a monk from the nearby monastery at St. Pachomius, took the banned books and hid them from destruction—in the jar where they remained buried for almost 1600 years."[7] And due to a series of events that read like a detective story, it took another thirty-four years after the discovery of these suppressed Gnostic gospels before scholars completed their study and Pagels's book at last brought them to public attention in 1979.

According to Professor Helmut Koester of Harvard University, some of these recently discovered sacred Christian writings are older than the Gospels of the New Testament. He writes that they date to "possibly as early as the second half of the first century (50–100)—as early as, or earlier, than Mark, Matthew, Luke, and John."[8]

The Gnostic gospels were thus written at a time when androcracy had already been the Western norm for a very long time. They are not gylanic documents. And yet, what we find in them is a powerful challenge to the norms of a dominator society.

The term *gnostic* derives from the Greek word *gnosis*, or knowledge. This is in contrast to the still widely used term *agnostic*, for one who believes such knowledge cannot be known with certainty, or is unknowable. Like other mystical Western and Eastern religious traditions, Gnostic Christianity held the seeming unheretical view that the mystery of higher or divine truth is knowable to all of us through religious discipline and moral living.

What then was so heretical about Gnosticism that it had to be banned? Specifically, what we find in these Gnostic gospels is the same idea that caused the Hebrew priesthood to revile and seek to do away with Jesus. This is that access to the deity need *not* go through a religious hierarchy headed by a chief rabbi, high bishop, or pope. It is, rather, available *directly* through gnosis, or divine knowledge—without having to pay homage or tithes to an authoritarian priesthood.

What we also find in these scriptures that were suppressed by the "orthodox" Christian priesthoods is the confirmation of something long suspected both from a reading of the official scriptures and from Gnostic fragments discovered earlier. This is that Mary Magdalene was one of the most important figures in the early Christian movement.

In the *Gospel of Mary* we again read that she was the first to see the risen Christ (as is also recorded in passing in the official Gospels of Mark and John).[9] Here we also read that Christ loved Mary Magdalene more than all the rest of the disciples, as is also confirmed in the Gnostic *Gospel of Philip*.[10] But just how important a part Mary may have played in the history of early Christianity only comes to light in these suppressed scriptures. What we read in the *Gospel of Mary* is that after the death of Jesus Mary Magdalene was the Christian leader who had the courage to challenge the authority of Peter as the head of a new religious hierarchy based on the claim that only he and his priests and bishops had a direct line to the godhead.[11]

"Consider the political implications of the *Gospel of Mary*," comments Pagels. "As Mary stands up to Peter, so the gnostics who take her as their prototype challenge the authority of those priests and bishops who claim to be Peter's successors."[12]

There were other related, and equally fundamental, doctrinal differences between the emerging and increasingly hierarchic church headed by Peter and other early Christian communities, such as most Gnostics and sects like the Montanists and Marcionites. Not only did these sects, in contrast to the men now described as the fathers of the church, honor women as disciples, as prophets, and as founders of Christianity; as part of their firm commitment to Jesus' teachings of spiritual equality, they also included women in their leadership.[13]

To even further emphasize the basic gylanic principle of linking and to avoid permanent rankings some Gnostic sects chose their leadership at each meeting by lot. This we actually know from the writings of such enemies of Gnosticism as Bishop Irenaeus, who supervised the church in Lyons circa 180 C.E.[14]

"At a time when the orthodox Christians increasingly discriminate between clergy and laity," writes Pagels, "this group of gnostic Christians demonstrated that, among themselves, they refused to acknowledge such distinction. Instead of ranking their members into superior and inferior 'orders' within a hierarchy, they followed the principle of strict equality. All initiates, men and women alike, participated equally in the drawing: anyone might be selected to serve as *priest, bishop,* or *prophet.* Furthermore, because they cast lots at each meeting, even the distinctions established by lot could never become permanent 'ranks.' "[15]

For the androcratic Christians who were everywhere seizing power on the basis of rank, such practices were horrible abominations. For example, Tertullian, who wrote circa 190 C.E. for the "orthodox" position, was outraged that "they all have access equally, they listen equally, they pray equally—even pagans if they happen to come." He was similarly outraged that "they also share the kiss of peace with all who come."[16]

But what outraged Tertullian most—as well it might, since it threatened the very foundation of the hierarchic infrastructure he and his fellow bishops were trying to impose in the church—was the equal position of women. "Tertullian protests especially the participation of 'those women among the heretics' who shared with men positions of authority," notes Pagels. " 'They teach, they engage in discussion; they exorcise; they cure'—he suspects that they might even baptize, which meant that they also acted as bishops!"[17]

To men like Tertullian only one "heresy" was even greater than the idea of men and women as spiritual equals. This was the idea that most fundamentally threatened the growing power of the men who were now setting themselves up as the new "princes of the church": the idea of the divine as female. And this—as we can still read in the Gnostic gospels and other sacred Christian documents not included in the official or New Testament scriptures—was precisely what some of the early followers of Jesus preached.

Following the earlier, and apparently still remembered, tradition in which the Goddess was seen as the Mother and Giver of All, the followers of Valentinus and Marcus prayed to the Mother as the "mystical and eternal Silence," as "Grace, She who is before all things," and as "incorruptible Wisdom."[18] In another text, the Trimorphic Protennoia (literally translated, the Triple-Formed Primal Thought) we find a celebration of such powers as thought, intelligence, and foresight as feminine—again following the earlier tradition in which these powers were seen as attributes of the Goddess. The text opens as a divine figure speaks: "I am Protennoia the Thought that dwells in the Light . . . She who exists before the All. . . . I move in every creature. . . . I am the Invisible One within the All. . . . I am perception and Knowledge, uttering a Voice by means of Thought. I am the real Voice."[19]

In another text, attributed to the Gnostic teacher Simon Magus, paradise itself—the place where life began—is described as the Mother's womb.[20] And in teachings attributed to Marcus or Theodotus (circa 160 C.E.), we read that "the male and female elements together constitute the finest production of the Mother, Wisdom."[21]

Whatever form these "heresies" took, they clearly derived from the earlier religious tradition when the Goddess was worshiped and priestesses were her earthly representatives. Accordingly, almost uniformly divine wisdom was personified as female—as it still is in such feminine words as the Hebrew *hokma* and the Greek *sophia*, both meaning "wisdom" or "divine knowledge," as well as in other ancient mystical traditions, both Eastern and Western.[22]

Another form these heresies took was the "unorthodox" way they depicted the holy family. "One group of gnostic sources claims to have received a secret tradition from Jesus through James and through Mary Magdalene," reports Pagels. "Members of this group prayed to both the divine Father and Mother: 'From Thee, Father, and through Thee, Mother, the two immortal names, Parents of the divine being, and thou, dweller in heaven, humanity, of the mighty name.' "[23]

Similarly, the teacher and poet Valentinus taught that although the deity is essentially indescribable, the divine can be imaged as a dyad consisting of both the female and the male principles.[24] Others were more literal, insisting that the divine is to be considered androgynous. Or they described the holy spirit as feminine, so that in conventional Catholic Trinity terms, out of the union of the Father with the Holy Spirit or Divine Mother, came their Son, the Messiah Christ.[25]

The Gylanic Heresies

These early Christians not only threatened the growing power of the "fathers of the church"; their ideas were also a direct challenge to the male-dominated family. Such views undermined the divinely ordained authority of male over female on which the patriarchal family is based.

Biblical scholars have frequently noted that early Christianity was perceived as a threat by both Hebrew and Roman authorities. This was not just because of the Christians' unwillingness to worship the emperor and give loyalty to the state. Professor S. Scott Bartchy, former director of the Institute for the Study of Christian Origins at Tübingen, West Germany, points out that an even more compelling reason the teachings of Jesus and his followers were perceived as dangerously radical was that they called into question existing family traditions. They considered women persons in their own right. Their fundamental threat, Bartchy concludes, was that the original Christians "disrespected" both the Roman and the Jewish family structures of their day, both of which subordinated women.[26]

If we look at the family as a microcosm of the larger world—and as the only world a small and pliable child knows—this "disrespect" for the male-dominated family, in which father's word is law, can be seen as a major threat to a system based on force-backed ranking. It explains why those who in our time would force us back to the "good old days" when women and "lesser men" still knew their place make a return to the "traditional" family their top priority. It also sheds new light on the struggle that tore apart the world two thousand years ago when Jesus preached his gospel of compassion, nonviolence, and love.

There are many interesting similarities between our time and those turbulent years when the mighty Roman Empire—one of the most powerful dominator societies of all time—began to break down. Both are periods of what "chaos" theorists call states of increasing systems disequilibrium, times when unprecedented and unpredictable systems changes can come about. If we look at the years immediately before and after the death of Jesus from the perspective of an ongoing conflict between androcracy and gylany, we find that, like our own time, this was a period of strong gylanic resurgence. This is no great surprise, for it is during such periods of great social disruption that, as the Nobel-Prize-winning thermodynamicist Ilya Prigogine writes, initially small "fluctuations" can lead to systems transformation.[27]

If we look at early Christianity as an initially small fluctuation that first appeared on the fringes of the Roman Empire (in the little province of Judaea), its potential for our cultural evolution acquires new meaning and its failure an even greater poignancy. Moreover, if we look at early Christianity within this larger framework, which views what happens in all systems as interconnected, we may also see there were other manifestations of gylanic resurgence, even within Rome itself.

In Rome, for example, education was changing so that aristocratic girls and boys were sometimes offered the same curriculum. As the historical theologian Constance Parvey writes, "within the Roman Empire in the first century A.D. many women were educated, and some were highly influential and exercised great freedom in public life."[28] There were still legal restrictions. Roman women had to have male guardians and were never given the right to vote. But, particularly in the upper classes, women increasingly entered public life. Some took up the arts. Others went into professions such as medicine. Still others took part in business, court, and social life, engaged in athletics, went to theaters, sporting events, and concerts, and traveled without being required to have male escorts.[29] In other words, as both Parvey and Pagels note, there was during this period a movement toward the "emancipation" of women.

There were other challenges to the androcratic system, such as slave rebellions and rebellions of outlying provinces. There was the Jewish uprising under Bar Kokhba (132–135 C.E.) that was to mark the end of Judaea.[30] But as androcracy's force-based rankings were challenged, as early Christians espoused nonviolence and spoke of compassion and peace, Rome became even more despotic and violent.

As the excesses of its emperors (including the Christian Constantine) and the famous circuses of the Roman Empire all too hideously reveal, the gylanic challenge to this bloody dominator society failed. Indeed, even within Christianity itself, gylany was not to succeed.

The Pendulum Swings Back

"Despite the previous public activity of Christian women," Pagels observes, "by the year 200, the majority of Christian communities endorsed as canonical the pseudo-Pauline letter of Timothy, which stresses (and exaggerates) the anti-feminist element in Paul's views: 'Let a woman learn in silence with all submissiveness. I permit no woman to teach or to have authority over men: she is to keep silent.'. . . By the end of the second century, women's participation in worship was explicitly condemned: groups in which women continued on to leadership were branded as heretical."[31]

As Pagels further writes, "Whosoever investigates the early history of Christianity (the field called 'patristics'—that is, study of 'the fathers of the Church') will be prepared for the passage that concludes the Gospel of Thomas: 'Simon Peter said to them (the disciples): Let Mary leave us, for women are not worthy of Life.' Jesus said, 'I myself shall lead her, in order to make her male, so that she too may become a living spirit, resembling you males. For every woman who will make herself male will enter the Kingdom of Heaven.' "[32]

Such an outright exclusion of one half of humanity from being worthy of life—even more ironically, the half from whose body life itself comes forth—makes sense only in the context of the androcratic regression and repression that now set in. It serves to verify what so many of us have known deep inside without being able to pinpoint just what it was: something went terribly wrong with Christianity's original gospel of love. How otherwise could such a gospel be used to justify all the torture, conquest, and bloodletting carried out by devout Christians against others, and against one another, that makes up so much of our Western history?

For in the end, there was in the Western world an unpredictable and dramatic systems change. Out of the chaos of the breakdown of the classical world of Rome, a new era took form. What began as a minor mystery cult became the new Western religion. But although its continual message was of the transformation of both self and society, instead of transforming society this "peripheral invader" was itself transformed. Like others before it and most since then, Christianity became an androcratic religion. The Roman Empire was replaced by the Holy Roman Empire.

Already by 200 C.E., in this classic case of spirituality stood on its head, Christianity was well on its way to becoming precisely the kind of hierarchical and violence-based system Jesus had rebelled against. And after Emperor Constantine's conversion, it became an official arm, that is, the servant, of the state. As Pagels writes, when "Christianity became an officially approved religion in the fourth century, Christian bishops, previously victimized by the police, now commanded them."[33]

According to Christian histories, it is said that in 312 C.E., on the day before Constantine defeated and killed his rival Maxentius and was proclaimed emperor, he saw in the setting sun a divinely sent vision: a cross inscribed with the words *in hoc signo victor seris* (in this sign you will be victor). What Christian historians usually fail to report is that it is also said that this first Christian emperor had his wife Fausta boiled alive and ordered the murder of his own son Crispus.[34] But the bloodshed and repression that ushered in the Christianization of Europe was not confined to Constantine's private acts. Nor was it confined to his public acts and those of his Christian successors, such as later edicts that heresy to the Church was now a treasonous act punishable by torture and death.

It was now to become standard practice for Church leaders themselves to command the torture and execution of all who would not accept the "new order."[35] It was also to become standard practice to methodically suppress all "heretical" information that could conceivably threaten this new androcratic hierarchy's rule.

Rather than being pure spirit and both mother and father, God was now explicitly male. And, as Pope Paul VI was still to assert nearly two thousand years later, in 1977, women were barred from the priesthood "because our Lord was a man."[36] At the same time, the Gnostic gospels and other texts like them, which had circulated freely in the Christian communities at the beginning of the Christian era, were denounced and destroyed as heresies by those who now called themselves the orthodox, that is, the only legitimate, church.

As Pagels writes, all these sources—"secret gospels, revelations, mystical teachings—are among those *not* included in the select list that constitutes the New Testament collection. . . . Every one of the secret texts which gnostic groups revered was omitted from the canonical collection, and branded as heretical by those who called themselves orthodox Christians. By the time the process of sorting the various writings ended—probably as late as the year 200—*virtually all the feminine imagery for God had disappeared from orthodox tradition.*"[37]

This branding as heretical by Christians of Christians who believed in equality is particularly ironic in view of the fact that in the early apostolic communities women and men had lived and worked as Jesus had commanded, practicing *agape,* or brotherly and sisterly love. It is even more ironic if we consider that many of these women and men who lived and worked hand in hand had gone to their death as Christian martyrs. But for the men who were now everywhere using Christianity to establish their rule, Christian life and Christian ideology had to be made to fit into the androcratic mold.

As the years went by, the Christianization of Europe's heathens became the excuse for once again firmly reinstating the dominator tenet that might makes right. This not only required the defeat or forceful conversion of all who did not embrace official Christianity; it also required the systematic destruction of "pagan" temples, shrines, and "idols" and the closing of the ancient Greek academies where "heretic" inquiry was still pursued. So successful was the Church's proof of "moral" right by might that until the Renaissance, over a thousand years later, any artistic expression or pursuit of empirical knowledge that was not "blessed" by the Church was practically nonexistent in Europe. And so thorough was the systematic destruction of all extant knowledge, including the mass burning of books, that it even spread outside of Europe, to wherever Christian authority could reach.

Thus, in 391 C.E., under Theodosius I, the now thoroughly androcraticized Christians burned the great library in Alexandria, one of the last repositories of ancient wisdom and knowledge.[38] And aided and abetted by the man who was later to be canonized Saint Cyril (the

Christian bishop of Alexandria) Christian monks barbarously hacked to pieces with oyster shells that remarkable mathematician, astronomer, and philosopher of Alexandria's school of Neoplatonic philosophy, Hypatia. For this woman, now recognized as one of the greatest scholars of all time, was according to Cyril an iniquitous female who had even presumed, against God's commandments, to teach men.[39]

In the officially sanctioned writings, Paulist—or as scholars are increasingly discovering, pseudo-Paulist—dogmas authoritatively reasserted that woman and all that is labeled feminine is inferior and so dangerous that it must be strictly controlled. There were still a few exceptions, notably the writings of Clement of Alexandria, who still characterized God as both feminine and masculine and wrote that "the name 'humanity' is common to both men and women."[40] But in the main, the model for human relations proposed by Jesus in which male and female, rich and poor, Gentile and Jew are all one was expurgated from the ideologies as well as the day-to-day practices of the orthodox Christian Church.

The men in control of the new orthodox Church might in ritual raise the ancient Chalice, now become the cup of Holy Communion filled with the symbolic blood of Christ, but in fact the Blade was once again ascendant over all. Under the sword and fire of the alliance of Church and ruling class fell not only pagans, such as Mithraists, Jews, or devotees of the old mystery religions of Eleusis and Delphi, but also any Christian who would not knuckle under and accept their rule. They still claimed their goal was to spread Jesus' gospel of love. But through the savagery and horror of their holy Crusades, their witch-hunts, their Inquisition, their book burnings and people burnings, they spread not love but the old androcratic staples of repression, devastation, and death.

And so, ironically, Jesus' revolution of nonviolence, in the course of which he died on the cross, was converted into rule by force and terror. As the historians Will and Ariel Durant noted, in its distortion and perversion of Jesus' teachings, medieval Christendom was actually a moral setback.[41] Rather than being any longer a threat to the established androcratic order, Christianity became what practically all this earth's religions, launched in the name of spiritual enlightenment and freedom, have also become: a powerful way of perpetuating that order.

Nonetheless, the struggle of gylany against androcracy was far from over. At certain times and places during the dark centuries of androcratic Christianity—and the despotic kings and popes who ruled Europe in its name—the gylanic urge to resume our cultural evolution would reemerge. As we shall see in the chapters that follow, this continuing struggle has been the major unseen force shaping Western history and is once again in our time coming to a head.

CHAPTER 10

The Patterns of the Past: Gylany and History

History as taught in most schools is largely a matter of the struggle for power among men and nations. It is the dates of battles and the names of kings and generals noted for alternately constructing and destroying fortresses, palaces, and religious monuments. But if we look again at history in light of the new information we have examined and the new theoretical framework we have been developing, a very different kind of struggle emerges. Now, behind all the bloody dates and names can be seen some of the same underlying processes being studied by scientists such as Ilya Prigogine, Isabel Stengers, Edward Lorenz, and Ralph Abraham in the natural world:[1] fluctuation, or apparently patternless movement; oscillation, or cyclic movement; and systems transformation at critical "bifurcation points," when, as Prigogine and Stengers write, "the system can 'choose' between or among more than one possible future."[2]

Looking at the surface, we may, first, observe fluctuations throughout history from warlike to more peaceful times, from authoritarian to freer and more creative times, from periods when women are more repressed to times when, at least for some women, there is a broadening of educational and life opportunities. For the traditional historian these kinds of fluctuations hold no real surprise, being simply what exists, not necessarily of any great meaning.

But is this really only random, patternless movement? If we look more deeply, we see that there are patterns to these historic fluctuations. From the perspective we are developing, it can be seen that the times of war usually are also times of greater authoritarianism. More peaceful times usually are also times of greater equality and may also be times of cultural evolution and high creativity. And if we look still deeper, oscillations, or movements in cycles, also become apparent. Moreover, we see that behind these cyclical movements is an underlying dynamic that has received only cursory or peripheral study until now.

If we look at history from a holistic perspective, taking into account both halves of humanity and the full span of our cultural evolution, we see how these cyclical patterns relate to the fundamental transformation we have examined: the systems shift in our prehistory that set us upon a radically different course of cultural evolution. And if we look at what happened after this shift from a partnership to a dominator model of social organization in light of the new principles about systems stability and systems change being discovered in the natural sciences, recorded history acquires both a new clarity and a new complexity.

Mathematicians studying the dynamics of systems processes speak of what they term *attractors*. Roughly analogous to magnets, these may be "point" or "static" attractors, which govern the dynamics of systems in equilibrium; "periodic" attractors, which govern cyclical or oscillatory movements; and "chaotic" or "strange" attractors, which are characteristic of far-from-equilibrium, or disequilibrium, states.[3] Somewhat like Gould and Eldredge's peripheral isolates, chaotic or strange attractors may sometimes with relative rapidity and unpredictability become the nuclei for the buildup of a whole new system. But there may also be more gradual or "subtle" transformations when point attractors lose some of their attractiveness and periodic attractors become progressively more attractive.[4]

Similarly, Prigogine and Stengers speak of fluctuations that are first localized in a small part of a system. If the system is stable, the new mode of functioning represented by these fluctuations will not survive. But if these "innovators" multiply fast enough, the whole system may adopt a new mode of functioning.[5] In other words, if the fluctuations exceed what Prigogine and Stenger call a "nucleation threshold," they will "spread to the whole system." As these initially small fluctuations are amplified, critical "bifurcation points," in effect, paths to possible systems transformations, open up. When these bifurcation points are reached, "deterministic description breaks down," and which "branch" or "future" will be chosen can no longer be predicted.[6]

How may we apply to social processes these observations of natural processes? There are obviously important differences between chemical, biological, and social systems—not only far greater complexity, but, most notably, a progressively greater element of choice. But although it is essential not to try to reduce what happens in social systems to what happens at simpler levels of organization, if we closely look at all living systems, some striking isomorphisms, or similarities in patterns governing both stability and change at all levels become evident. And if we look at history from the dynamic perspective afforded by this newly evolving view of systems and systems change, we can begin to formulate a new theory of cultural transformation, or more specifically, androcratic/gylanic systems change.

Rather than being random, fluctuations in recorded history can be seen to reflect periodic movement in the prevailing androcratic system toward the "attractor" of a partnership model of social organization. On the structural level, this is reflected in periodic alterations in the way human relations are organized—particularly the relations between the female and male halves of humanity. On the level of values, it is reflected (in everything from literature to social policies) in the periodic struggle between the stereotypically hard "masculine" values, symbolized by the Blade, and the stereotypically soft or "feminine" values symbolized by the Chalice.

Moreover, these historical dynamics can be seen from a larger evolutionary perspective. As we saw in preceding chapters, the original cultural direction of our species during the formative years for human civilization was toward what we may call an early partnership, or proto-gylanic, model of society. Our cultural evolution was initially shaped by this model and reached its early peak in the highly creative culture of Crete. Then came a period of increasing disequilibrium or chaos. Through wave after wave of invasions and through the step-by-step replicative force of sword and pen, androcracy first acted as a "chaotic" attractor and later became the well-seated "static" or "point" attractor for most of Western civilization. But all through recorded history, and particularly during periods of social instability, the gylanic model has continued to act as a much weaker but persistent "periodic" attractor. Like a plant that refuses to be killed no matter how often it is crushed or cut back, as the history we will now reexamine shows, gylany has again and again sought to reestablish its place in the sun.

The "Feminine" as a Force in History

The idea of history as the dialectical movement of conflicting forces has shaped Hegelian, Marxist, and other analyses. Historical cycles have also been observed by Arnold Toynbee, Oswald Spengler, Arthur

Schlesinger, Sr., and others.[7] However, in conventional male-centered histories there is characteristically no mention of the powerful alternation between periods of gylanic ascendancy and androcratic regression. To understand this cyclical alternation—now critical because one more shift from peace to war could be our last—we must therefore turn to the works of unconventional historians.

One such historian is Henry Adams. Although in some respects a visionary, Adams was essentially a conservative man who argued that we must return to older, more religious values. But if we look beneath the surface of Adams's work, we find recognition of a powerful and traditionally ignored "feminine" force in history. Adams asserted that "without understanding movement of sex" history is "mere pedantry." He criticized American history for mentioning "hardly the name of a woman" and British history for handling women "as timidly as though they were a new and undescribed species."[8] Indeed, the main thrust of Adams's analysis was that the civilizing force in Western history had been what he termed the Virgin. "All the steam in the world," he wrote, "could not, like the Virgin, build Chartres," for it is the Virgin who has been "the greatest force the western world ever felt."[9] Counterposed to the positive power of the Virgin was a negative and destructive power: the harsh force Adams called the Dynamo, or rampant dehumanizing technology.

Adams couched his observations in a mix of androcratic sexual stereotypes and mystical generalizations. But what emerges once one transcends these barriers is actually the same conflict we have identified as the struggle between the two views of power represented by androcracy and gylany, the dominator and the partnership models, or the Blade and the Chalice. In fact, Adams's symbolism of the Virgin and the Dynamo closely parallels that of the Chalice and the Blade. Both the Chalice and the Virgin are symbols of the "feminine" power to create and nurture. And both the Blade and the Dynamo are "masculine" symbols of insensate, destructive technology.

An even more remarkable forerunner of the analysis of history in terms of the struggle between so-called feminine and masculine values is G. Rattray Taylor's *Sex in History*.[10] But, as with Adams, to use Taylor's data we must go beyond what he says he is describing to what he is in fact describing. Following the well-known theories of Wilhelm Reich[11] and other psychologists who primarily see patriarchal societies as sexually repressive, Taylor argues that historical swings from sexually permissive to sexually repressive attitudes are what underlie the alternation between freer, more creative and more authoritarian, less creative periods.[12] But what his book in fact documents is that under-lying these cycles are shifts between values he himself refers to as either mother- or father-identified.

Indeed, Taylor's terms *matrism,* or mother-identification, and *patrism,* or father-identification, which he had to devise because of the lack of words for what he was looking at, describe the same configurations as *gylany* and *androcracy.* Matrist periods are those when women and "feminine" (what Taylor calls mother-identified) values are accorded higher status. These periods are characteristically intervals of greater creativity, less social and sexual repression, more individualism, and social reform. Conversely, in patrist periods the derogation of women and femininity is more pronounced. These periods, when father-identified, or "masculine," values are once again on the ascendant, are more socially and sexually repressive, with less emphasis on the creative arts and social reform.[13]

Taylor uses the troubadour period in southern France as a medieval example of a matrist period—or, in our terms, a period of gylanic resurgence. This was a time when out of the twelfth-century courts of Eleanor of Aquitaine and her daughters Marie and Alix, courtly love and reverence for women emerged as the central themes of both poetry and life.[14] The troubador view of woman as powerful and honored rather than dominated and despised, and of man as honorable and gentle rather than dominating and brutal, was not new. As we have seen, it echoes both Crete and the Neolithic. But in an age when male savagery and debauchery was the norm, the troubadours' concepts of chivalry, gentleness, honor, and romantic love were, as Taylor notes, truly revolutionary.

Taylor also brings out that there can be no question that the "feminine" (or, in his terms, "mother-identified")[15] values of the troubadours profoundly humanized Western history. Not only did these values later "flower whenever matrists were in the ascendant"; to a certain extent "even the patrist came to accept the ideal of gentleness to the weak, to children, and to women, provided the women were of his own class."[16]

"They were innovators and progressives," Taylor writes of the troubadors, "interested in the arts and sometimes pressing for social reforms; they eschewed the use of force: they delighted in gay and colorful clothes. Above all, they erected the Virgin Mary into their especial patron: many of their poems are addressed to her, and in 1140 a new feast was instituted at Lyons—a feast which, as Bernard of Clairvaux protested, was 'unknown to the custom of the Church, disapproved

by reason and without sanction from tradition'—the feast of the Im-
maculate Conception."[17]

Bernard's charge that there was no traditional sanction for the worship of a mother who gives birth to a divine son was, of course, totally
unfounded. The worship of Mary was a return to the ancient worship
of the Goddess. And the Church's fierce resistance to Mary worship
was not only tacit recognition of the lingering power of this earlier
religion; it was also an expression of patrist resistance to the strong
resurgence of gylanic values that characterized the troubadour movement.

If as we read we substitute for Taylor's terms *matrist* and *patrist* our
terms *gylanic* and *androcratic*, much that otherwise seems incompre-
hensible in medieval history acquires a specific political meaning. The
Church's condemnation of women to subordinate and "silent" status
can be seen not as a minor historical mystery but a *primary* expression
of the Church's possession by the androcratic/dominator model. It was
essential to subordinate and silence women—along with the "feminine" values originally preached by Jesus—if androcratic norms, and
with them, the medieval Church's power, were to be maintained.

Another otherwise inexplicable aspect of medieval history acquires
a comprehensible—and critical—political meaning. This is the
Church's extreme vilification of women, in the words of the *Malleus
Maleficarum* or *Hammer of Witches* (the Church-blessed Inquisitor's man-
ual for the hunting of witches), as the "carnal source of all evil."[18]

In most history books, the intermittent witch-hunts over several
centuries when, on orders of the Church, men sadistically inflicted hideous tortures on many thousands, possibly millions, of "witches," are
at most mentioned in passing. When these barbaric persecutions of
women (most of whom were ultimately condemned to the excruciating
pain of slowly burning to death) are noted at all, they are usually explained as the result of mass hysteria. We are told that from the thirteenth to the sixteenth centuries the European peasantry simply went
mad, or alternatively, that the witches themselves were insane—as
Gregory Zilboorg wrote, that "millions of witches, sorcerors, possessed
and obsessed were an enormous mass of severe neurotics [and] psy-
chotics."[19] But as Barbara Ehrenreich and Deirdre English point out,
"The witch-craze was neither a lynching party nor a mass suicide by
hysterical women. Rather, it followed well-ordered, legalistic proce-
dures. The witch-hunts were well organized campaigns, initiated, financed, and executed by Church and State."[20]

One impetus for these persecutions was that, beginning with their treatment of monarchs and nobility in the thirteenth century, church-educated male "physicians" (who in fact were given absolutely no practical training for healing) began to compete with the traditional "wise-women," who were now accused of having "magical powers" affecting health—and often burned at the stake for the "crime" of using these gifts to help and heal.[21] Another impetus, reflected in the accusation that there were organized witches' covens where pagans met in the woods to consort with devils, was that many of these women evidently clung to earlier religious beliefs, probably including the worship of a female deity and/or her son-consort, the ancient bull god (now the cloven-hoofed devil). But the most repeated, and revealing, charge is that the witches were quite simply accused of being sexual; for in the eyes of the Church, all the witches' power was ultimately derived from their "sinful" female sexuality.[22]

Typically, this pathologically misogynistic view of women as a sex is presented as merely an irrationality of sexually frustrated men. But the Church's "moral" condemnation of women was far more than a psychological quirk. It was a justification for male dominance—an appropriate, and in that sense of the word also rational, response by the androcratic system not only to the remnants of earlier gylanic traditions but also to the recurrent gylanic surges that, as Taylor writes, threatened to "overturn the father's authority."[23]

In other words, the officially sanctioned witch-hunts, as well as the Church's repeated denunciation of women as a sex, were neither eccentric nor unrelated phenomena. They were essential elements in first the imposition and then the maintenance of androcracy: necessary, and in that sense, reasonable, means of countering recurring gylanic resurgences.

In focusing on the Church's hysterical antisexuality and violent repressiveness—which made the "moral" Middle Ages "a cross between a charnel house and an insane asylum"[24] Taylor tends to miss the essentially antifeminist character of the Church's condemnation of sex. Nonetheless, the data he presents leave little question of what, above all else, the Church viewed as "heretical." Time and time again Taylor shows that the common thread uniting the various heretical sects the Church so cruelly persecuted was their identification with so-called feminine values. These sects typically worshiped the Virgin as Our Lady of Thought. And like the earlier Christian sects that played such an important part in the gylanic resurgence of their time, they also often accorded high status, and even positions of leadership, to women.[25]

As Taylor himself writes, "the question we are bound to ask is why did the Church feel, however obscurely, that there was some common factor uniting the Troubadours, the Cathars, the Baghards, and the various minor sects which preached a chaste love? . . . The answer can only be that there was such a common factor: . . . While their dogma and ritual differed greatly and some of them claimed to be still within the Church, psychologically they had one thing in common: mother identification. This is the only heresy in which the medieval Church was really interested."[26]

History Repeats Itself

In *Sex in History* we see that the essential quality of the medieval Church was its patrism or father-identification—in our terms, its androcractic or dominator character. We also begin to see that behind the oscillating swings of history lie specific conflicts between dominator and partnership values.

For example, Taylor notes how in the Elizabethan age, when a woman, Queen Elizabeth I, sat on the English throne, "mother-identified" or "feminine" values were in the ascendancy. There was in Elizabethan England "an awakening conscience of responsibility for others, expressed, for instance, in the institution of the poor law." There was also "a new love of free learning, finding expression in scholarship and the founding of colleges for students" and "a flood of creative energy, especially in poetry and the drama, England's preferred form of art, but also in painting, architecture, and music."[27]

It is also significant—and as we will see, in systems terms, critical—that during periods of gylanic resurgence such as the Elizabethan age, the time of the troubadors, and the Renaissance, upper-class women obtain relatively more freedom and greater access to education.[28] For example, Portia and other Shakespearean heroines were notably learned women, reflecting the somewhat higher status of women in the period. But, as the treatment of Shakespeare's heretically rebellious Kate in *The Taming of the Shrew* and other literary works indicates, even before the Elizabethan age drew to a close, the violent reassertion of male control was already under way.

Indeed, one of the most telltale signs that the pendulum is about to swing back is the revival of misogynist dogmas. Along with the introduction of new "facts" justifying the subordination of women, this is a signal of what Taylor calls "the permanent self-delusion of patrists to suppose that standards of behavior are declining" and that the reimposition of "father-identified" values must be accomplished at all cost.[29] Most important, it is an early warning signal that a more repressive and bloody period of androcratic regression is about to set in.

Of particular relevance here is the much more recent work of the psychologist David Winter. Along with other well-known modern scholars, Winter has been studying what in his book of the same title he calls "the power motive."[30] As a social psychologist he set out to uncover historical patterns through objective measurements. And although again we must look beyond what Winter stressed from the conventional male-centered psychological perspective, his findings dramatically document that more repressive attitudes toward women are predictors of periods of aggressive warfare.

Focusing on one of literature's and opera's most famous romantic figures, the dashing "lady-killer" Don Juan, Winter's social-psychological analysis is largely based on a study of the frequency of certain themes in literary documents. Winter observes that despite obligatory condemnations of Don Juan's actions as "wicked" and "damned," Don Juan is in fact idealized as the "greatest seducer of Spain." He also points out that aggression, hate, and the desire to humiliate and punish women—not sexual drives—are Don Juan's underlying motives. He further notes something of profound psychological and historical importance: extremely hostile attitudes toward women are characteristic of times when women are most rigidly suppressed by men. The classic case in point he cites is the Spain out of which the Don Juan legend arose, when upper-class Spaniards had adopted the "Moorish custom of keeping their women folk secluded."[31] The psychological reason behind this heightened hostility, Winter explains, is that in such periods the mother-son relationship—along with female-male relations in general—becomes particularly tense.[32]

In context, it is evident Winter's "power motive" is, in our terms, the androcratic drive to conquer and dominate other human beings. Having established that Don Juan's debasement of women is a manifestation of this "power motive," Winter then charts the frequency of stories about Don Juan in a nation's literature in relation to periods of imperial expansion and war. What his findings document is what we would predict using the gylanic-androcratic alternation model: that stories about this most famous archetype of masculine domination over women historically increase in frequency before and during periods of increased militarism and imperialism.[33]

Winter confirms that in systems terms male dominance is inextricably interrelated with the male violence of warfare. He also confirms an aspect of the gylanic-androcratic alternation that pioneering feminist scholars such as Kate Millett and Theodore Roszak observed earlier: the reidealization of male supremacy signals a shift toward the values and behaviors that historically fuel the violence of androcratic regressions.[34]

Millett's brilliant *Sexual Politics* was a pioneering study of what she intuitively saw as the most important factor in our political history: male dominance.[35] And though Roszak is best known for his more conventional male-centered analyses of society, his essay "The Hard and the Soft: The Force of Feminism in Modern Times," is also a pioneering work for the analysis of history from the perspective of a developing theory of androcratic-gylanic systems change.[36]

Looking between the lines and behind the surface of hundreds of studies seeking to understand the escalating violence and militarism that culminated in the terrible carnage of World War I, Roszak detected what he called the "historical crisis of masculine dominance."[37] The nineteenth-century feminist movement, he noted, had not only challenged the conventional sexual stereotypes of male dominance and female submission; for the first time in recorded history, it also offered a sizable frontal challenge to the prevailing system, going straight to its ideological core. Typically, this nineteenth-century challenge is almost unreported in our conventional histories. But it was as hotly debated and passionately argued about as the women's liberation movement of our time. For it not only challenged the traditional dominance of men over women; it also challenged the most fundamental values of our system, in which traits like tenderness, compassion, and peacefulness are considered feminine, thus totally inappropriate for real or "masculine" men—and for social governance.[38]

The androcratic system's response to that challenge was the violent reassertion of the masculine stereotypes and all their manifestations. As Roszak wrote of the late nineteenth and early twentieth century preceding World War I, "compulsive masculinity was written all over the political style of the period." In the United States, Theodore Roosevelt spoke of "a cancer of unwarlike and isolated ease" and of "manly and adventurous virtues." In Ireland, the revolutionary poet Patrick Pearse proclaimed that "bloodshed is a cleansing and sanctifying thing, and the nation which regards it as a final horror has lost its manhood." In Italy, Filippo Marinetti announced: "We are out to glorify war, the only health-giver of the world! Militarism! Patriotism! The Destructive Arm of the Anarchist! Contempt for women!"[39]

As with the hallowed legend of Don Juan, this brutal contempt for women and anything considered feminine was a signal. The message (permeating writings that bridged all national and ideological barriers) was that a shift to an "unwarlike" and "unmanly" world—a world no longer governed by the "masculine" Blade—was *not* to be tolerated.

Probing beneath the surface of all their national and ideological differences, Roszak showed an underlying commonality among the men who at the turn of this century—and throughout history—plunged the world into war. This is the equation of masculinity with violence that is required if a system of force-based rankings is to be maintained. He also dramatically confirmed the dynamic that Winter observed in his research: the re-idealization of the "masculine" stereotype signals not only a regressive shift of values but also a shift from peace to war.

An equally compelling corroboration of this still generally overlooked social dynamic is found in the research of the psychologist David McClelland. In *Power: The Inner Experience*, McClelland reports how he set out to see whether one might predict periods of warfare, or of peace, by looking for indicators in writings and statements preceding the times in question.[40] His findings confirm what we would predict in charting historical alterations using the gylanic-androcratic model of history.

McClelland studied literary and historical materials in American history. He found that periods when what he called the "affiliation motive" (or we would call more "feminine" peaceful and compassionate values) gained strength were followed by times of peace. For instance, McClelland found the "affliliation motive" rising before the peaceful years from 1800 to 1810 and from 1920 to 1930.[41] Conversely, periods when writings again showed a shift to what he called the "imperial power" motivation (what we call the "masculine" dominator motivation) almost invariably culminated in wars. In English history, too, a combination of high "imperial power" motivation and low "affiliation" motivation preceded times of historical violence, for example 1550, 1650, and 1750.[42] On the other hand, periods of low power and high affiliation motivation in English history preceded more peaceful times.

Like Taylor's work, McClelland's verifies another important point. This is that the "softer," more "feminine" values characteristic of a partnership model of society are part of a particular social and ideological configuration that stresses creation rather than destruction. As we saw in the Neolithic era and in the delightful murals and palaces of ancient Crete, as well as in the periods Taylor calls matrist, such as the Elizabethan age, more gylanic periods are also characteristically periods of great cultural creativity.

McClelland's shorthand for his motivational system refers to the need for affiliation as "n Affiliation," need for power as "n Power," and so on. In these terms, he observes that "what is really remarkable about the Elizabethan period is that the motivational indicators all attest this must have been a good time to be alive, just as historians have always argued. Need for Affiliation had risen, Power had dropped a bit, symbolizing an era of relative peace, and Achievement had remained high, presaging some prosperity."[43] But soon thereafter came the all-too-familiar shift. "During the Cavalier and Roundhead struggles and civil war n Power rose again and n Affiliation dropped sharply, indicating that this should have been a period of great violence and ruthlessness, as indeed it was."[44] Or in our terms, the movement toward higher levels of cultural evolution could, under the prevailing male-dominant system, only go so far and no further. To maintain the system, there had to be cultural regression, again plunging the system into the "normal" dynamics of androcratic violence.

Completing the characteristic androcratic systems configuration we have observed throughout this book, McClelland's analysis also confirms that during times when aggressive power motivations again became dominant this system's third major component, authoritarianism, is strengthened. "High n Power combined with low n Affiliation," he writes, "has been associated among modern nations with dictatorships, with ruthlessness, suppression of liberty, and domestic and international violence."[45]

The new feminist scholarship has also focused on the study of power in newly illuminating ways. The exceptional works of the noted sociologist Jessie Bernard, the Harvard psychologist Carol Gilligan, and the psychiatrist Jean Baker Miller document how in male-dominated societies *affiliation* is associated with femininity whereas *power*—in the conventional sense of control over others—is associated with masculinity.[46]

These works also reveal something else of the greatest importance: the configuration of values that McClelland called affiliation, Taylor called matrist, and we have called gylanic are in male-dominated systems generally confined to a separate world subordinate or ancillary to the larger "men's" or "real" world—the world of women.

It is here that the gylanic definition of power as *enabling*—the power to give and to create so characteristic of the ancient partnership ethos—can still be seen. As Miller notes, this is still the way women define power, as the responsibility of mothers to help their children, particularly their sons, develop their talents and abilities.[47] It is here that what Bernard calls 'the female ethos of love/duty" remains the primary model for thought and action—but only for women.[48] And it is here that what Gilligan calls the feminine morality of caring—of a positive duty to do unto others as we would want them to do unto us—also governs.[49] But again, it is only as the model of thought and action for those who are not supposed to govern society: women.

Taking into account these new studies of the conventionally ignored half of humanity, what we begin to see is how periods of warfare and repression can be predicted from a weakening of the gylanic values of affiliation or *linking* and the corresponding strengthening of the androcratic values of aggressive power, or force-based *ranking*. We can also glimpse how beneath the seemingly inexplicable shifts that punctuate recorded history lies the basic resistance to our cultural evolution: a social system in which the female half of humanity is dominated and repressed.

Women as a Force in History

But why, if these androcratic/gylanic systems dynamics seem so obvious, have they received so little formal study? Indeed, since women are half of our species, why have their behaviors, activities, and ideas been given so little sustained study? Again we confront one of these omissions that scientists and historians will marvel over in ages to come.

The door to a holistic study of human society is only slightly ajar at this time. It opened a crack when historians began to recognize, as Lynn White, Jr., observed, that the recording of history has been very selective—characteristically done by, for, and about the historically dominant groups.[50] But it is only now, when the missing female half of history is starting to be seriously considered, that we can begin to develop a new theory of history, and of cultural evolution, that takes into account the *totality* of human society.

It is hardly surprising that our conventional histories systematically omit anything relating to women or "femininity" when only a very short time ago not one American university even had a women's studies program. There still is no such thing in the vast majority of our high schools and grammar schools. Even now, where they exist, women's studies programs are given miniscule budgets, low status, and even lower priority in the college and university hierarchy. Only in a handful of places is even a single women's studies class a graduation requirement. It is thus also not surprising that most "educated" people still find it hard to believe there were any women who mattered in history or that anything as peripheral as women and "feminine" values could be a force central, not only to our past, but also to our prospects for a better future.

One of the first twentieth-century works to try to redress this pathological omission of women from what has conventionally been written as history is Mary Beard's *Woman as a Force in History*.[51] Showing how, despite male dominance, women have in fact been important shapers of Western society, this pioneering woman historian led the way back into prehistory as a source of the lost human heritage. Of particular relevance here is Beard's documentation of something that to conventional historians would seem even more outrageous than the correlations shown by Winter and McClelland between "feminine" and "masculine" values and critical historical alternatives. This is that periods of the rising status of women are characteristically periods of cultural resurgence.

From the perspective of the Cultural Transformation theory we have been developing, it is hardly surprising to find a correlation between the status of women and whether a society is peaceful or warlike, concerned with people's welfare or indifferent to social equity, and generally hierarchical or equalitarian. For, as we have seen throughout this book, the way a society structures the relations between the two halves of humanity has profound, and highly predictable, systems implications. What is surprising is that, without any such theoretical framework, writing at the beginning of this century, Beard could see these patterns and remark on them in what is still one of few attempts to chart the activities of women in Western history.

In *Women as a Force in History*, Beard remarks on "the wide-reaching, and influential activities of Italian women in the promotion of humanistic learning" during the Renaissance. She notes that this was a time when women—along with "effeminate" values like artistic expression and inquiry—were beginning to free themselves from medieval church control. She documents that in the French Enlightenment of the seventeenth and eighteenth centuries women played similarly critical roles. Indeed, as we will see, during this period—which launched the secular revolt against what Beard calls "the barbarisms and abuses" of the old regime—it was in the "salons" of women like Madame Rambouillet, Ninon de Lenclos, and Madame Geoffrin that the ideas for what later became the more humanist, or in our terms more gylanic, modern ideologies first germinated.[52]

This is not to say that women have not also helped to keep men and "masculine" values in power. Despite the emergence of great figures here and there, women's part in our recorded past was by necessity largely played in the androcratically prescribed role of the male's "helper." But as Beard repeatedly shows, although women have helped men fight wars, and sometimes even fought in them, theirs has generally been a very different role. For not being socialized to be tough, aggressive, and conquest-oriented, women in their lives, actions, and ideas have characteristically been "softer," that is, less violent and more compassionate and caring. For example, as Beard remarks, "one of the earliest—and perhaps the first—rivals of the hymnology of war, hatred, and revenge made immortal by Homer was the poetry of an Aeolian woman called Sappha by her people but uniformly known in later times as Sappho."[53]

This insight is also found in another pioneering work focusing on the role of women in history: Elizabeth Gould Davis's *The First Sex.*[54] Like books by other women trying to reclaim their past with no institutions or learned colleagues for support, Davis's book has been criticized for veering into strange, if not downright esoteric, flights of fancy. But despite their flaws—and perhaps precisely because they did not conform to accepted scholarly traditions—books like this intuitively foreshadow a study of history in which the status of women and so-called feminine values would become central.

Like Beard's, Davis's book puts women back into the places from which they were erased by androcratic historians. It also provides data that make it possible to see the connection at critical historical junctures between the suppression of women and the suppression of feminine values. For instance, Davis contrasts the Elizabethan age with the Puritan regression that followed, marked by virulent measures to repress women, including "witch" burnings.

But it is primarily in the works of today's more exacting feminist historians and social scientists that we can find the data needed to flesh out and develop a new holistic theory of gylanic-androcratic transformation and alternation. These are the works of women such as Renate Bridenthal, Gerda Lerner, Dorothy Dinnerstein, Eleanor Leacock, JoAnn McNamara, Donna Haraway, Nancy Cott, Elizabeth Pleck, Carroll Smith-Rosenberg, Susanne Wemple, Joan Kelly, Claudia Koonz, Caroline Merchant, Marilyn French, Francoise d'Eaubonne, Susan Brownmiller, Annette Ehrlich, Jane Jaquette, Lourdes Arizpe, Itsue Takamure, Rayna Rapp, Kathleen Newland, Gloria Orenstein, Bettina Aptheker, Carol Jacklin, and La Frances Rodgers-Rose and men such as Carl Degler, P. Steven Sangren, Lester Kirkendall, and Randolph Trumbach, who, painstakingly, often using obscure, hard-to-find sources like women's diaries and other hitherto ignored records, are gradually reclaiming an incredibly neglected half of history.[55] And in the process, they are producing the missing building blocks required to construct the kind of historical paradigm needed to understand, and move beyond, the one-step-forward-and-one-step-back alternations of recorded history. For it is in the new feminist scholarship that we begin to see the reason behind something the French philosopher Charles Fourier observed over a century ago: the degree of emancipation of women is an index of the degree of a society's emancipation.[56]

The Female Ethos

We have already glimpsed how in periods of rigid androcratic control the softer, more "feminine" values are more rigidly confined to the subordinate world of women, the private world of the home ruled by individual men. Conversely, we have seen how in periods of gylanic ascendancy these values press out into the larger public, or man's world, thereby effecting some measure of social progress.

What the findings of the new feminist scholarship now make possible is documentation that this happens not because of some mystical, cyclical, and inexorable principle or "fate" (e.g., Adams's juxtaposition of the "Virgin" and the "Dynamo"). It happens for a very simple and practical reason that would have been apparent to historians had they included women in the history they studied. In times and places when women are not strictly confined to the private world of the home—in times when they can move more freely into the public world en masse, as carriers and disseminators of the "female ethos"—they inject a more gylanic worldview into the mainstream of society.

As we saw in classical Greece, and then again in the days of Jesus, women have in fact had a great impact in the bettering of society. But perhaps the most striking case in point is the most profoundly humanizing social movement of modern times, which is, again, except in feminist sources, almost completely ignored. This is the feminist movement that first flared up in the nineteenth century and is now again catching fire in the twentieth century.

Although even this is generally omitted from our standard history books, the unknown or ignored work of hundreds of nineteenth-century feminists like Lucy Stone, Margaret Fuller, Mary Lyon, Elizabeth Cady Stanton, and Susan B. Anthony obviously greatly improved the situation of the female half of humanity. Domestically, these "mothers" of modern feminism liberated women from laws that sanctioned wife beating. Economically, they helped free women from laws that gave husbands control over their wives' property. They opened up professions like law and medicine to women and won women access to higher education, thus vastly enriching their, and their families', lives.[57]

But in freeing women from blatantly oppressive forms of male dominance, the nineteenth-century feminist movement helped set in motion the gylanic thrust of our time in still another way that, characteristically, only becomes evident if we look outside our standard history books. In making it possible for more women than ever before to gain at least a partial foothold in the world outside their homes, this movement vastly humanized society as a whole. For it was through the impact of the "female ethos" embodied by women like Florence Nightingale, Jane Addams, Sojourner Truth, and Dorothea Dix, who were now beginning to enter the "public world" en masse, that new professions like organized nursing and social work emerged, that the abolitionist movement to free slaves gained massive grass roots support, that the treatment of the insane and mentally deficient became more humane.[58]

Moreover, it is this same more "feminine" or partnership view of human relations, defined by affiliation rather than by violence-based rankings, that spread into the mainstream of society through the twentieth-century feminist movement. Like the nineteenth-century feminist movement, the women's liberation movement has also vastly improved the situation of women. At a time when technological changes are increasingly shifting women from subservient roles in the household to subservient roles in the labor force, the women's liberation movement has pressed for new laws to protect women both inside and outside the home. But, once again, this second wave of modern feminism has also greatly upgraded the situation of *both* women and men by injecting a more gylanic consciousness into spheres of activity that were once solidly under male control.

Just as in the nineteenth century women played a major role in the movement to free black slaves, in the twentieth century women have again provided massive grass roots support, and have even died, to strengthen blacks' civil rights. Similarly, all over the Western world today organizations by the hundreds, large and small, that are trying to bring about a more just, peaceful, and ecologically harmonious social order are heavily female in composition.[59]

Clearly, not all women bring gylanic values into public life. For example, the lone women who occasionally make it to the top of male hierarchies, like Indira Gandhi or Margaret Thatcher, often do so precisely because they keep proving that they are *not* too "soft" or "feminine." And clearly many men are today also working for social betterment and peace—as they have in other times of gylanic resurgence. But one of the reasons they do so is that these are times when more "feminine" values—along with women—are less "privatized."

The developments of the late 1960s and early 1970s, when so many Americans rejected the "masculine" idea that the war in Vietnam was "patriotic" and "noble," illustrate this point. Not only was this a time when many women rejected confinement to the private sphere of men's homes; it was also a time when many men rejected the "masculine" stereotypes demanding that, particularly in their public behavior, "real men" may not be "womanly"—that is, gentle, peaceful, and caring.

This is not to say there is a simple, linear cause-and-effect relation between changes in the status of women and the rise of "feminine" values. Indeed, by the time a sizable number of women forcefully demand or achieve any gains, an androcratic backlash is generally already under way.

During the counterculture movement of the 1960s and 1970s, for example, young men were rejecting warfare as "heroic" and "manly" and switching to more effeminate styles of dress and hair and women were making important gains in equal rights. But at the same time that the old sexual stereotypes were powerfully challenged, the forces of the so-called conservative and male backlash were already gathering steam in anti-ERA, Moral Majority, and other rightist groups. Similarly, in Renaissance and Elizabethan times, where we find strong gylanic resurgences, we also find clear signs of simultaneous androcratic resistance. On one hand, a trend can be seen toward equal education for women of the ruling classes. Along with this, we see the beginnings of modern feminist literature in works like Christine de Pisan's *Book of the City of Ladies*.[60] On the other hand, vilification of women intensifies; new laws restrict their economic and political power; and a genre of literature devoted to showing women in appropriately "feminine"— that is, submissive—roles erupts.

All this leads to a final and fundamental point. Despite some periodic weakening in the androcratic infrastructure during periods of gylanic ascendance, until very recent times the subordinate status of women has remained substantially unchanged. Correspondingly, so also has the subordinate status of values like affiliation, caring, and nonviolence, stereotypically associated with women.

The End of the Line

As we have seen, throughout recorded history the androcratic system's first line of "defense" has been the reassertion of male control. Even more precisely, we have seen that a regression toward more suppression of women is an early predictor that a generally repressive and bloody period of history is setting in. As the research of Mc-Clelland, Roszak, and Winter so vividly documents, what this all points to is the grim conclusion that unless the systems relationship between the suppression of women and of affiliative and caring values is finally addressed, we are inevitably moving toward another period of massive bloodletting through war.

McClelland's research shows how the upsurge of violent themes in literature and art predicts periods of warfare and repression. Winter's research on the rapist Don Juan shows that the theme of repressive violence against women is an even more specific predictor of times of violence and war. And today there is a massive worldwide upsurge in violence against women—not only in fiction, but in fact.

Ideologically, our world is in the throes of a major regression to the woman-hating dogmas of both Christian and Islamic fundamentalism. There is in literature and film an unprecedented barrage of violence against women, of graphic portrayals of woman-murder and rape compared to which the earlier literary violence (of a *Taming of the Shrew* or a *Don Juan*) pales to insignificance. Also unprecedented is the current proliferation of hard-core pornography that, through a multi-billion-dollar industry, blares out into the home from books, magazines, comic strips, movies, and even cable television the message that sexual pleasure lies in violence, in the brutalization, enslavement, torture, mutilation, degradation, and humiliation of the female sex.[61]

As Theodore Roszak noted, the resistance to the nineteenth-century feminist movement was marked by an increase in what crime records term *aggravated assault*, severe, bone-breaking domestic beatings, the setting of a wife on fire, the putting out of her eyes.[62] Because throughout recorded history violence against women has been the androcratic system's response to any threat of fundamental change, in the wake of the twentieth-century women's liberation movement has come a substantial rise in violence against women. Examples are Indian bride burnings, Iranian public executions, Latin American imprisonments and tortures, worldwide wife batterings, and the global terrorism of rapes—which scholars estimate now occur in the United States at the rate of one every thirteen seconds.[63]

Viewed from the perspective of Cultural Transformation theory, the systems function of the massive and brutal violence against women today is not hard to see. If androcracy is to be maintained, women must be suppressed at all cost. And if this violence—and the incitements to violence through the revival of religious calumnies against women and the equation of sexual pleasure with the killing, raping, and torturing of women—is mounting all over our globe, it is because never before has male dominance been as vigorously challenged through a global, mutually reinforcing, synergistic women's movement for human liberation.[64]

Never before has the world seen such a mushrooming of governmental and nongovernmental organizations with memberships in the millions—groups ranging from the official All China Women's Federation to the National Women's Studies Association, the National Organization for Women, and the Older Women's League in the United States—all dedicated to improving the status of women. Never before has there been a United Nations Decade for Women. Never before have there been global conferences attracting thousands of women from every corner of the world to address the problems stemming from male supremacy. Never before in all of recorded history have women from every nation on this earth come together to work for a future of sexual equality, development, and peace—the three goals of the First United Nations Decade for Women.[65]

The growing recognition by women—and men—that these three goals are related stems from the intuitive perception of the dynamics we have been examining. For once the function of male violence against women is perceived, it is not hard to see how men who are taught they must dominate the half of humanity that is not as physically strong as they are will also think it their "manly" duty to conquer weaker men and nations.

Be it in the name of national defense, as in the USA and USSR, or in the holy name of God, as in the Muslim world, war or the preparation for war serve not only to reinforce male dominance and male violence but, as illustrated by both Hitler's Germany and Stalin's Russia, also to reinforce androcracy's third major systems component, authoritarianism. Times of war provide justification for "strongman" leadership. They also justify the suspension of civil liberties and rights—as illustrated by the news blackout during the U.S. invasion of Grenada in 1983 and the chronic martial law in embattled nation after nation in Africa, Asia, and Latin America.

In the past, the pendulum has always swung back from peace to war. Whenever more "feminine" values have risen for a time, threatening to transform the system, an aroused and fearful androcracy has thrust us back. But must the current swing backward inevitably bring on more and more domestic and international violence and, with it, more and more suppression of civil liberties and rights?

Is there really no way out of another—now, nuclear—war? Is this to be the end for the cultural evolution that began with such hope in the age of the Goddess, when the power of the life-giving Chalice was still supreme? Or are we now close enough to gaining our freedom to avert that end?

CHAPTER 11

Breaking Free: The Unfinished Transformation

Ours was to be the modern era, the Age of Reason. Enlightenment was to replace superstition; humanism was to replace barbarism; empirical knowledge was to take the place of cant and dogma. Yet perhaps never before had such magical powers been attributed to the Word. For it was through words, through the stuff that makes possible the conscious logical thinking processes of the human mind, that all the old irrationalities, all the old errors and maladies of humanity, were now to be cured. And never before had words, particularly written words, reached so far and so wide.

One reason was that never before had so many people been literate, and never before had so many new media of communication spread words to so many inhabitants of our globe. The move into what the philosophical historian Henry Aiken calls the Age of Ideology[1] came along with a major socio-technological shift. This was a shift, or "second wave," in Alvin Toffler's terms, comparable in proportion to the "first wave" of the agrarian revolution many millennia earlier.[2] The industrial revolution, although still primarily limited to the West, brought with it a barrage of new technologies, among them the printing press, which made possible the first large-scale distribution of books, journals, and newspapers. Then came the auditory media, the telegraph, telephone, and radio. These were followed by visual mass media, movies and television, which along with the gargantuan proliferation of magazines, newspapers, and books literally inundated every nook and cranny of our globe with words.

But there was, particularly in the West, another reason for this ideological explosion. As religious ideologies weakened in the wake of advancing industrialization, there was a great hunger, indeed almost a desperation, for new ways of perceiving, ordering, and valuing reality, in other words, for new ideologies.

Soon the voices of what some have called a secular clergy—philosophers and scientists—were making themselves heard throughout the Western world. By the nineteenth century they were everywhere, reinterpreting, reordering, and revaluing reality according to the modern gospels of Kant and Hegel, Copernicus and Galileo, Darwin and Lavoisier, Mill and Rousseau, Marx and Engels, to name but a few of the early prophets of the secular Word.

The Failure of Reason

These were to be the prophets of a cultural transformation. With the liberation of the human mind by reason, "rational man"—the product of the eighteenth-century Enlightenment—would now leave behind the barbarism of the past.

Through the industrial revolution, our technological evolution had been moving upward by leaps and bounds. Soon, so also would our cultural evolution. In the same way that new material technologies such as machines and medicines were bringing about seemingly miraculous changes, new social technologies, such as better ways of organizing and guiding human behavior, would speed the realization of humanity's higher potentials and aspirations. At long last, the age-old human striving for justice, for truth, for beauty could bring our ideals to reality.

But gradually this great hope and promise began to wane. For during the nineteenth and twentieth centuries "rational man" continued to oppress, kill, exploit, and humiliate his fellow and sister humans at every turn. Justified by such new "scientific" doctrines as the social Darwinism of the nineteenth century, the economic slavery of "inferior" races continued. Instead of being fought to "save heathens" or for the greater glory and power of God and king, colonial wars were now waged for "rational" economic and political purposes, such as the promotion of "free trade" and the "containment" of rival economic and political powers. And if male control of women could no longer be based on such irrational grounds as Eve's disobedience of the Lord, it would now be justified by new "rational scientific" dogmas proclaiming that male dominance was a biological and/or social law.

"Rational man" now spoke of how he would "master" nature, "subdue" the elements, and—in the great twentieth-century advance—"conquer" space. He spoke of how he had to fight wars to bring about peace, freedom, and equality, of how he had to murder children, women, and men in terrorist activities to bring dignity and liberation to oppressed peoples. As a member of the elites in both the capitalist and communist worlds, he continued to amass property and/or privilege. To make more profits or to meet higher quotas, he also began to systematically poison his physical environment, thereby threatening other species with extinction and causing severe illness in human adults and deformities in human babies. And all the while he kept explaining that what he was doing was either patriotic or idealistic and—above all—rational.

Finally, after Auschwitz and Hiroshima, the promise of reason began to be questioned. What was one to make of the "rational" and efficient use of human fat for soap? Or the highly efficient use of the hygienic shower for poison gas? How could one explain the carefully reasoned military experiments of the effect of atomic bombs and radiation on living and totally helpless human beings? Could all this superefficient mass destruction be called an advance for humanity?

Was explosive industrial overexpansion, the regimentation of whole populations into assembly lines, the computerization of individuals into numbers a step forward for our species? Or were these modern developments, along with the increasing pollution of land, sea, and air, signs of cultural regression rather than cultural progress? Since "rational man" seemed bent on desecrating and destroying our planet, would it not be better to turn back to "religious man," to the time before scientific advances plunged us into our secular-technological age?

By the last quarter of the twentieth century, philosophers and social scientists were not only questioning reason but all the progressive modern ideologies. Neither capitalism nor communism had fulfilled its promise. Everywhere there was talk of "the end of liberalism" as "realists" asserted that a free and equal society was never anything but a utopian dream.

Disillusioned by the purported failure of the progressive secular ideologies, all over the world people were returning to fundamentalist Christian, Muslim, and other religious teachings. Frightened by increasing signs of impending global chaos, masses of people were turning back to the old androcratic idea that what really matters is not life here on earth but whether, by disobeying God—and the commands of the men speaking for him on earth—we will be violently punished through all eternity.

Given the reality of the threat of global annihilation posed by nuclear bombs, from the perspective of a worldview that offers no realistic alternatives to the prevailing system, there do seem only three ways to respond to what increasingly look like insoluble global crises. One way is to go back to the old religious view that the only way out is in the next world, where—as born-again Christians or Shiite Muslims assert—God will reward those who obeyed his orders and punish those who did not. The second is through more immediate forms of escape: the nihilism, desensitization, and hopelessness that fuel the angry disillusionment of punk rock, the mind-numbing excesses of drugs, liquor, or mechanical sex, the decadence of grasping overmaterialism, and the deadening of all compassion through a modern "entertainment" industry that begins to resemble the bloody circuses of the last days of the Roman Empire. The third way is to try to drive society back to an imaginary better past—to the "good old days" before women and "inferior" men questioned their proper place in the "natural order."

But from the perspective we have been developing, based on the careful reexamination of our present and past, all this hopelessness is unfounded. All is not hopeless if we recognize it is not human nature but a dominator model of society that in our age of high technology inexorably drives us toward nuclear war. All is not futile if we recognize that it is this system, not some inexorable divine or natural law, that demands the *use* of technological breakthroughs for better ways of dominating and destroying—even if this drives us to global bankruptcy and ultimately to nuclear war. In short, if we look at our present from the perspective of Cultural Transformation theory, it becomes evident that there are alternatives to a system founded on the force-based ranking of one half of humanity over the other. What also becomes evident is that the great transformation of Western society that began with the eighteenth-century Enlightenment did not fail but is merely incomplete.

The Challenge to the Androcratic Premises

The ideas that came out of the eighteenth-century Enlightenment are in fact only partly new. Rooted in the deep past we examined in our first chapters, they are gylanic ideas: ideas suitable for a partnership rather than a dominator system of social organization. These were the kinds of ideas that in more modern forms reemerged during the Enlightenment to find new growth in the intellectual salons of women like Madame du Châtelet and Madame Geoffrin. At first, after so many centuries of disuse or misuse, they were little more than novelties, intellectual entertainment for a small, educated elite. But then, through better technologies of mass communication like the printing press, and later also through mass education, these ideas—which did not fit a dominator model of society—began to be replicated everywhere.

One of the earliest and most important of these ideas was the idea of progress. For if the universe was not, as religious dogma had it, an immutable entity controlled by an all-powerful deity, and if "man" was not after all created in God's image, improvements in nature, in society, and in "man" became real possibilities. This is a point usually stressed by those who argue that the great break in Western culture was the replacement of religious with secular ideas. But the point that is ignored is that what was being rejected was not religion, but the androcratic premise that a static and hierarchic social order was the will of God.[3]

When in 1737 Abbé de Saint-Pierre wrote his *Observations on the Continuous Progress of Human Reason,* he expressed, perhaps for the first time in such definite terms, the idea that ahead of humanity lies "the vista of an immensely long progressive life."[4] This idea of vast opportunities for the improvement of social and individual life here on earth was an outright rejection of Christian beliefs that this earth is a kind of testing ground where human beings, under a divine plan, are trained and disciplined for their ultimate destination—not here on earth, but in an afterlife. No longer supportive of an authoritarian status quo, but rather of ever-advancing human ideals and aspirations, the idea of progress was integral to much of the legal, social, and economic progress that in fact did occur in the eighteenth and nineteenth centuries.

Two related ideas, equality and freedom, also represented a fundamental break with androcratic ideology. In 1651 Thomas Hobbes had written in his *Leviathan* that "nature hath made men so equal in the faculties of body and mind, as that . . . when all is reckoned together the difference between man and man is not so considerable, as that one man can thereupon claim to himself any benefit to which another may not pretend as well."[5]

In the following century in France Jean Jacques Rousseau wrote that not only were "men" born free and equal, but that this was a "natural right" that entitled them to "sever their chains"[6]—a view of reality that was to be central to the American and French revolutions. And in the same century in England, Mary Wollstonecraft asserted that this "natural right" belongs to women as well as men—a view that was to be central to the still ongoing feminist revolution.[7]

Then in the nineteenth century Auguste Comte wrote of positivism and the law of human development. John Stuart Mill wrote of representative government as best suited to foster desirable moral and intellectual qualities. And Karl Marx, in part influenced by the first discoveries of the preandrocratic era, wrote of a classless society in which "the free development of each is the condition for the free development of all."[8]

Overriding all the many differences among these modern secular philosophers was the common antiandrocratic assumption that under the proper social conditions, human beings could and would live in free and equitable harmony. In other words, although not articulated in those terms, what these women and men envisioned was the possibility of a partnership rather than a dominator society.

The term *human being* was then, as now, generally equated with "men" or "mankind." Thus, the new eighteenth- and nineteenth-century commitment to human rights was generally seen as applicable only to men. In fact, this commitment was at first only to men who were white, free, and propertied. Nonetheless, along with these fundamental ideological breaks with the past came equally fundamental changes in social realities, which profoundly affected the lives of all women and men.

In first the American and then the French revolutions, the institution of Kingship—for many centuries a cornerstone of androcratic social organization—was challenged. In the minds of more and more people words like *equality, freedom,* and *progress* replaced words like *fealty, order,* and *obedience.* In most of the Western world, republics gradually replaced monarchies, secular schools replaced religious ones. And less autocratic families began to replace rigidly male-dominated households in which the word of father and husband, like the word of kings, had been absolute law.

Today the continued weakening of male control within the family is presented by many as part of a dangerous decline in the family. But the gradual erosion of the absolute authority of the father and husband was a critical prerequisite for the entire modern movement toward a more equalitarian and just society. As the sociologist Ronald Fletcher, one of few to focus on this critical point, writes in *The Family and Its Future,* "The fact is that the modern family has been created as a necessary part of this larger process of approximating to the central ideals of social justice in the entire reconstitution of society."[9]

A recent work shedding light on these critical, but still generally overlooked, psychohistorical dynamics is Randolph Trumbach's *The Rise of the Equalitarian Family.*[10] Trumbach shows that the fact that the modern equalitarian family appeared earlier in England than it did on the continent may have been an important factor in explaining why England, unlike France, Russia and Germany, did not have violent antimonarchic upheavals in the eighteenth and nineteenth centuries. His research shows how the rising power of women in the families of the British ruling classes brought important changes in the men who governed England. And these changes made these men more ready to accept social reforms, such as the move to parliamentary government with the monarch retained only as titular head—in sharp contrast to the lingering despotism of the Russian, German, and French kings.

The Secular Ideologies

If we pursue the analysis of modern history from the perspective of the underlying conflict between androcracy and gylany as two different paths for our cultural evolution, the emergence of the progressive modern secular ideologies acquires a new, and far more hopeful, meaning. By using the new analytic tools provided by Cultural Transformation theory, we can see how the replication of ideas like equality and freedom gradually led to the formulation of new ways of looking at the world. Acting as "attractors," such gylanic ideas served as the nuclei for the formation of new systems of belief, or ideologies, which were gradually disseminated through the social system and, at least in part, replaced the androcratic paradigm. In bits and pieces, these ideologies challenged a pyramidal world ruled from the very top by a male God, with men, women, children, and finally the rest of nature in a descending dominator order.

Ironically, one of the earliest of these progressive ideologies is one of those most heavily criticized by progressives today: capitalism. The ideological ground for capitalism had already been paved by the seventeenth-century Protestant Reformation. With its stress on the mercantile virtues of industry, individual attainment, and wealth—and conversely on the mercantile sins of sloth, individual failure, and poverty—the Protestant ethic was a prerequisite to the rise of capitalism.[11] But it was not until the eighteenth century that capitalism as a secular ideology emerged. By all accounts, its principal author is the first of the so-called worldly philosophers, Adam Smith.[12] The first economist, Smith extolled a free market as the cornerstone of a free and prosperous society.

In its radical departure from the older view in which men's social position and wealth were basically a function of birth, of being born a nobleman, a craftsman, or a serf, capitalism was in fact a move toward a freer society. It fundamentally challenged the rigid hierarchies of the earliest or protoandrocratic social organization in which the strongest, most brutal and violent men, the warrior-conquerors, and their descendants, the nobles and kings, exerted despotic powers justified by religious ideologies as divinely ordained.

Capitalism, the first modern ideology founded primarily on an economic or material base, was thus an important step in the move from a dominator to a partnership society. It also provided much of the impetus for new and more socially responsible political forms, such as constitutional monarchies and republics. Certainly capitalist economics was infinitely preferable to feudal economics, which was based primarily on violence: on those endless back and forth killings and pillagings of lords and kings in their seemingly insatiable drive for more real estate as a basis for power. But in its emphasis on individual acquisitiveness, competitiveness, and greed (the profit motive), its inherent hierarchism (the class structure), and its continued reliance on violence (e.g., colonial wars), capitalism remained fundamentally androcratic.

Most critically, as modern capitalist ideologues like George Gilder openly state, capitalism as we know it rests on male supremacy. In his book *Wealth and Poverty*, hailed by President Reagan as one of the most important works on capitalism since Adam Smith's *The Wealth of Nations*, Gilder specifically extols what he terms "the male's superior aggression" as the greatest of all social and economic values.[13]

Socialism and communism were the next major ideologies to emerge. Their early theorists rejected many of the androcratic premises espoused by capitalism. The works of "utopian socialists" such as Charles Fourier and the "scientific socialism" of Marx and Engels were powerful factors in promoting the ideal of equality; that is, a social organization based on linking or affiliation rather than ranking or domination.[14] And although it was only a sidelight in their voluminous writings, Marx and Engels explicitly acknowledged the critical importance of the oppression of women by men, which Engels called "the first class oppression" or "the world historical defeat of the female sex."[15]

But while in many parts of the world socialist ideas (such as free public education and a graduated income tax) helped achieve greater social equality and brought relief from brutal poverty for millions of peasants and industrial workers, socialism and communism also retained important androcratic components. Part of the problem lay in communist theory. Marxism, which developed into one of the most influential ideologies of modern times, did not abandon the androcratic tenet that power is to be attained through violence, as attested by its well-known adage "The end justifies the means." And part of the problem lay in how Marxism was applied in the first nation that adopted communism as its official ideology: the Soviet Union. Marx and Engels had recognized that a profound alteration of relations between women and men during prehistoric times ushered in the class society they so abhorred. Consequently, in the early years of the Russian Revolution there were some efforts to equalize the position of women. But in the end, men—and just as critically, "masculine" values—remained in control.[16]

Indeed, one of the most instructive lessons of modern history is how the massive regression to violence and authoritarianism under Stalin coincided with the reversal of earlier policies to replace patriarchal family relations with an equal relationship between women and men. As Trotsky was to remark (but only after his fall from power and exile), the failure of the communist revolution to achieve its goals in large part stemmed from the failure of its leadership to bring about a change in patriarchal relations within the family.[17] Or in our terms, it lay in the failure to bring about any fundamental changes in the relations between the two halves of humanity, which continued to be based on ranking rather than linking.

During the nineteenth and into the twentieth century other modern humanist ideologies—abolitionism, pacifism, anarchism, anticolonialism, environmentalism—also emerged. But like the proverbial blind men describing the elephant, they each described different manifestations of the androcratic monster as the totality of the problem. At the same time, they failed to address the fact that at its heart lies a male-dominator, female-dominated model of the human species.

The only ideology that frontally challenges this model of human relations, as well as the principle of human ranking based on violence, is, of course, feminism. For this reason it occupies a unique position both in modern history and in the history of our cultural evolution.

Seen from the long view of cultural evolution detailed in earlier chapters, feminism is clearly not a new ideology. Whereas the idea of our affiliation or linking with other human beings can be given only lip service in androcratic systems, for millennia of cultural evolution this idea was operationally expressed in more equalitarian and peaceful societies. And throughout recorded history—in ancient Greece and

Rome, during the troubador and Elizabethan eras, during the Renaissance and the Enlightenment—the "woman question," as Marx and Engels called it, has been a recurrent issue.

But feminism as a modern ideology did not emerge until the middle of the nineteenth century. Although many of the philosophical foundations for feminism had been articulated earlier by women like Mary Wollstonecraft, Frances Wright, Ernestine Rose, George Sand, Sarah and Angelina Grimké, and Margaret Fuller, its formal birthdate is July 19, 1848, at Seneca Falls, New York.[18] Here, at the first convention in recorded history held for the express purpose of launching women's collective struggle against subordination and degradation, Elizabeth Cady Stanton made a pivotal statement. "Among the many important questions which have been brought before the public," Stanton said, "there is none that more vitally affects the human family than that which is technically called 'Women's Rights.' "[19]

Though the mounting expression of this statement now challenges our system with greater strength and certainty than ever before, feminism still is perceived by many people as "just a women's issue." And as a consequence—because feminism continues to be split off from the ideological mainstream—the other progressive ideologies, from middle to left, continue to be riddled by massive internal inconsistencies.

By contrast, in a fourth group of modern ideologies there is no such difficulty, no problem with contradictory backward and forward pulls. These are the ideologies that began to evolve in the eighteenth- and nineteenth-century works of men like Edmund Burke, Arthur Schopenhauer, and Friedrich Nietzsche, who were squarely and unabashedly androcratic.[20]

Nietzsche, whose philosophy reidealizes primitive or protoandrocracy, is still much cited and admired. Openly and without any pretense or dissembling, Nietzsche declared that just as men must rule over women, a few "naturally selected," "socially pure" men must rule over the rest of mankind. For him, religion was a vile and despicable form of superstition, and he based his opposition to such "degenerate" and "effeminate" ideas as equality, democracy, socialism, women's emancipation, and humanitarianism on strictly "rational" and nonreligious grounds.[21]

Nietzsche's philosophy, under which the "noble and powerful" "may act toward persons of a lower rank just as they please," is the forerunner of modern fascism. Going back to Indo-European myths, Nietzsche despised the Judeo-Christian tradition as not androcratic enough because it contained what he called an "effeminate" "slave-

THE CHALICE AND THE BLADE

morality": ideas like "selflessness," "charity," "benevolence," and "neighborly love." As in the "noble" days of Aryan or Indo-European warriors, Nietzsche's ideal moral order was a world in which "the rulers" alone determined what is "goodness" and "supermen" heroes fought glorious wars. It was a world ruled by men who say, "I like that, I take it for my own," who know how to "keep hold of a woman and punish and overthrow insolence," and to whom the weak "willingly submit . . . and naturally belong." In short, it was a world very much like that imagined in that twentieth-century neoandrocratic document par excellence, Hitler's *Mein Kampf.*[22]

The Dominator Model of Human Relations

The modern rise of fascism and other rightist ideologies is much lamented by those who still harbor hope that we may continue our cultural evolution. They note with alarm that rightist ideologies would reimpose authoritarianism and push us back to a time of even greater injustice and inequality. They are particularly alarmed by the militarism of rightists and neorightists, their idealization of violence, bloodshed, and war, recognizing the imminent danger this way of thinking poses to our safety and survival. But there is a third aspect of rightist ideology that is rarely noted. This is that rightists—all the way from the American Right at the end of this century to the Action Française at its start—not only accept, but openly recognize the systems relationships between male dominance, warfare, and authoritarianism.[23]

If we objectively reexamine the political regimes of modern times, we see that it is no accident that rigid male dominance, and with it the dominance of "masculine" values, have marked some of the most violent and repressive modern regimes. This was the case in Hitler's Germany, in Franco's Spain, and in Mussolini's Italy. Such repressive regimes as those of Idi Amin in Africa, Zia-ul-Haq in Pakistan, Trujillo in the West Indies, and Ceausescu in Romania further illustrate the point.[24]

Most instructive (and sobering) is that in the "cradle of modern democracy," the same U.S. administration that holds itself above the law, carries out covert wars, and slashes public welfare spending to fund the highest military budget in American history, also opposes the constitutional amendment that would grant women legal equality, backing instead an amendment to deprive women of reproductive freedom of choice. Moreover, if we look closely at the two most visible religious neoandrocratic ideologies—that of American fundamentalist preachers like Jerry Falwell (a good friend and spiritual advisor of President Reagan) and that of the Ayatollah Khomeini in Iran—the link between institutionalized violence, the suppression of women, and the suppression of liberty becomes even more vividly apparent.

In the United States, Jerry Falwell preached to millions of television viewers that God is against the Equal Rights Amendment. His stand against freedom of speech, reproductive freedom of choice, and freedom to worship or not worship according to one's conscience constituted a threat to liberty. And his support for a more militaristic and "strong" America, for the brutally repressive South African government, and for other regimes that kill and torture their own people with weapons provided by "God-fearing American leaders" put the stamp of the will of God upon violence. In such ways, the Falwells of androcratic Christianity demonstrate their "bread and butter" recognition of the connection between male dominance, authoritarianism, and male violence.

A similar recognition of these connections was displayed by the Ayatollah Khomeini when he proclaimed the *chuddar*, the full-length dress that traditional Muslim women are required to wear, as the symbol of Iran's return to a theocratic androcracy run from the top by Khomeini and his mullahs.[25] Indeed, seen from the perspective of cultural transformation theory, the so-called Islamic resurgence is in fact a resurgence of the androcratic system, violently resisting the strong gylanic thrust of modern times.

The Ayatollah Khomeini was originally expelled from Iran after he led a two-day riot in protest against the more equal treatment of women. Upon his return one of his first official acts was to suspend the Family Protection Act of 1967, which gave women greater equality in divorce, marriage, and inheritance, and to exhort his followers to reinstate the veil.[26] At the same time, rigid new laws sexually segregating schools and beaches and lowering the minimum marriage age for girls to thirteen were also swiftly imposed.[27]

In Khomeini's new "moral" order that condoned, and indeed commanded, the violent taking of American diplomats as hostages and plunged Iran into a "holy war" against Iraq, any disobedience of the men now in power was proclaimed a crime against Islam, punishable by imprisonment, torture, even death. Neither freedom of speech nor press was tolerated. Any attempt to create a rival party was branded heretical.[28] And for the crime of believing in a faith that encourages equality between women and men, and for organizing women, in 1983 ten Baha'i women, including Iran's first woman physicist, a concert pianist, a nurse, and three teen-age college students were killed at a public execution.[29]

In sum, those who would reimpose strongman rule over *both* women and men see so-called women's issues like reproductive freedom of choice and equal rights under the law as primary issues. Indeed, if we look at rightist actions—from the American New Right to their religious counterparts in both West and East—we see that to them the return of women to their traditional subservient place is a top priority.[30]

Yet ironically, for the majority of those committed to ideals like progress, equality, and peace, the connection between "women's issues" and the attainment of progressive goals remains invisible. For liberals, socialists, communists, and others from middle to left the liberation of women is a secondary or peripheral issue—to be addressed, if at all, after the "more important" problems facing our globe have been resolved.

Much of the ideological confusion, as well as the one-step-forward, two-steps-back cultural movement of modern times can be traced to the failure of those working for progress to perceive the logical impossibility of creating a just and equal society as long as a dominator-dominated model of human relations remains in place. To the extent that we still fail to see that an equalitarian society and inequality between the two halves of humanity are contradictory, reason indeed seems to have failed us. One is reminded of Hans Christian Andersen's tale of the emperor with no clothes, whose nudity is only perceived by a small, as yet untutored, child. Having been tutored in the views of reality required to maintain the prevailing system, even the great logical powers of our minds have difficulty making the seemingly self-evident connection between a dominator model of human relations and a dominator society.

The two basic human types are male and female. The way the relationship between women and men is structured is thus a basic model for human relations. Consequently, a dominator-dominated way of relating to other human beings is internalized from birth by every child brought up in a traditional, male-dominated family.[31]

In the case of racism, this model of human relations is generalized from members of a different sex to members of a different race. In the related phenomenon of colonialism, it is generalized one step further, to members of a different nation (and usually also race). It is a model that has throughout history lent itself to the rationalization of all possible variations of social and economic exploitation.

Forward or Back?

Once we transcend the older ideological labels of liberal versus conservative, religious versus secular, or left versus right, modern history becomes in many critical respects radically clarified. The progressive modern ideologies can be seen as part of one mounting and continuing revolution against androcracy.

The rebellions first of burghers, workers, and peasants (Marx's bourgeoisie and proletariat), and later of black slaves, colonials, and women are also part of this still evolving movement to replace androcracy with gylany. For all these mass rebellions were and are fundamentally against a system in which ranking is the primary principle of social organization.

But until now the ideological challenge to androcracy has been fragmented. Rightist or neoandrocratic ideology provides an internally consistent and all-encompassing vision of both personal and public life. But of the progressive ideologies, only feminism avoids internal inconsistency by applying principles such as equality and freedom to all humanity—not just its male half. Only feminism offers the vision of a reordering of the most fundamental social institution: the family. And only feminism makes the explicit systems connection between the male violence of rape and wife beating and the male violence of war.[32]

In terms of our modern ideological system, feminism may be seen as a powerful attractor. While still on the system's periphery, during the nineteenth and twentieth centuries feminism has acted as a periodic attractor, guiding intellectual movement toward a worldview in which women and femininity are no longer devalued. But in our time of growing systems disequilibrium, feminism could become the nucleus for a new, fully integrated gylanic ideology. Incorporating the humanistic elements of both our religious and our secular ideologies, this modern gylanic worldview would at long last provide the internally consistent, overarching ideology required to replace a dominator with a partnership society.

There is already movement toward such an ideology. For example, at a 1985 New Paradigm Symposium sponsored by Fritjof Capra's Elmwood Institute, new paradigm thinking was specifically described as "postpatriarchal," and the new epistemology was seen as representing a "shift from domination and control of nature to cooperation and nonviolence."[33] Male futurists such as Robert Jungk, David Loye, and John Platt also recognize the link between equality for women and peace.[34] The 1985 Statement of the Baha'i Universal House of Justice, presented to world heads of state, expressly recognizes that "the achievement of full equality between the sexes" is a prerequisite for world peace.[35]

Feminist philosophers and activists from all over the world have called for a new ethic for both women and men based on "feminine" values like nonviolence and caring: women such as Wilma Scott Heide, Helen Caldicott, Betty Friedan, Alva Myrdal, Elise Boulding, Fran Hosken, Hilkka Pietila, Charlene Spretnak, Celina Garcia, Gloria Steinem, Dame Nita Barrow, Patricia Ellsberg, Patricia Mische, Barbara Deming, Mara Keller, Bella Abzug, Pam McAllister, Allie Hixson, and Elizabeth Dodson-Gray.[36] And innumerable feminist artists, writers, theologians, and scientists are providing both new theories and new images suitable for a partnership rather than a dominator world: Jessie Bernard, Carol Christ, Abida Khanum, Susan Griffin, Karen Sacks, Judith Plaskow, June Brindel, Gita Sen, Rosemary Radford Ruether, Dale Spender, Nawal El Saadawi, Jean O'Barr, Betty Reardon, Starhawk, Paula Gunn Allen, Carol Gilligan, Charlotte Bunche, Judy Chicago, Mayumi Oda, Alice Walker, Margaret Atwood, Georgia O'Keeffe, Peggy Sanday, Holly Near, Ursula Le Guin, E. M. Broner, Marge Piercy, Ellen Marie Chen, Alix Kates Shulman to name but a few.[37]

There are also attempts to found what are essentially gylanic political movements based on linking rather than ranking. For example, Petra Kelly's vision of an ecology-feminism-peace party provided much of the impetus for the West German Greens.[38] And Sonia Johnson's Citizen's Party Platform for the 1985 U.S. presidential elections clearly articulated the centrality of feminism to any significant social, economic, and political change.

These are all steps toward the fully integrated and coherent re-vision of reality necessary to effectively actualize a partnership society. Although we don't usually think of them this way, most social realities—schools, hospitals, stock exchanges, political parties, churches—are actualizations of ideas that once existed only in the minds of a few women and men. This also is true of the abolition of slavery, the replacement of monarchies with republics, and all the other progress we have made in the last few hundred years.[39] Even physical realities—tables, books, pots, airplanes, violins—are actualizations of human ideas. But for new ideas to be translated into new realities requires not only clarity of vision but also the opportunity to change old realities.

The ferment of our modern age as a time of unprecedented technological change is providing the opportunity for social change—and potentially for a fundamental social transformation. As we may see all around us, rapid technological change creates social instability. And, as transformation theory shows, when there are unstable states a shift from one system to another can occur.

The modern rebellions of women and men against a dominator society have come along with great technological advances. Moreover, every major technological change has given impetus to the gylanic thrust by forcing changes in the roles of both women and men. Now even nature seems to be rebelling against androcracy: in soil erosion, resource depletion, acid rain, and environmental pollution. But this rebellion of nature is not, as is sometimes argued, a rebellion against technology. Rather, it is a rebellion against the exploitive and destructive *uses* to which technology is put in a dominator society, in which men must keep conquering—be it nature, women, or other men.

It is said that modern technology is a danger not only to our cultural but also to our biological evolution. To the extent that androcracy remains in place, advanced technology does pose a major threat to our survival. Yet even this threat provides further impetus for a fundamental systems transformation.

On this most basic level, the modern gylanic thrust may be seen as an adaptive process impelled by the survival impulse of our species. As we will examine in the chapter that follows, the evidence mounting from every quarter is that the prevailing system is rapidly nearing its logical evolutionary end, the end of the line for a five thousand-year androcratic detour. What may lie ahead is the final bloodbath of this dying system's violent efforts to maintain its hold. But the death throes of androcracy could also be the birth pangs of gylany and the opening of a door into a new future.

CHAPTER 12

The Breakdown of Evolution: A Dominator Future

What was once merely a science fiction scenario for our future is now a serious possibility. This is that after humanity has wiped itself out in a nuclear war our earth will be taken over by cockroaches, one of few life-forms immune to radiation. If that should happen it would be a fitting finale for androcracy—and a grim evolutionary joke on us. The system that has stunted our cultural evolution would finally have succeeded in producing the kinds of creatures it is best suited for: insects rather than humans.

In his pioneering work *The Human Use of Human Beings* Norbert Wiener points out that the rigidly hierarchic organization of social insects such as ants and bees is perfectly appropriate for these less evolved life-forms.[1] Insects, Wiener observes, have bodies that are imprisoned in hard outer skeletons, or shells. Their minds too are imprisoned, in miniscule brains with little room for the memory storage or the complex information processing that is the basis of learning. Therefore a social organization in which each member fulfills a narrowly circumscribed and predetermined role and the sexes are completely specialized is appropriate for social insects like bees and ants. Here the queen bee's or ant's only function is the laying of eggs. The drone's only function is impregnation. And the worker bees or ants, as their names imply, do nothing except the nonreproductive work that keeps the insect colony fed and housed.

By contrast, humans are the life-forms with the most flexible and least specialized physical structures. Both women and men have the erect posture that frees our hands to make and use tools. Both sexes have the highly evolved brains, with the immense memory storage and extraordinary information processing capacity, that make us as flexible, as versatile—in short, as human—as we are.[2]

Thus, although a rigidly hierarchical social structure like androcracy, which imprisons both halves of humanity in inflexible and circumscribed roles, is quite appropriate for species of very limited capacity like social insects, it is truly *in*appropriate for humans.[3] And at this juncture in our technological evolution, it may also be fatal.

The Insoluble Problems

Wiener's book on cybernetic processes was a forerunner of the dynamic new way of understanding our world now being advanced in the natural sciences. In his work he stressed that what gives our species its evolutionary edge is our vastly superior ability to change our behavior in response to what he called feedback: changing information about the effectiveness or lack of effectiveness of past behavior and new information about present conditions.[4]

Moreover, as Wiener writes, we have a further evolutionary advantage in that we can change our behavior quickly. Other species also evolve new patterns of behavior in response to changing conditions. If they don't, they die out. But for most species these changes occur in the course of their biological evolution and involve changes in their bodily and mental structure. By contrast, we humans can if necessary change our patterns of behavior very fast, even instantly, by using our vastly superior minds.

But to do so successfully requires three things: that we perceive the feedback, that we interpret it correctly, and that we use it to change.

The feedback now bombarding us about present conditions on our globe is summed up by futurists in one phrase: *the world problematique*.[5] On the basis of computerized data analyses like the first and second Club of Rome reports, government reports like *Global 2000*, and a multitude of United Nations and other international studies, what most scientists project if present trends continue is that we are moving toward an even more chaotic time, when our world will see increasingly massive political, economic, and environmental dislocations.[6]

Already we are seeing serious ecological imbalances and environmental damage. We are seeing the effects of acid rain, rising levels of radioactivity, and toxic dumps and other forms of industrial and military pollution. Scientists fear increasing concentrations of ozone-depleting chemicals could even alter the world's climate. The rapid destruction of tropical rain forests is also grave cause for concern. Many species are dying out, and predictions are that by the year 2000 hundreds of thousands, perhaps as many as 20 percent of all species, will be irretrievably lost.[7]

Serious losses of arable soil are another problem, particularly in famine-torn Africa, as each year areas of crop and grasslands approximately the size of Maine become barren wasteland. And forecasts are that the spread of desertlike conditions is likely to accelerate.[8]

Famine and poverty are already catastrophic. In 1983, eleven million babies died before their first birthday. Two billion people lived on incomes below five hundred dollars per year. Four hundred fifty million suffered from hunger and severe malnutrition. Two billion had no dependable supply of safe water to drink.[9] In the United States, one of the richest nations of the world, the national poverty rate was the highest in seventeen years, with thirty-four million people, about one fifth of the population, classified as poor under official poverty standards.[10]

On the basis of current trends, projections are that conditions will worsen, not improve. The gap between rich and poor and between poor and rich nations will continue to widen. And despite greater material output, because of population growth, the lives of the world's growing numbers of poor will in coming years be even worse than they are today.[11]

In short, from all around us we are getting danger signals: feedback that our global system is beginning to break down. Of these signals, the most urgent is what futurists call the population explosion. As more and more people are born and in turn give birth to more and more people, population is growing at a fantastic rate.[12] In fact, if the present rate of population growth continues, it is projected that more people would be added to our planet in *one year* during the middle of the twenty-first century than during the entire first *fifteen hundred years* after the death of Christ![13]

The population crisis—the fact that present policies have failed to slow down growth rate significantly—lies at the heart of the seemingly insoluble complex of problems futurists call the *world problematique*. For behind soil erosion, desertification, air and water pollution, and all the other ecological, social, and political stresses of our time lies the pressure of more and more people on finite land and other resources, of increasing numbers of factories, cars, trucks, and other sources of pollution required to provide all these people with goods, and the worsening tensions that their needs and aspirations fuel.[14] And it is in connection with this population explosion that we can most clearly see how and why under an androcratic system our worsening problems are in fact insoluble.

Human Issues and Women's Issues

Looking at our past, we saw how the prevailing paradigm so blinded scholars that in prehistoric figures of the Mother Goddess they could see only fat Venuses—obese sex objects for men. Looking at our future through this same mind-set, the troubles afflicting our globe are also seen in a distorted way.

The problem begins with the fact that the information gathered by most experts chronically leaves out women. Thus, most policymakers work with only half a data base. But even if the data is before their eyes, policymakers still cannot take appropriate action if the present system is maintained.

For example, in many overpopulated and economically underdeveloped Muslim nations, high birthrates are not considered a problem. Leaders like the Ayatollah Khomeini and Zia-ul-Haq seem to make no connection between the terrible poverty of their people and the fact that in these cultures women are viewed as male-controlled technologies of reproduction. Similarly, at the 1984 Population Conference in Mexico City—held in the world's most notoriously overpopulated city, in a country from which every year millions of illegal migrant workers flee north to escape the terrible poverty caused by burgeoning overpopulation—Reagan administration representatives flatly announced that there is no population problem.[15]

The implication from the world's press, and even most scholarly studies, is that instances such as these mainly show a lack of intelligence or awareness on the part of the governments involved. But this impression can be dangerously misleading. For in actuality they reflect an acute awareness of what is required to maintain the androcratic system worldwide.

Ironically, in this time of massive androcratic regression, a dramatic example of such policies comes from a nation that was once an example of a very different kind in its striving toward the gylanic ideals of justice, equality, and social progress. The United States—which both exerts a disproportionate influence on the policies of overpopulated nations and consumes a disproportionate percentage of world resources—recently regressed to policies that would increase rather than decrease birthrates. Not only did the Reagan administration radically cut funding for Third World family planning programs; at the same time that hunger and poverty were increasing in the United States, this administration also pressed for a constitutional amendment that would again outlaw abortion. And in a move calculated to deny women fair and equal access to nonbreeding life options, the Reagan administration also firmly opposed the proposed Equal Rights Amendment to the U.S. Constitution and ignored or effectively repealed earlier laws designed to equalize women's employment and educational opportunities.[16]

Elsewhere in the world, with the notable exception of nations like China, Indonesia, Taiwan, and more recently Kenya and Zimbabwe, family planning is rarely a top priority. On the contrary, in communist Romania, one of the poorest Eastern bloc countries, President Nicolae Ceausescu declared it women's "patriotic duty" to bear four children, requiring women to undergo monthly pregnancy tests at their workplace and provide medical explanations for "persistent nonpregnancy."[17] And in many of the most overpopulated and poorest nations of the developing world, women are specifically denied access to birth control.[18]

Although in a historic first the 1984 International Conference on Population declared "improving the status of women" worldwide an important goal both for its own sake and because of its significance in lowering fertility,[19] policies creating the opportunities and motivations for women to limit birth are almost everywhere extremely low priorities.[20] Moreover, this continues to be the case—despite the clear message from population experts worldwide that if population planning is to succeed, creating satisfying and socially rewarded roles for women other than those of wives and mothers is even more important than the availability of birth control education.[21]

Logically, the alternatives are simple. The traditional means of stemming population growth have been disease, hunger, and war. Giving top priority to reproductive freedom and equality for women is the only other way to halt the population explosion. But to give these "women's issues" top priority would mean the end of the present system. It would mean a transformation from a dominator to a partnership society. And to the androcratic mind—the mind of many of our world's present leaders—this is not a possibility.

So these men find and fund "think tanks" that tell them what they want to hear. Funded by extremely conservative interests in the United States is the Heritage Foundation, which in turn funded studies by the well-known futurist Herman Kahn, by economist Julian Simon, and others that argue there is no global population problem.[22] In essence, they project that, short-range, widespread famine will help reduce excess population, and long-range, the men who run the world's economic empires will, through unbridled, aggressive competition, produce so much wealth that enough will "trickle down" to feed as many billions as come.[23]

These modern successors of the men who in our prehistory stood reality on its head use the same approach to the problem of "solutions" for hunger and poverty. As a first step, the existence of global hunger and poverty is either denied or minimized.[24] If then presented with irrefutable evidence—for example, that every minute thirty children die for want of food and inexpensive vaccines[25]—they retort that this "unfortunate situation" is only temporary. Poverty and hunger too will gradually go away as the "free market" takes over.[26]

Even those who seem less callous about human suffering, and are in fact deeply concerned, often fall into the conventional traps that obscure and distort reality. They continue to talk of hunger and poverty in general terms—when the evidence clearly shows that, in keeping with the rank-ordering for the androcratic/dominator system, poverty and hunger are in fact primarily "women's issues."[27]

According to U.S. government figures, families headed by women are the poorest in America, with a poverty rate triple that of other families, and two out of three older Americans living in poverty are women.[28] In the developing world the realities are even grimmer.[29] In Africa, inside and outside refugee camps where thousands are starving, the poorest of the poor and the hungriest of the hungry are women and their children.[30] And as the United Nations *State of the World's Women 1985* report and many other official and unofficial reports document, the situation in Asia and Latin America is the same.[31]

Again, logic would dictate that national and international policies would make programs dealing with the poverty and hunger of women a top priority. But what is the response to these realities?

In the United States, despite heavy female unemployment, the unemployment relief programs passed in the 1970s and 1980s characteristically created only a fraction of the jobs outside male-dominated occupations like construction and road repair. In Africa, despite famines and despite the fact that women do from 60 to 80 percent of the food growing, technical agricultural aid, loans, land grants, and money subsidies go almost exclusively to men. In Asia and Latin America, despite the fact that women are doomed by unequal education and training to the lowest paid occupations, economic development and foreign aid programs are likewise geared almost exclusively to men.[32]

The androcratic system's rationale is that it is men who as "heads of households" take care of women and children. But this rationale is based on a model of reality that, once again, ignores masses of data. For there are more than ample data demonstrating that a major reason so many women and children all over our globe live in abject misery is that in *both* "intact" and "broken" families men do *not* adequately provide for their wives and children.

The problem is not only that in industrialized countries like the United States over one half of divorced fathers fail to obey court orders to pay child and spousal support.[33] Nor is it only that in many parts of Africa and Asia men now flock to cities leaving the women and children behind to fend as they may—returning only occasionally to sire still another child.[34]

The problem is that in male-dominated societies women's poverty and hunger is far more deeply rooted. It is not only confined to families headed by women. It is integral to a family organization in which the male "head" of household has the socially sanctioned power to determine how resources or money are to be distributed and used.

For example, in our own Western history, be it among Russian serfs, Irish miners, or American "hard hats," many men considered it an affront to their masculinity to "hand over" their wages so that their wives could buy food for the family. Instead, as many Western men still do today, they drank up or gambled away these earnings, beating their wives for "nagging" if, by objecting, the women challenged their male authority. This also is still a frequent pattern in many Latin American countries and in large regions of Africa.

Moreover, in much of the developing world the women who prepare—and frequently also grow—the food for their families do not get to eat until after the men have had their fill.[35] Once again, there is a rationale for such sexually discriminatory eating patterns. Often in places where women do backbreaking work from dawn to dusk it is argued that men need more food, or that these are "ethnic traditions" that should not be tampered with by Western outsiders. These are also the rationales for food taboos that forbid women, particularly pregnant ones, from eating the very foods they need to maintain their health. As a consequence, World Health Organization studies show that nutritional anemia afflicts close to half of all Third World women of childbearing age and 60 percent of pregnant women![36]

But such sexually discriminatory patterns in the distribution of resources do not "only" seriously affect women. They also have horrendous implications for men—and for human evolution. It is well known that mothers suffering from malnutrition tend to give birth to children who are more prone to debility and disease. This obviously affects both male and female children, who are born physically under par and often also mentally defective, or at best endowed with lower intelligence than they would have had if their mothers had been adequately fed.

Thus, because our world systematically ignores those human issues that are still called "women's issues," millions of human beings of *both* sexes are deprived of their birthright: the chance to lead healthy, productive, and rewarding lives. And because the rights of women are not considered human rights, not only our cultural evolution, but also our biological evolution, is unnecessarily stunted.

Again, it would seem logical to take immediate steps to change sexually discriminatory patterns of food distribution. But as in the case of population policies and development policies, there are in androcracies overriding systems constraints.

The basic problem is that in male-dominated societies there are two fundamental obstacles to formulating and implementing the kinds of policies that could effectively deal with our mounting global problems. The first obstacle is that the models of reality required to maintain male dominance require that all matters relating to no less than half of humanity be ignored or trivialized. This monumental exclusion of data is an omission of such magnitude that, in any other context, scientists would immediately pounce upon it as a fatal methodological flaw. But even when this first obstacle is somehow overcome and policymakers are provided with complete and unbiased data, a second and even more fundamental obstacle remains. This is that the first policy priority in a male-dominated system has to be the preservation of male dominance.

Hence, policies that would weaken male dominance—and most policies that offer any hope for the human future will—cannot be implemented. Even if they are formulated, such policies must be shelved, given inadequate funding, or otherwise diverted from being effective.

The Totalitarian Solution

When their elected leaders fail to solve economic, social, and political problems, people look to others for answers. In the androcratic mind, valuing above all rank-orderings and conditioned to equate right with might, these answers tend to be equated with violence and strong-man rule.

It is thus not surprising that besides progressive systems breakdown and/or nuclear holocaust, a frequent futures scenario is global totalitarianism. This has been the theme of many science fiction stories, from Orwell's prophetic *1984* to movies like *Rollerball* and *Fahrenheit 451*. It has also been the subject of scholarly futurist studies such as Jacques Ellul's prediction of a dehumanized world ruled by inhuman technocrats.[37] Even the "optimistic" scenario predicted by The Hudson Institute's Herman Khan of a future of incredible prosperity resulting from the business-as-usual course of the institute's giant corporate and military clients is of a world ruled by what Kahn called a new "Augustinian Empire."[38]

It has often been suggested that the great psychic appeal of a totalitarian future is its promise of a "strong leader" who, like the "strong father" of childhood, will "take care of things" in return for faithful obedience. Certainly a mind socialized to submit to male authority will tend to turn to this "protection" in times of crisis. But there is another reason for the strong appeal—and great danger—of modern totalitarianism.

The conventional view of totalitarianism is that it is an entirely modern affliction, a special horror of our secular, scientific age.[39] It is true the technological efficiency of German mass extermination camps was unprecedented. But, as prehistory and history amply demonstrate, attempts to slaughter entire populations are far from unusual. And neither is the reign through terror that is the hallmark of modern totalitarian regimes.

What we may now see through our repossession of our lost past is that, in its methods of control and its basic structure, modern totalitarianism is the logical culmination for a cultural evolution based on the dominator model of social organization. In the efficiency of its control through terror, it is the ultimate advancement for this type of society. In essence, it is a technologically advanced version of the rigidly androcratic city-states that first emerged in our prehistory.

The twentieth-century totalitarian state is the modern successor of the theocratic city-state of antiquity where, as the cultural historian Lewis Mumford writes, the mass of people were no more than rigidly controlled cogs in giant social machines.[40] And the elites of fascist and communist totalitarian state hierarchies are in essence the successors of the old warrior/priest dominator castes. Both claim a direct and exclusive line to the Word—be it the Word of God, Marx, the Führer,

Stalin, or Mao. Both also claim the exclusive right to interpret that Word through law and to impose it by force or the threat of force.

As in androcratic theocracies, where there was no separation between Church and State, the men who rule fascist and communist societies wield both spiritual and temporal power. Like androcratic religions, neither communism nor fascism tolerate any deviation from the "true" faith. And unlike other modern political ideologies, but like androcratic religions, both offer a comprehensive worldview, encompassing most, if not all, aspects of familial, social, and political life. Extreme rightists still cite the Bible as authority for male-dominated families. In Nazi Germany the Führer proclaimed that not only women but also "weak" and "effeminate" men like Jews were the natural inferiors to his new race of "supermen." And in the Soviet Union, the official model for family relations, replicated in endless stories and pictures of women serving meals to their men, is the same as that of the German *hausfrau* idealized in Nazi propaganda.[41]

In communist and fascist totalitarian states, as in the Bible, the Koran, and other traditional scriptures, obedience and conformity are the supreme virtues. And in both, violence is not only permitted but also ordered if it is in the service of the officially approved ideology—be it through the reign of terror of a medieval priesthood, with its book burnings and people burnings, or the more efficient technologies of brainwashing and torture of modern totalitarian regimes.

The charismatic or hypnotic leader who successfully rallies his followers to "destroy the enemy" is another integral feature of both modern and traditional totalitarianism. In medieval Europe, for example, androcratic religious fervor and greed were successfully whipped up in mammoth pageant-filled rallies by men like Pope Urban II and Bernard of Clairvaux, catapulting Europe and Asia Minor into the centuries-long bloodbath of the Crusades.[42] In Nazi Germany, at equally long and pageant-filled torchlight rallies, Hitler's fiery speeches catapulted the modern world into World War II. More recently, reaching into millions of homes through the hypnotic medium of television, a new breed of charismatic demagogues have been exhorting Americans to go out and battle the "heathen and immoral humanists, feminists, and communists"—whom they blame for all our world's ills.

Both traditional and modern totalitarian regimes require the constant study of holy or officially sanctioned scriptures—be it a Bible or a Koran, or a *Mein Kampf*, or *Quotations from Chairman Mao*. These provide all the answers: the ultimate "truth." And, serving the same purpose as the rigid religious censorship of androcratic prehistory and history, all the mass media are rigidly controlled in modern totalitarian regimes.

In fact, although it is on a much smaller scale than during the prehistoric imposition of androcracy, perhaps the most striking characteristic of modern totalitarian societies is that (as in Orwell's *1984*) one of their main industries is the manufacture of myths. In Nazi Germany, Adolf Hitler, an unattractive dark-haired man, was successfully mythologized into the Führer, the strong-man leader of the "racially pure," blond, blue-eyed, and beautiful Aryan supermen. In Russia, God the Father and his surrogate, the tyrannical Little Father or Czar, were replaced by first Lenin, the Father of the Revolution, whose mummified body became an object of cult veneration, and then Stalin, who coldbloodedly butchered millions of his own people.

In both communist and fascist mythologies, we may see exactly the same processes at work as were used during the first androcratic takeover to stand reality on its head. Not only new myths, but also new symbols were created. For example, the swastika and the hammer and sickle have in the twentieth century been almost as powerful as the symbol of Christ on the Cross in mobilizing men for "holy" crusades and wars. And in place of the old religious ceremonies and rituals have come new ceremonies and rituals: mass rallies, torchlight parades, rhythmic marches, and the righteous thunder and fury of the Leader's words exhorting the "enlightened" to go forth and violently spread the "truth."

New Realities and Old Myths

If we reexamine Nazi myths from the perspective of Cultural Transformation theory, we see it is not coincidental that they were a return to the mythology of the Indo-European or Aryan invasions. For Nazi Germany was a return to Kurgan times not only in its myths, but in its realities.

In their wholesale slaughter of Jews—whose homes, businesses, private possessions, and even the gold in their teeth served to fill official coffers and to reward party faithfuls—the Nazis were simply repeating the way the Kurgans had gone about obtaining wealth. They killed, plundered, and looted.

The Nazi view of women as male-controlled property was likewise a throwback to Kurgan norms. In Nietzsche's words, for the new Aryan supermen of Germany, women were to be like some "often pleasant domestic animal," to be used by men for sexual enjoyment, personal service, entertainment, and procreation.[43] Even beyond that, as in Hitler's plan to reward decorated soldiers with the right to have more than one wife, basically women were for the Nazi what they were for Kurgan men: warrior's booty.[44]

The rule of the all-powerful Führer or Leader on a larger scale duplicated the autocratic strongman rule of the Kurgan chief. In the same way, the Nazi elite corps, the feared S.S. and S.A., duplicated the Kurgan warrior caste, who as living exemplars of "manly" virtues sought glory, honor, and power by unleashing destruction and terror.

In its faithful replication of rigid male dominance, authoritarianism, and a high degree of institutionalized male violence, Nazi Germany was one of the most violent reactions to the gylanic thrust. It was also one of the first modern regressions to the earliest and most brutal form of proto-androcracy—and the foreshadower of a neo-androcratic future.

For be it rightist or leftist, Christian or Muslim, the totalitarian solution is nothing more nor less than an updating of the androcratic solution. Its basic premises are contempt for "effeminate," or peaceful, approaches, a conviction that obedience to orders, be they divine or temporal, is the ultimate virtue, and a creed that—starting with male and female— divides humanity into in-groups and out-groups that must forever be at war.

That this solution was, and still is, accepted by so many people is not because it offers any viable answer to the mounting problems of our world. Its attraction comes from the entrenched power of androcratic and neoandrocratic symbols and myths. For these images and stories continue to inculcate in our unconscious minds the fear that even to contemplate any deviation from androcratic premises and solutions will be severely punished, not only in this life but also in the next.

An important lesson to be learned from the rise of modern totalitarianism is that it can be a fatal error to underestimate the power of myth. The human psyche seems to have a built-in need for a system of stories and symbols that "reveal" to us the order of the universe and tell us what our place within it is. It is a hunger for meaning and purpose seemingly beyond the power of any rationalistic or logical system to provide.

Modern history shows that the way to stop the horrors that have been humanity's lot under the guidance of androcratic myths is *not* to suppress everything that cannot be reduced to "masculine" reason. It is not to try to hold down the intuitive, nonlinear, nonrational functions

of our mind that in neoandrocratic dogma have so often been called
"the feminine."[45] For the problem is not that symbols and myths are
of a lower and therefore less desirable order than logic or rationality.
The problem is rather what *kinds* of symbols and myths are to fill and
guide our minds: prohuman or antihuman, gylanic or androcratic.

Just as the Kurgan invasions truncated our early cultural evolution,
totalitarians and would-be totalitarians still block our cultural evolution
at every turn today, aided by both old and new androcratic myths. In
the last few centuries, the partial shift from a dominator to a partnership society has partly freed humanity, allowing some movement toward a more just and equalitarian society. But at the same time there
has been a strong countermovement, on both left and right, to more
deeply entrench the dominator society in its modern or totalitarian
form.

Given the strong inertial pull of androcratic social and ideological
organization and the new technologies of both body and mind control
(modern propaganda, drugs, nerve gases, and even experiments in
psychic control), a totalitarian future is a real possibility. Such a world
order, however, probably would not last very long.

For be they religious or secular, modern or ancient, Eastern or Western, the basic commonality of totalitarian leaders and would-be leaders
is their faith in the power of the lethal Blade as the instrument of our
deliverance. A dominator future is therefore, sooner or later, almost
certainly also a future of global nuclear war—and the end of all of
humanity's problems and aspirations.

CHAPTER 13

Breakthrough in Evolution: Toward a Partnership Future

Science fiction writers' visions of the future are filled with incredible technological inventions. But by and large, theirs is a world singularly bereft of new social inventions. In fact, more often than not, what they envision takes us backward while seeming to go forward in time. Be it in Frank Herbert's *Dune*[1] or George Lucas's *Star Wars*, what we frequently find is actually the social organization of feudal emperors and medieval overlords transposed to a world of intergalactic high-tech wars.

After five thousand years of living in a dominator society, it is indeed difficult to imagine a different world. Charlotte Perkins Gilman tried in *Herland*.[2] Written in 1915, this was a tongue-in-cheek utopia about a peaceful and highly creative society in which the most valued and rewarded work—and the top social priority—was the physical, mental, and spiritual development of children. The catch was that this was a world where all the men had wiped themselves out in a final orgy of war, and the handful of surviving women had, in an amazing mutation, saved their half of humanity by learning to reproduce themselves all by themselves.

But as we have seen, the problem is not men as a sex, but men and women as they must be socialized in a dominator system. There were men and women in the Neolithic and in Crete. There are men and women among the peaceful !Kung and BaMbuti. And even in our male-dominated world not all women are peaceful and gentle, and many men are.

Clearly both men and women have the biological potential for many different kinds of behaviors. But like the external armor or shell that encases insects and other arthropods, androcratic social organization encases both halves of humanity in rigid and hierarchic roles that stunt their development. If we look at our evolution from the perspective of androcracy and gylany as the two possibilities for human social organization, we see that it is not by accident that the sociobiologists who are today trying to revitalize androcratic ideology with yet another infusion of nineteenth-century social Darwinism so frequently cite insect societies to support their theories. Neither is it accidental that their writings reinforce the view that the normative model for rigidly hierarchic social rankings—the male-dominator/female-dominated model of human relations—is preprogrammed in our genes.[3]

As many scientists have pointed out, evolution is not predetermined.[4] On the contrary, from the very beginning we have been active co-creators in our own evolution. For example, as Sherwood Washburn wrote, our invention of tools was both the cause and effect of the bipedal locomotion and erect posture that freed our hands to fashion ever more complex technologies.[5] And, as both technology and society have grown more complex, the survival of our species has become increasingly dependent on the direction, not of our biological, but of our cultural evolution.

Human evolution is now at a crossroads. Stripped to its essentials, the central human task is how to organize society to promote the survival of our species and the development of our unique potentials. In the course of this book we have seen that androcracy cannot meet this requirement because of its inbuilt emphasis on technologies of destruction, its dependence on violence for social control, and the tensions chronically engendered by the dominator-dominated human relations model upon which it is based. We have also seen that a gylanic or partnership society, symbolized by the life-sustaining and enhancing Chalice rather than the lethal Blade, offers us a viable alternative.

The question is how do we get from here to there?

A New View of Reality

Scientists like Ilya Prigogine and Niles Eldredge tell us that bifurcations or evolutionary branchings in chemical and biological systems involve a large element of chance.[6] But as the evolutionary theorist Erwin Laszlo points out, bifurcations in human social systems also involve a large element of choice. Humans, he points out, "have the ability to act consciously, and collectively," exercising foresight to "choose their own evolutionary path." And he adds that in our "crucial epoch" we "cannot leave the selection of the next step in the evolution of human society and culture to chance. We must plan for it, consciously and purposefully."[7] Or as the biologist Jonas Salk writes, our most urgent and pressing need is to provide that wonderful instrument, the human mind, with the wherewithal to image, and thereby create, a better world.[8]

Initially this may seem an impossibly difficult task. But as we have seen, our views of reality—of what is possible and desirable—are a product of history. And perhaps the best proof that our ideas, symbols, myths, and behaviors can be changed is the evidence that such changes were in fact effected in our prehistory.

We have seen how the image of woman was once venerated and respected in most of the ancient world and how images of women as merely sexual objects to be possessed and dominated by men became predominant only after the androcratic conquests. We have also seen how the meaning of symbols such as the tree of knowledge and the serpent that sheds its skin in periodic renewal were completely reversed after that critical bifurcation in our cultural evolution. Now seemingly firmly associated with terrible punishment for questioning male dominance and autocratic rule, these same symbols were not so long ago in evolutionary time seen as manifestations of the human thirst for liberation through higher or mystical knowledge.

We have seen that even after the imposition of androcratic rule, the meaning of our most important symbols has often shifted radically through the impact of gylanic resurgence or androcratic regression. A striking example is the cross. The original meaning of the crosses incised on prehistoric figurines of the Goddess and other religious objects appears to have been her identification with the birth and growth of plant, animal, and human life. This was the meaning that survived into Egyptian hieroglyphics, where the cross stands for life and living, forming part of such words as *health* and *happiness*.[9] Later, after impaling people on stakes became a common way to execute them (as shown in Assyrian, Roman, and other androcratic art), the cross became a symbol of death. Later still, the more gylanic followers of Jesus again tried to transform the cross on which he was executed into a symbol of rebirth—a symbol associated with a social movement that set out to preach and practice human equality and such "feminine" concepts as gentleness, compassion, and peace.[10]

In our time, centuries after this movement was co-opted by the androcratic/dominator system, the way we interpret ancient symbols and myths still plays an important part in how we shape both our present and our future. At the same time that some of our religious and political leaders would have us believe a nuclear Armageddon may actually be the will of God,[11] we are seeing a vast reaffirmation of the desire for life, not death, in an accelerated, and indeed unprecedented, movement to restore ancient myths and symbols to their original gylanic meaning.[12]

For instance, artists like Imogene Cunningham and Judy Chicago are for the first time in recorded history using female sexual imagery in ways that are strikingly reminiscent of Paleolithic, Neolithic, and Cretan symbolisms of birth, rebirth, and transformation.[13] Also for the first time in recorded history, images from nature, such as seals, birds, dolphins, and the green forests and grasses—in earlier times symbols of the unity of all life under the Goddess's divine power—are being used by the ecology movement to reawaken in us the consciousness of our essential link with our natural environment.[14]

Often unconsciously, the process of unraveling and reweaving the fabric of our mythical tapestry into more gylanic patterns—in which "masculine" virtues such as "the conquest of nature" are no longer idealized—is in fact already well under way.[15] What is still lacking is the "critical mass" of new images and myths that is required for their actualization by a sufficient number of people.

Perhaps most important is that women and men are increasingly questioning the most basic assumption of androcratic society: that both male dominance and the male violence of warfare are inevitable. Among studies by anthropologists bearing on this point, a cross-cultural study conducted by Shirley and John McConahay found a significant correlation between the rigid sexual stereotypes required to maintain male dominance and the incidence of not only warfare, but wife beating, child beating, and rape.[16] As will be detailed in a second book continuing our reports, these systems correlations are verified by a growing number of new studies undertaken precisely because scientists in many disciplines are beginning to question the prevailing models of reality.[17] Moreover, by studying *both* halves of humanity, scientists are today in ground-breaking ways expanding our knowledge about the possibilities for human society, as well as for the evolution of human consciousness.[18]

Indeed, from the perspective of Cultural Transformation theory, the much written about modern "revolution in consciousness" can be seen as the transformation of androcratic to gylanic consciousness.[19] An important index of this transformation is that, for the first time in recorded history, many women and men are frontally challenging destructive myths, such as the "hero as killer."[20] They are becoming aware of what "heroic" stories ranging from those of Theseus to Rambo and James Bond actually teach us and demanding that children of both sexes be taught to value caring and affiliation instead of conquest and domination.[21] In Sweden, laws have already been enacted to phase out the sale of war toys, which have traditionally served to teach boys lack of empathy with those they hurt, as well as all the other attitudes and behaviors that men require for killing others of their kind.[22] And peace demonstrations by millions of people all over this planet are dramatic evidence of a renewed consciousness of our connectedness with all of humanity.

Women and men all over the world are, for the first time in such large numbers, frontally challenging the male-dominator/female-dominated human relations model that is the foundation of a dominator worldview.[23] At the same time that the idea of the "war of the sexes" is being exposed as a consequence of this model, its further result of seeing "the other" as "the enemy" is also being challenged.[24] There is, most significantly, a growing awareness that the emerging higher consciousness of our global "partnership" is integrally related to a fundamental reexamination and transformation of the roles of both women and men.[25]

As the psychiatrist Jean Baker Miller writes, in society as presently constituted only women are "geared to be carriers of the basic necessity for human communion"[26]—and to in fact value their affiliations with others more highly than even themselves. In contrast to men, who are generally socialized to pursue their own ends, even at the expense of others, women are socialized to see themselves primarily as responsible for the welfare of others, even at the expense of their own well-being.[27]

This dichotomization of human experience, as Miller extensively documents, creates psychic distortions in both women and men. Women tend to be so overidentified with others that the threatened loss, or even disruption, of an affiliation can be, as she writes, "perceived not as just a loss of a relationship but as something closer to a total loss of self." Men, on the other hand, often tend to see their human need for affiliation as "an impediment" or "a danger." Thus, they can perceive service to others not as something central but rather secondary to their self-image, something a man "may desire or can afford *only* after he has fulfilled the primary requirements of manhood."[28]

These views of gender roles and of reality are, as we have seen, fundamental to androcratic society. But, as Miller writes, "it is extremely important to recognize that the pull toward affiliation that women feel in themselves is not wrong or backward. . . . What has not been recognized is that this psychic starting point contains the possibilities for an entirely different (and more advanced) approach to living and functioning—very different, that is, from the approach fostered by the dominant culture. . . . It allows for the emergence of the truth: that for everyone—men as well as women—individual development proceeds *only* by means of affiliation."[29]

These new ways of imaging reality for both women and men are giving rise to new models of the human psyche. The older Freudian model saw human beings primarily in terms of elemental drives such as the need for food, sex, and safety. The newer model proposed by Abraham Maslow and other humanistic psychologists takes these elemental "defense" needs into account but also recognizes that human beings have a higher level of "growth" or "actualization" needs that distinguish us from other animals.[30]

This shift from defense needs to actualization needs is an important key to the transformation from a dominator to a partnership society. Hierarchies maintained by force or the threat of force require defensive habits of mind. In our type of society, the creation of enemies for man begins with his human twin, woman, who in prevailing mythology is blamed for nothing less than our fall from paradise. And for both men and women, this ranking of one half of humanity over the other, as Alfred Adler noted, poisons all human relations.[31]

Freud's observations bear out that the androcratic psyche is indeed a mass of inner conflicts, tensions, and fears.[32] But as we move from androcracy to gylany, more and more of us can begin to move from defense to growth. And as Maslow observed in studying self-actualizing and creative people, as this happens, rather than becoming more selfish and self-centered, more and more of us will move toward a different reality: the "peak-experience" consciousness of our essential interconnectedness with all of humanity.[33]

A New Science and Spirituality

This theme of our interconnectedness—which Jean Baker Miller calls affiliation, Jessie Bernard calls the "female ethos of love/duty," and Jesus, Gandhi, and other spiritual leaders have simply called love—is today also a theme of science. This developing "new science"—of which "chaos" theory and feminist scholarship are integral parts—is for the first time in history focusing more on relationships than on hierarchies.

As the physicist Fritjof Capra writes, this more holistic approach is a radical departure from much of Western science, which has been characterized by a hierarchic, overcompartmentalized, and often mechanistic approach.[34] It is in many ways a more "feminine" approach, as women are said to think more "intuitively," tending to draw conclusions from a totality of simutaneous impressions rather than through step-by-step "logical" thinking.[35]

Salk writes of a new science of empathy, a science that will use both reason and intuition "to bring about a change in the collective mind that will constructively influence the course of the human future."[36] This approach to science—successfully used by the geneticist Barbara McClintock, who in 1983 won a Nobel Prize—will focus on human society as a living system of which all of us are a part.[37] As Ashley Montagu said, it will be a science congruent with the true, and original, meaning of education: to draw forth and cause to grow the innate potentialities of the human being.[38] Above all else, as Hillary Rose writes in "Hand, Brain, and Heart: A Feminist Epistemology for the Natural Sciences," it will no longer be a science "directed toward the domination of nature or of humanity as part of nature."[39]

Evelyn Fox Keller, Carol Christ, Rita Arditti, and other scholars point out how, under the protective mantle of "objectivity" and "field-independence," science has often negated as "unscientific" and "subjective" the caring concerns considered overly feminine by the traditional view.[40] Thus, science has until now generally excluded women as scientists and focused its study almost entirely on men. It has also excluded what we may call "caring knowledge": the knowledge that, as Salk writes, we now urgently need to select those human forms that are "in cooperation with evolution, rather than those that are antisurvival or antievolutionary."[41]

This new science is also an important step toward bridging the modern gap between science and spirituality, which is in large part the product of a worldview relegating empathy to women and "effeminate" men. Scientists are further beginning to recognize that—like the artificial conflict between spirit and nature, between woman and man, and between different races, religions, and ethnic groups fostered by the dominator mentality—the way we view conflict itself needs to be reexamined.

As Miller writes, focusing her research on actualization rather than defense, the question is *not* how to eliminate conflict, which is impossible. As individuals with different needs and desires and interests come into contact, conflict is inevitable. The question directly bearing on whether we can transform our world from strife to peaceful coexistence is how to make conflict productive rather than destructive.[42]

As a result of what she terms productive conflict, Miller shows how individuals, organizations, and nations can grow and change. Approaching each other with different interests and goals, each party to the conflict is forced to reexamine its own goals and actions as well as those of the other party. The result for both sides is productive change rather than nonproductive rigidity. Destructive conflict, by contrast, is the equation of conflict with the violence required to maintain domination hierarchies.

Under the prevailing system, Miller points out, "conflict is made to look as if it *always* appears in the image of extremity, whereas, in fact, it is actually the lack of recognition of the need for conflict and provision of appropriate forms for it that leads to danger. This ultimate destructive form is frightening, but it is also *not* conflict. It is almost the reverse; it is the end result of the attempt to avoid and suppress conflict."[43]

Although this suppressive dominator approach to conflict still overwhelmingly prevails, the success of less violent and more "feminine" or "passive" approaches to conflict resolution offers concrete hope for change. These approaches have ancient roots. In recorded history Socrates and later Jesus both used them. In modern times they are best known as embodied by men like Gandhi and Martin Luther King, Jr.—whom androcracy handled by killing and canonizing. But by far their most extensive use has been by women. A notable example is how in the nineteenth and twentieth centuries women nonviolently fought against unjust laws. For access to family planning information, birth control technologies, and the right to vote, they permitted themselves to be arrested and chose to go on hunger strikes, rather than using force or the threat of force to gain their ends.[44]

This use of nonviolent conflict as a means of attaining social change is not merely passive or nonviolent resistance. By refusing to cooperate with violence and injustice through the use of violent and unjust means, it is the creation of the positive transformative energy Gandhi called *satyagraha* or "truth force." As Gandhi said, the aim is to *transform* conflict rather than to suppress it or explode it into violence.[45]

Just as critical in recharting the course of cultural evolution is the current reexamination of the way we define power. Writing about the still prevailing view of power, Miller notes how the so-called need to control and dominate others is psychologically a function *not* of a feeling of power but rather of a feeling of powerlessness. Distinguishing between "power *for* oneself and power *over* others," she writes: "The power of another person, or group of people was generally seen as dangerous. You had to control them or they would control you. But in the realm of human development, this is not a valid formulation. Quite the reverse. In a basic sense, the greater the development of each individual the more able, more effective, and less needy of limiting or restricting others she or he will be."[46]

A central motif of twentieth-century feminist literature has been the probing not only of existing power relations but also of alternative ways of perceiving and using power: of power as affiliation. This theme has been explored by Robin Morgan, Kate Millett, Elizabeth Janeway, Berit Aas, Peggy Antrobus, Marielouise Janssen-Jurreit, Tatyana Mamonova, Kathleen Barry, Devaki Jain, Caroline Bird, Birgit Brock-Utne, Diana Russell, Perdita Huston, Andrea Dworkin, Adrienne Rich, to name but a few.[47] Described in such phrases as "sisterhood is powerful," this nondestructive view of power is one that women are increasingly bringing with them as they move into the "men's" world from their "women's" place. It is a "win-win" rather than a "win-lose" view of power, in psychological terms, a means of advancing one's own development *without* at the same time having to limit the development of others.

In visual or symbolic terms, this is the representation of power as linking. It has from time immemorial been symbolized by the circle or oval—the Goddess's cosmic egg or Great Round—rather than by the jagged lines of a pyramid where, as gods or as the heads of nations or families, men rule from the top. Long suppressed by androcratic ideology, the secret of transformation expressed by the Chalice was in earlier times seen as the consciousness of our unity or linking with one another and all else in the universe. Great seers and mystics have continued to express this vision, describing it as the transformative power of what early Christians called *agape*. This is the elemental linking between humans that in the distortion characteristic of androcracy is called "brotherly" love. In essence, it is the kind of selfless love a mother has for her children, once mythically expressed as the divine love of the Great Mother for her human children.

In this sense, our reconnection with the earlier spiritual tradition of Goddess worship linked to the partnership model of society is more than a reaffirmation of the dignity and worth of half of humanity. Nor is it only a far more comforting and reassuring way of imaging the powers that rule the universe. It also offers us a positive replacement for the myths and images that have for so long blatantly falsified the most elementary principles of human relations by valuing killing and exploiting more than giving birth and nurturing.

In the early chapters of this book we saw how at the outset of our cultural evolution the feminine principle embodied in the Goddess was the image not only of the resurrection or regeneration of death into life, but also of the illumination of human consciousness through divine revelation. As the Jungian psychoanalyst Erich Neumann notes, in ancient mystery rites the Goddess represented the power of physical transformation of the "godhead as the whirling wheel of life" in its "birth-bringing and death-bringing totality." But she was also the symbol of spiritual transformation: "the force of the center, which within this cycle passes toward consciousness and knowledge, transformation and illumination—the higher goals of humanity from time immemorial."[48]

A New Politics and Economics

In our time, a good deal is being said and written about transformation. Futurists like Alvin Toffler write of great technological transformations from "first wave," or agrarian, to "second wave," or industrial, and now to "third wave," or postindustrial society.[49] Indeed, we have in recorded history seen major technological transformations. But within the perspective of the Cultural Transformation theory we are developing, it can be seen that what have often been described as major cultural transformations—for example, the shift from classical to Christian times and more recently to the secular or scientific age—have only been changes within the androcratic system from one type of dominator society to another.

There have been other bifurcation points, points of social disequilibrium when a fundamental systems transformation could have occurred, when new fluctuations or more gylanic patterns of functioning appeared. But these have never gone beyond the nucleation thresholds that would signal a shift from androcracy to gylany. To use a familiar analogy, until now the androcratic system has been like a rubber band. During periods of strong gylanic resurgence, for example, in Jesus' time, the band has stretched quite far. But always in the past, when the boundaries or limits of androcracy were reached, it snapped back toward its original shape. Now, for the first time in recorded history, instead of snapping back this band may break—and our cultural evolution may at last transcend the confines that have for millennia held us back.

What, at our level of technological development, would be the political and economic implications of a complete shift from a dominator to a partnership society? We have the technologies that in a world no longer governed by the Blade could vastly accelerate our cultural evolution. As Ruth Sivard records in her yearly report *World Military and Social Expenditures*, the cost of developing one intercontinental ballistic missile could feed 50 million children, build 160,000 schools, and open 340,000 health care centers. Even the cost of a single new nuclear submarine—equal to the annual education budget of twenty-three developing countries in a world where 120 million children have no school they can go to and 11 million babies die before their first birthday—could open new opportunities for millions of people now doomed to live in poverty and ignorance.[50]

What we lack, as futurist writings stress again and again, is the social guidance system, the governing values, that would redirect the allocation of resources, including our advanced technological know-how, to higher ends.

Willis Harman, who has headed major futurist studies at the Stanford Research Institute, writes that what is needed—and evolving—is a "metamorphosis in basic cultural premises and all aspects of social roles and institutions." He describes this as a new consciousness in which competition will be balanced with cooperation and individualism will be balanced with love. It will be a "cosmic consciousness," a "higher awareness," which "relates self-interest to the interests of fellow man and of future generations." And it will entail nothing short of a fundamental transformation of "truly awesome magnitude."[51]

Similarly, in the second Club of Rome report we read that in order "to avoid major regional and ultimately global catastrophe," we must develop a new world system "guided by a rational master plan for long-term organic growth," held together by "a spirit of truly global cooperation, shaped in free partnership."[52] This world system would be governed by a new global ethic based on a greater consciousness of and identification with future as well as present generations and will require that cooperation, rather than confrontation, and harmony with, rather than conquest of, nature become our normative ideals.[53]

A striking aspect of these projections is that these futurists do *not* see technology or economics as the main determinants of our future. They recognize instead that our roads to the future will be shaped by human values and social arrangement, in other words, that our future will be primarily determined by the way we human beings conceive its possibilities, potentials, and implications. In the words of the futurist John McHale, "Our mental blueprints are its basic action programs."[54]

But what is most remarkable is that what many futurists are actually saying—practically in so many words—is that we must leave behind the hard, conquest-oriented values traditionally associated with "masculinity." For is not the need for a "spirit of truly global cooperation, shaped in free partnership," "a balancing of individualism with love," and the normative goal of "harmony with rather than conquest of nature," the reassertion of a more "feminine ethos"? And to what end could "drastic changes in the norm stratum" or a "metamorphosis in basic cultural premises and all aspects of social institutions" relate if not to the replacement of a dominator with a partnership society?

The transformation from a dominator to a partnership society would obviously bring with it a shift in our technological direction: from the use of advanced technology for destruction and domination to its use for sustaining and enhancing human life. At the same time, the wastefulness and overconsumption that now robs those in need would also begin to wane. For as many social commentators have observed, at the core of our Western complex of overconsumption and waste lies the fact that we are culturally obsessed with getting, buying, building— and wasting—*things*, as a substitute for the satisfactory emotional relationships that are denied us by the child-raising styles and the values of adults in the present system.[55]

Above all, the shift from androcracy to gylany would begin to end the politics of domination and the economics of exploitation that in our world still go hand in hand. For as John Stuart Mill pointed out over a century ago in his ground-breaking *Principles of Political Economy*, the way economic resources are distributed is a function not of some inexorable economic laws, but of political—that is, human—choices.[56]

Many people today recognize that in their present form neither capitalism nor communism offers a way out of our growing economic and political dilemmas. To the extent that androcracy remains in place, a just political and economic system is impossible. Just as Western nations like the United States, where slates of candidates are financed by powerful special interests, have not yet reached political democracy, nations like the USSR, ruled by a powerful, privileged, and mostly male managerial class, are still far from economic democracy.

In particular, the politics of domination and the economics of exploitation are in *all* androcracies exemplified by a "dual economy" in which women's unpaid, or at best low paid, productive activities are systematically exploited. As the United Nations *State of the World's Women 1985* points out, globally women are half the population, perform two thirds of the world's work in terms of hours, earn one tenth as much as men earn, and own one hundredth the property that men own.[57] Moreover, the unpaid labor of women—who in Africa do most of the food growing and who worldwide provide as many health services for free as all formal health care sectors combined—is routinely excluded from calculations of national productivity.[58] The result, as the futurist Hazel Henderson points out, is global economic projections based on "statistical illusions."[59]

In *The Politics of the Solar Age*, Henderson describes a positive economic future in which the roles of women and men are fundamentally rebalanced. This will entail facing up to the fact that our "masculine" militarism is the "most energy-intensive entropic activity of humans, since it converts stored energy directly into waste and destruction without any useful intervening fulfillment of basic human needs." Following the present period "marked by the decline in systems of patriarchy," Henderson predicts neither economic nor ecological reality will be governed by the "masculinized" values "now deeply associated with male identity."[60]

Similarly, in *The Sane Alternative*, the British writer James Robertson contrasts what he terms the "hyper-expansionist" or HE future with a "sane, humane, ecological" or "SHE future."[61] And in Germany Professor Joseph Huber describes his negative economic scenario for the future as "patriarchic." By contrast, in his positive scenario, "the sexes are on a socially equal standing. Men and women share in paid positions, as well as household tasks, child rearing, and other social activities."[62]

The central theme unifying these and other economic analyses, though of critical importance for our future, still remains largely unarticulated. This is that traditional economic systems, be they capitalist or communist, are built upon what, borrowing from Marxist analyses, may be called the *alienation of caring labor*.[63] As this caring labor—the life-sustaining labor of nurturing, helping, and loving others—is fully integrated into the economic mainstream, we will see a fundamental economic and political transformation.[64] Gradually, as the female half of humanity and the values and goals that in androcracy are labeled feminine are fully integrated into the guidance mechanisms of society, a politically and economically healthy and balanced system will emerge. Then, unified into the global family envisioned by the feminist, peace, ecology, human potential, and other gylanic movements, our species will begin to experience the full potential of its evolution.

Transformation

The move to a new world of psychological and social rebirth will entail changes we cannot yet predict, or even envision. Indeed, because of so many failures following earlier hopes for social betterment, projections of a positive future elicit skepticism. Yet we know that changes in structure are also changes in function. Just as one cannot sit in the corner of a round room, as we shift from a dominator to a partnership society, our old ways of thinking, feeling, and acting will gradually be transformed.

For millennia of recorded history, the human spirit has been imprisoned by the fetters of androcracy. Our minds have been stunted, and our hearts have been numbed. And yet our striving for truth, beauty, and justice has never been extinguished. As we break out of these fetters, as our minds, hearts, and hands are freed, so also will be our creative imagination.

For me, one of the most evocative images of the transformation from androcracy to gylany is the caterpillar metamorphosed into the butterfly. It seems to me a particularly fitting image to express the vision of humanity soaring to the heights it can attain, as the butterfly is an ancient symbol of regeneration, an epiphany of the transformative powers attributed to the Goddess.

Two further books, *Breaking Free* and *Emergence*, will explore this transformation in depth. They will lay out a new blueprint for social actualization—not for a utopia (which literally means "no place" in Greek), but for a *pragmatopia*, a realizable scenario for a partnership future. Though a few pages obviously cannot even begin to cover what will be developed in two books, I would like to close this chapter by briefly sketching some of the changes I envision as we resume our interrupted cultural evolution.[65]

The most dramatic change as we move from a dominator to a partnership world will be that we, and our children and grandchildren, will again know what it means to live free of the fear of war. In a world rid of the mandate that to be "masculine" men must dominate, and along with the rising status of women and more "feminine" social priorities, the danger of nuclear annihilation will gradually diminish. At the same time, as women gain more equality of social and economic opportunities—so that birthrates can come into better balance with our resources—the Malthusian "necessity" for famine, disease, and war will progressively lessen.[66]

Since they also are to a large extent related to overpopulation, to "man's conquest of nature," and to the fact that environmental "house-keeping" is not in androcracies a "masculine" policy priority, our problems of environmental pollution, degradation, and depletion should likewise begin to lessen during the years of transformation. So also should their consequences in shortages of energy and other natural resources and in health problems from chemical pollution.[67]

As women are no longer systematically excluded from financial aid, land grants, and modernization training, Third World economic development programs for advancing education and technology and raising standards of living will become much more effective. There will also be far less economic inefficiency and less of the terrible human suffering that is the lot of millions of people, in both the developed and developing world today. For, as women are no longer treated as breeding animals and beasts of burden and have greater access to health care, education, and political participation, not only the female half of humanity, but all of humanity will benefit.[68]

Along with more rational measures aimed at successfully reducing the poverty and hunger of the mass of the world's poor—women and children—the growing consciousness of our linking with all other members of our species should gradually also narrow the gulf between rich and poor nations. Indeed, as billions of dollars and work hours are rechanneled from technologies of destruction to technologies that sustain and enhance life, human poverty and hunger could gradually become memories of a brutal androcratic past.[69]

The changes in woman-man relations from the present high degree of suspicion and recrimination to more openness and trust will be reflected in our families and communities. There will also be positive repercussions in our national and international policies. Gradually we will see a decrease in the seemingly endless array of day-to-day problems that now plague us, ranging from mental illness, suicide, and divorce to wife and child battering, vandalism, murder, and international terrorism. As research to be detailed in the second book of our report shows, these types of problems in large part derive from the high degree of interpersonal tension inherent in a male-dominated social organization and from dominator child-rearing styles heavily based on force. Thus, with the move to more equal and balanced relations between women and men and the reinforcement of gentler, more prohuman and caring behavior in children of both sexes, we may realistically expect fundamental psychic changes. These, in a relatively short time, will in turn exponentially accelerate the tempo of transformation.

In the world as it will be when women and men live in full partnership, there will, of course, still be families, schools, governments, and other social institutions. But like the already now emerging institutions of the equalitarian family and the social-action network, the social structures of the future will be based more on linking than ranking. Instead of requiring individuals that fit into pyramidal hierarchies, these institutions will be heterarchic, allowing for both diversity and flexibility in decision making and action. Consequently, the roles of both women and men will be far less rigid, allowing the entire human species a maximum of developmental flexibility.[70]

In keeping with present trends, many of our new institutions will also be more global in scope, transcending national boundaries. As the consciousness of our linking with one another and our environment firmly takes hold, we can expect to see the old nation-state as a self-absorbed political entity wither away. However, rather than more uniformity and conformity, which is the logical projection from the dominator system viewpoint, there will be more individuality and diversity. Smaller social units will be linked in matrices or networks for a variety of common ends, ranging all the way from the cooperative cultivation and harvesting of oceans and space exploration to the sharing of knowledge and the advancement of the arts.[71] There will also be other, as yet unforeseeable, global ventures to develop more equitable and efficient ways of utilizing all our natural and human resources, as well as new material and social inventions that we at this point in our development cannot yet foresee.

With the global shift to a partnership society will come many technological breakthroughs. There will also be adaptations of existing techniques to new social requirements. Some of these may, as Schumacher, and others have predicted, be better, more labor-intensive technologies in areas of craft—for example, a return to the pride of creativity and individuality in weaving, carpentry, pottery, and other applied arts. But at the same time, since the goal is to free humanity from insectlike drudgery, this will *not* mean a return to more labor-intensive technologies in all fields. On the contrary, allowing us the time and energy to actualize our creative potentials, we can expect that mechanization and automation will play an even more life-supporting role. And both small- and large-scale methods of production will be utilized in ways that encourage, and indeed require, worker participation, rather than, as required in a dominator system, turning workers themselves into machines or automatons.

The development of safer and more reliable birth control methods will be a top technology priority. We will also see much more research on understanding and slowing down the aging process, ranging from already emerging techniques to replace worn-out body parts to means of regenerating body cells. We might also see the perfection of laboratory-created life. But rather than replacing women, or converting women into incubators for artificially developed cells, such new technologies of reproduction would be carefully evaluated by both women and men to ensure they serve to actualize both sexes' full human potential.[72]

Since technologies of destruction would no longer consume and destroy such a vast portion of our natural and human resources, as yet undreamed (and presently undreamable) enterprises will be economically feasible. The result will be the generally prosperous economy foreshadowed by our gylanic prehistory. Not only will material wealth be shared more equitably, but this will also be an economic order in which amassing more and more property as a means of protecting oneself from, as well as controlling, others will be seen for what it is: a form of sickness or aberration.

In all this, there will be a number of economic stages. The first of these, already emerging, will be what is termed a mixed economy, combining some of the best elements of capitalism and communism— and in the sense of a variety of decentralized cooperative units of production and distribution—also anarchism.[73] The socialist concept that human beings have not only basic political but basic economic rights will certainly be central to a gylanic economy based on caring rather than domination. But as a partnership society replaces a dominator one, we can also expect new economic inventions.

At the heart of this new economic order will be the replacement of the presently failing "dual economy," in which the male-dominated economic sector that is rewarded by money, status, and power must in its industrial stages, as Henderson documents, "cannibalize both social and ecological systems." Instead we can expect that the non-monetized "informal" economy—of household production and maintenance, parenting, volunteer community service, and all the cooperative activities that permit the now "over-rewarded competitive activities to appear successful"—will be appropriately valued and rewarded.[74] This will provide the now-missing basis for an economic system in which caring for others is not just given lip service but is the most highly rewarded, and therefore most highly valued, human activity.

Practices like female sexual mutilation, wife beating, and all the other more or less brutal ways through which androcracy has kept women "in their place" will of course be seen not as hallowed traditions but as what they are—crimes spawned by man's inhumanity to woman.[75] As for man's inhumanity to man, as male violence is no longer glorified by "heroic" epics and myths, the so-called male virtues of dominance and conquest will also be seen for what they are—the brutal and barbaric aberrations of a species turned against itself.

Through the reaffirmation and celebration of the transformative mysteries symbolized by the Chalice, new myths will reawaken in us that lost sense of gratitude and the celebration of life so evident in the artistic remnants of the Neolithic and Minoan Crete. By reconnecting us with our more innocent psychic roots—before warfare, hierarchism, and male dominance became our ruling norms—this mythology will not move us back psychically to the world as it was in the technological childhood of our species. On the contrary, by intertwining our ancient heritage of gylanic myths and symbols with modern ideas, it will move us forward toward a world that will be much more rational, in the true sense of the word: a world animated and guided by the consciousness that both ecologically and socially we are inextricably linked with one another and our environment.

Along with the celebration of life will come the celebration of love, including the sexual love between women and men. Sexual bonding through some form of what we now call marriage will most certainly continue. But the primary purpose of this bonding will be mutual companionship, sexual pleasure, and love. Having children will no longer be connected with the transmission of male names and property. And other caring relationships, not just heterosexual couples, will be fully recognized.[76]

All institutions, not only those specifically designed for the socialization of children, will have as their goal the actualization of our great human potentials. Only a world in which the quality rather than the quantity of human life is paramount can have such a goal. Hence, as Margaret Mead predicted, children will be scarce, and thus highly valued.[77]

The life-formative years of childhood will be the active concern of both women and men. Not just biological parents, but many other adults will take various responsibilities for that most precious of all social products: the human child. Rational nutrition as well as physical

and mental exercises, such as more advanced forms of yoga and med-
itation, will be seen as elementary prerequisites for healthy bodies and
minds. And rather than being designed to socialize a child to adjust
to her or his place in a world of rank orderings, learning will be—as
we are already beginning to see—a lifelong process for maximizing
flexibility and creativity at all stages of life.

In this world, where the actualization of our higher evolutionary
potentials—our greater freedom through wisdom and knowledge—will
guide social policy, a primary focus of research will be the prevention
of personal and social illness, of both body and mind. Beyond this,
our as yet untapped, but increasingly recognized, mind powers will be
extensively researched and cultivated. The result will be that as yet
undreamed of mental and physical potentials will be uncovered and
developed.[78]

For above all, this gylanic world will be a world where the minds
of children—both girls and boys—will no longer be fettered. It will be
a world where limitation and fear will no longer be systematically
taught us through myths about how inevitably evil and perverse we
humans are. In this world, children will not be taught epics about men
who are honored for being violent or fairy tales about children who
are lost in frightful woods where women are malevolent witches. They
will be taught new myths, epics, and stories in which human beings
are good; men are peaceful; and the power of creativity and love—
symbolized by the sacred Chalice, the holy vessel of life—is the governing principle. For in this gylanic world, our drive for justice, equality, and freedom, our thirst for knowledge and spiritual illumination,
and our yearning for love and beauty will at last be freed. And after
the bloody detour of androcratic history, both women and men will at
last find out what being human can mean.

Notes

Introduction: The Chalice and the Blade (pp. xiii–xxiii)

1. See, e.g., Fritjof Capra, *The Turning Point: Science, Society, and the Rising Culture* (New York: Simon & Schuster, 1982); Marilyn Ferguson, *The Aquarian Conspiracy: Personal and Social Transformation in the 1980s* (Los Angeles: Tarcher, 1980); George Leonard, *The Transformation: A Guide to the Inevitable Changes in Humankind* (New York: Delta, 1972).

2. The first paper to advance the theory that Minoan civilization was destroyed by earthquakes and tidal waves was Spyridon Marinatos, "The Volcanic Destruction of Minoan Crete," *Antiquity* 13 (1939): 425–39. Since then, it appears more likely that these natural disasters so weakened Crete as to make possible the takeover by Achaean (Mycenaean) overlords, as there is no evidence that this takeover was through a full-scale armed invasion.

3. James Mellaart, *The Neolithic of the Near East* (New York: Scribner, 1975).

4. P. Steven Sangren, "Female Gender in Chinese Religious Symbols: Kuan Yin, Ma Tsu, and the 'Eternal Mother,' " *Signs* 9 (Autumn 1983): 6.

5. In connection with the dominator model, an important distinction should be made between domination and actualization hierarchies. The term *domination hierarchies* describes hierarchies based on force or the express or implied threat of force, which are characteristic of the human rank orderings in male-dominant societies. Such hierarchies are very different from the types of hierarchies found in progressions from lower to higher orderings of functioning—such as the progression from cells to organs in living organisms, for example. These types of hierarchies may be characterized by the term *actualization hierarchies* because their function is to maximize the organism's potentials. By contrast, as evidenced by both sociological and psychological studies, human hierarchies based on force or the threat of force not only inhibit personal creativity but also result in social systems in which the lowest (basest) human qualities are reinforced and humanity's higher aspirations (traits such as compassion and empathy as well as the striving for truth and justice) are systematically suppressed.

6. A fascinating analysis of the transformation of Aztec culture toward rigid male dominance, and with it, male violence, is found in June Nash, "The Aztecs and the Ideology of Male Dominance," *Signs* 4 (Winter 1978): 349–62. As noted in the text, some of the most ancient myths of many cultures refer to a more peaceful and just time when women had high status. For example, the Chinese *Tao Te Ching*, as R. B. Blakney notes, refers to a time before the imposition of male dominance (see, e.g., R. B. Blakney, ed. and trans., *The Way of Life: Tao Te Ching* [New York: Mentor, 1955]). Similarly, Joseph Needham tells of the Taoist doctrine of "regressive evolution" (in other words, cultural regression from an earlier and more civilized time). He also notes that some of the best-known statements of the earlier Taoist period of The Great Togetherness or *Ta Thung* occur in the second century B.C.E. *Hua Nan Tsu* and the later Confucian *Li Chi* (Joseph Needham, "Time and Knowledge in China and the West," in Julius T. Fraser, ed., *The Voices of Time* [New York: Braziller, 1966]).

7. Marija Gimbutas, "The First Wave of Eurasian Steppe Pastoralists into Copper Age Europe," *The Journal of Indo-European Studies* 5 (Winter 1977): 281.

8. For some works on human behavior not being genetically preprogrammed but the product of a complex interaction between biological and social/environmental factors, see, e.g., R. A. Hinde, *Biological Bases of Human Social Behavior* (New York: McGraw-Hill, 1974); Ruth Hubbard and Marian Lowe, eds., *Genes and Gender II* (New York: Gordian Press, 1979); Helen Lambert, "Biology and Equality: A Perspective on Sex Differences," *Signs* 4 (Autumn 1978): 97–117; Riane Eisler and Vilmos Csanyi, "Human Biology and Social Structure" (work in progress); Ethel Tobach and Betty Rosoff, eds., *Genes and Gender: I* (New York: Gordian Press, 1978); Ruth Bleier, *Science and Gender* (Elmsford, NY: Pergamon Press, 1984); Ashton Barfield, "Biological Influences on Sex Differences in Behavior," in M. Teitelbaum, ed., *Sex Differences: Social and Biological Perspectives* (New York: Doubleday Anchor, 1976); Linda Marie Fedigan, *Primate Paradigms: Sex Roles and Social Bonds* (Montreal: Eden Press, 1982); R. C. Lewontin, Steven Rose, and Leon Kamin, *Not in Our Genes* (New York: Pantheon, 1984). An excellent overview of aggressive behavior (and a very effective refutation of the current sociobiological revival of nineteenth-century social Darwinism) may be found in Ashley Montagu, *The Nature of Human Aggression* (New York: Oxford University Press, 1976).

   Even the question of instincts in animals is not as clear-cut as was once believed. For instance, new research indicates that even in birds learning or experience must take place if a capacity is to become an ability. See, e.g., Gilbert Gottlieb, *Development of Species Identification in Birds: An Inquiry into the Determinants of Prenatal Perception* (Chicago: University of Chicago Press, 1971); Daniel Lehrman, "A Critique of Konrad Lorenz's Theory of Instinctive Behavior,"*Quarterly Review of Biology* 28 (1953): 337–63; John Crook, ed., *Social Behavior in Birds and Mammals* (New York: Academic Press, 1970); Peter Klopfer, *On Behavior: Instinct Is a Cheshire Cat* (Philadelphia: Lippincott, 1973).

9. These systems configurations are examined in detail in a second book (Riane Eisler and David Loye, *Breaking Free*, work in progress). See also Riane Eisler and David Loye, "Peace and Feminist Thought: New Directions," in *The World Encyclopedia of Peace* (London: Pergamon Press, 1986); Riane Eisler, "Violence and Male Dominance: The Ticking Time Bomb," *Humanities in Society* 7 (Winter-Spring 1984): 3–18; Riane Eisler and David Loye, "The Failure of Liberalism: A Reassessment of Ideology from a New Feminine-Masculine Perspective," *Political Psychology* 4 (1983): 375–91.

10. See note 9. For more detailed anthropological data, see, e.g., Colin Turnbull, *The Forest People: A Study of the Pygmies of the Congo* (New York: Simon & Schuster, 1961); Pat Draper, "!Kung Women: Contrasts in Sexual Egalitarianism in Foraging and Sedentary Contexts," in *Toward an Anthropology of Women*, Raya Reiter, ed. (New York: Monthly Review Press, 1975). See also Richard Leakey and Roger Lewin, *People of the Lake* (New York: Doubleday Anchor, 1978). Please also note that in this book *equalitarian* is used instead of the more conventional *egalitarian*. The reason is that egalitarian has traditionally only described equality between men and men (as the works of Locke, Rousseau, and other "rights of man" philosophers, as well as modern history, evidence). Equalitarian describes social relations in a partnership society where women and men (and "masculine" and "feminine") are accorded equal value. This is why this usage is increasing among feminists.

11. See Riane Eisler, "The Blade and the Chalice: Technology at the Turning Point," paper presented at the General Assembly, World Futures Society, Washington, D.C., 1984; Riane Eisler, "Cultural Evolution: Social Shifts and Phase Changes," in Ervin Laszlo, ed., *The New Evolutionary Paradigm* (Boston: New Science Library, 1987); Riane Eisler, "Women, Men, and the Evolution of Social Structure," *World Futures* 23 (Spring 1987).

12. See, e.g., Alfred Marrow, *The Practical Theorist* (New York: Basic Books, 1969); Chris Argyris, *Action Science* (San Francisco: Jossey-Bass, 1985).

13. This approach to cultural evolution is based on the assumption, articulated in the nineteenth century by men such as Auguste Comte and Lewis Henry Morgan, that society must pass through a fixed and limited number of stages in a given sequence. For Morgan these stages were savagery, barbarism, and civilization, and this was

the evolutionary progression later also adopted by Marx and Engels (see, e.g., Frederick Engels, *The Origins of the Family, Private Property, and the State* [New York: International Publishers, 1972]). Herbert Spencer saw a social progression from small groups to large, from the homogeneous to the heterogeneous (*The Study of Sociology* [New York: Appleton, 1873], 471). See also Emile Durkheim, *The Division of Labor in Society* (Glencoe, IL: The Free Press, 1933), for an influential work that posited a two-stage social evolution progressing from the small and less specialized society to the larger and more specialized one in a scheme roughly paralleling the stages of *Gemeinschaft* (community) and *Gesellschaft* (corporate) types of societies earlier proposed by the German sociologist Ferdinand Tonnies. An interesting variation of this approach are the so-called cyclical theories of social evolution, such as Pitirim Sorokin's theory of the "ideational," "sensate," and "idealistic" phases of culture. In these theories, the stages may happen repeatedly, but each cycle invariably follows the earlier one in a given sequence (Pitirim Sorokin, *Social and Cultural Dynamics* [Boston: Sargent, 1957]).

14. Probably the best-known modern work based on technological stages of evolution is Alvin Toffler's *The Third Wave* (New York: Bantam, 1980). A number of anthropologists, such as Leslie White and William Ogburn, also base their theories of social evolution on technological stages, although they do not argue that each society necessarily goes through all of them (see, e.g., Leslie White, *The Science of Culture* [New York: Farrar, Strauss, 1949]; William Ogburn, *Social Change with Respect to Culture and Original Nature* [New York: Viking, 1950]). For a good recent work on technological evolution, see Bela Banathy, "Systems Inquiring and the Science of Complexity: Conceptual Bases" (ISI Monograph 84–2, Far West Laboratory, San Francisco, 1984).

15. These regressions lasted many hundreds of years. The Greek Dark Age spanned over three hundred years, from ca. 1100 to 800 B.C.E. and the Middle Ages in Europe lasted for almost a whole millennium.

16. See, e.g., Ilya Prigogine and Isabel Stengers, *Order Out of Chaos* (New York: Bantam, 1984); Ralph Abraham and Christopher Shaw, *Dynamics: The Geometry of Behavior* (Santa Cruz, CA: Aerial Press, 1984); Humberto Maturana and Francisco Varela, *Autopoeisis and Cognition: The Realization of the Living* (Boston: Reidel, 1980).

17. Fritjof Capra, *The Tao of Physics* (Boston: Shambhala New Science Library, 1975); *The Turning Point* (see n. 1).

18. Niles Eldredge and Stephen J. Gould, "Punctuated Equilibria: An Alternative to Phyletic Gradualism," in *Models of Paleobiology*, T. J. Schropf, ed. (San Francisco: Freeman, Cooper, 1972); Vilmos Csanyi, *General Theory of Evolution*, (Budapest: Akademiai Kiado, 1982); Ervin Laszlo, *Evolution: The Grand Synthesis* (Boston: New Science Library, 1987); Erich Jantsch, *The Self-Organizing Universe* (New York: Pergamon Press, 1980); David Loye and Riane Eisler, "Chaos and Transformation: Implications of Nonequilibrium Theory for Social Science and Society," *Behavioral Science* 32 (1987), 53–65.

19. These correspondences in findings across fields are in keeping with the earlier conclusions of general systems theorists, for instance, Ludwig von Bertalanffy, in *General Systems Theory* (New York: Braziller, 1968), and Ervin Laszlo, in *Introduction to Systems Philosophy* (New York: Gordon & Breach, 1972).

20. Niles Eldredge, *Time Frames* (New York: Simon & Schuster, 1985); Eldredge and Gould, "Punctuated Equilibria."

21. See, e.g., Jessie Bernard, *The Female World* (New York: Free Press, 1981); Ester Boserup, *Woman's Role in Economic Development* (London: Allen & Unwin, 1970); Dale Spender, *Feminist Theorists: Three Centuries of Key Women Thinkers* (New York: Pantheon, 1983); Gita Sen with Caren Grown, *Development, Crisis, and Alternative Visions: Third World Women's Perspectives* (New Delhi: Dawn, 1985); Mary Daly, *Gyn/Ecology: The Metaethics of Radical Feminism* (Boston: Beacon Press, 1978); Carol Gilligan, *In a Different Voice* (Cambridge: Harvard University Press, 1982); Catherine MacKinnon, "Feminism, Marxism, Method, and the State: An Agenda for Theory," *Signs* 7: 517–44; Wilma Scott Heide, *Feminism for the Health of It* (Buffalo: Margaretdaughters Press,

1985); Jean Baker Miller, *Toward a New Psychology of Women* (Boston: Beacon, 1976); Carol Christ and Judith Plaskow, *Womanspirit Rising: A Feminist Reader in Religion* (San Francisco: Harper & Row, 1979); Charlene Spretnak, ed., *The Politics of Women's Spirituality* (New York: Doubleday Anchor, 1982). I have tried in the course of this book to give recognition to many important feminist scholars. However, it is such a burgeoning list that many have of necessity not been mentioned.

22. Spender, *Feminist Theorists*. Feminism as a modern phenomenon dates to the eighteenth century. But there are much earlier instances of women scholars questioning the established knowledge of their time, for example, Christine de Pisan, who between 1390 and 1429 wrote twenty-eight books, some of them, like her *Cité des dames* (*Book of the City of Ladies*) questioning the misogynism of the scholarly men of her day.

CHAPTER 1: Journey into a Lost World (pp. 1–15)

1. Edwin Oliver James, *Prehistoric Religion* (New York: Barnes & Noble, 1957), 146. James was one of the earlier religious historians to criticize this view. For a more recent and excellent critique of the astonishing blindness of many scholars to the mythic significance of the Paleolithic female imagery, see Marija Gimbutas, "The Image of Woman in Prehistoric Art," *The Quarterly Review of Archaeology*, December 1981, 6–9. It should be noted that to avoid unnecessary complexity the terms *Paleolithic* and *Upper Paleolithic* are sometimes used interchangeably. This practice has been followed here, although most of the discussion pertains to the Upper Paleolithic: the period from ca. 30,000 to 10,000 B.C.E. It is to this period that most of the extraordinary cave paintings of animals and the carved statues and reliefs of figures described in the text date. The Paleolithic, or Stone Age, probably goes back to ca. 65,000 B.C.E., but very little is known about the earlier part of this era.

2. Edwin Oliver James, *The Cult of the Mother Goddess* (London: Thames & Hudson, 1959), 19.

3. Ibid., p. 16; James, *Prehistoric Religion*, 148.

4. James, *Cult of the Mother Goddess*, 16.

5. See note 10, Introduction.

6. See, e.g., Elizabeth Fisher, *Woman's Creation* (New York: McGraw-Hill, 1979), 140.

7. John Pfeiffer, *The Emergence of Man* (New York: Harper & Row, 1972), pp. 251–65. For a new model of human evolution that seems more consistent with the best available data, see Nancy Tanner, *On Becoming Human* (Boston: Cambridge University Press, 1981). Similar models characterize the work of Adrienne Zihlman, Jane Lancaster, and other feminist scholars, whose new scholarship is no longer constrained by the evolutionary model of "man the hunter." See, e.g., Adrienne Zihlman, "Women in Evolution, Part II: Subsistence and Social Organization among Early Hominids," *Signs* 4 (Autumn 1978): 4–20; Jane Lancaster, "Carrying and Sharing in Human Evolution," *Human Nature* 1 (February 1978): 82–89. See also chapter 5.

8. Gimbutas, "Image of Woman."

9. See, e.g., Gertrude Rachel Levy, *Religious Conceptions of the Stone Age* (New York: Harper & Row, 1963), first published as *The Gate of the Horn* (London: Faber & Faber, 1948). Levy notes that the cave itself was probably a symbol of the womb of the Goddess (the Creatrix, the Mother, the Earth), and that the rituals performed there were manifestations of the wish to partake in—and also influence—her creative acts. These would include giving birth to the animals that came out of her womb (which provided sustenance for the people of the Paleolithic). Thus animals would often be depicted on the cave walls.

   Another, more recent, female scholar is Z. A. Abramova, who published the official anthology of Upper Paleolithic engraving and sculpture in the territory of the USSR. Like the Soviet archaeologist A. P. Okladnikov, Abramova believes that "the two different aspects of the woman's image during the Paleolithic . . . do not contradict, but rather complement each other." She was depicted as "mistress of the home and hearth, protectress of the domestic fire . . . and woman as . . . the sovereign mistress of animals and especially of game animals" (Z. A. Abramova, "Paleolithic Art in the USSR," *Arctic Anthropology* 4 (1967): 1–179, ed. Chester S. Chard and trans. Catharine Page, quoted in Alexander Marshack, *The Roots of Civilization* [New York: McGraw-Hill, 1967], 338–39.

    A forthcoming book, Elinor Gadon, *The Once and Future Goddess: A Symbol for Our Time* (San Francisco: Harper & Row, 1988), provides cross-cultural evidence for the centrality of the Goddess in human intuitions of the sacred and in ritual practice since remote antiquity.

10. Marshack, *Roots of Civilization*, 219.
11. Peter Ucko and Andrée Rosenfeld, *Paleolithic Art* (New York: McGraw-Hill, 1967), 100, 174–95, 229.
12. Marshack, *Roots of Civilization*, 173, 219. Marshack also recognizes the importance of female figurines in Paleolithic art. Indeed, his *Roots of Civilization* is a ground-breaking and fascinating attempt to explore new models for the interpretation of Paleolithic art. His highly original analysis of Paleolithic time-sequenced notations provides an impressive data base for the exploration of time-sequenced stories involving cyclic phenomena (such as women's menstruation and the seasons and lunar and solar cycles) that, like women's nine-month pregnancy, our ancestors obviously observed and tried to explain (and probably also control) through seasonal and calendric myths and rites.
13. André Leroi-Gourhan, *Prehistoire de l'Art Occidental* (Paris: Edition D'Art Lucien Mazenod, 1971), 120.
14. Ibid. For a brief summary of his findings, see André Leroi-Gourhan, "The Evolution of Paleolithic Art," *Scientific American*, February 1968, 61.
15. James, *Prehistoric Religion*, 147–49. For a more recent and comprehensive analysis of this religious evolution and the culture it reflected, see Marija Gimbutas, *Evolution of Old Europe and Its Indo-Europeanization: The Prehistory of East Central Europe* (unpublished manuscript).

    As used in this book, the term *Goddess* refers to the ancient conceptualization of the powers governing the universe in female form. Hence, Goddess and terms such as Great Mother and Creatrix are capitalized.
16. James Mellaart, *Catal Huyuk* (New York: McGraw-Hill, 1967), 24.
17. Ibid., 23. Terms like "backward societies" to describe Australian aborigines and "fertility cults" to describe Goddess-centered religion are unfortunately ubiquitous in the literature and reflect cultural biases that demean and devalue tribal people and women.
18. Ibid., 23–24.
19. Merlin Stone, *When God Was a Woman* (New York: Harcourt Brace Jovanovich, 1976), 15.
20. James Mellaart, *The Neolithic of the Near East* (New York: Scribner, 1975), 152, 52, 53.
21. James, *Prehistoric Religion*, 157.
22. Ibid., 70–71; James, *Cult of the Mother Goddess*.
23. Mellaart, *Catal Huyuk*, 11.
24. Mellaart, *Neolithic of the Near East*, 275.
25. Ibid., 10.
26. Marija Gimbutas, *The Goddesses and Gods of Old Europe, 7000–3500 B.C.* (Berkeley and Los Angeles: University of California Press, 1982), 17. In its broader sense "Old Europe" covers all Europe west of the Pontic steppe before the incursions of the steppe (or Kurgan) pastoralists. See Marija Gimbutas, *The Language of the Goddess: Images and Symbols of Old Europe* (New York: Van der Marck, 1987). In a narrower sense, "Old Europe" applies to Europe's first civilization, which was focused in southeastern Europe. (See map in illustrations.)
27. Ibid., 18.

28. Ibid., 17.
29. Marija Gimbutas, *The Early Civilization of Europe* (Monograph for Indo-European Studies 131, University of California at Los Angeles, 1980), chap. 2, 17.
30. Mellaart, *Catal Huyuk*, 53.
31. Gimbutas, *Early Civilization of Europe*, chap. 2, 32–33.
32. Ibid., chap. 2, 33–34.
33. Ibid., chap. 2, 35–36.
34. Gimbutas, *Goddesses and Gods of Old Europe*, 11–12.

CHAPTER 2: Messages from the Past (pp. 16–28)

1. Marija Gimbutas, *Goddesses and Gods of Old Europe, 7000–3500 B.C.* (Berkeley and Los Angeles: University of California Press, 1982), 37–38.
2. See illustrations in James Mellaart, *Catal Huyuk* (New York: McGraw-Hill, 1967); Gimbutas, *Goddesses and Gods of Old Europe*.
3. *Goddesses and Gods of Old Europe*, plate 17 and text figure 148.
4. Nicolas Platon, *Crete* (Geneva: Nagel Publishers, 1966), 148.
5. For examples, see illustrations in Erich Neumann, *The Great Mother* (Princeton, NJ: Princeton University Press, 1955); Mellaart, *Catal Huyuk*; Gimbutas, *Goddesses and Gods of Old Europe*.
6. Gimbutas, *Goddesses and Gods of Old Europe*, examples (in order) from plates 58, 59, 105–7, 140, 144; plate 53, text figures 50–58 on pp. 95–103; 114, 181, 173, 108, 136.
7. Ibid., 66; plates 132, 341, 24, 25; pp. 101–7.
8. Mellaart, *Catal Huyuk*, 77–203.
9. In Gimbutas, *Goddesses and Gods of Old Europe*, see, e.g., plates 179–81 for bee Goddess, plates 183–85 for Goddess with animal mask, p. 146 for Minoan snake Goddess with a bird's beak.
10. The absence of these images is also striking in the art of Minoan Crete. See, e.g., Jacquetta Hawkes, *Dawn of the Gods: Minoan and Mycenaean Origins of Greece* (New York: Random House, 1968), 75–76. The double ax of the Minoan Goddess is reminiscent of the hoe axes used to clear farmland and was, according to Gimbutas, also a symbol of the butterfly, part of the Goddess's epiphany. As Gimbutas notes, the image of the Goddess as a butterfly continued to be engraved on double axes (Gimbutas, *Goddesses and Gods of Old Europe*, 78, 186).
11. Joseph Campbell, "Classical Mysteries of the Goddess" (workshop at Esalen Institute, California, May 11–13, 1979). The cultural historian Elinor Gadon also stresses this aspect of the prehistoric worship of the Goddess but takes it one important step further. Gadon writes that the reemergence of the Goddess in our time is a key to "the radical pluralism so urgently needed to counteract the prevailing ethnocentrism and cultural imperialism" (prospectus for Elinor Gadon, *The Once and Future Goddess: A Symbol for Our Time* [San Francisco: Harper & Row, 1988]; and private communications with Gadon, 1986).
12. Ibid.
13. See, e.g., Joseph Campbell, *The Mythic Image* (Princeton, NJ: Princeton University Press, 1974), 157, 77.
14. Gimbutas, *Goddesses and Gods of Old Europe*, 112–50, 112, 145; figs. 87, 88, 105, 106, 107; p. 149.
15. Mellaart, *Neolithic of the Near East* (New York: Scribner, 1975), 279.
16. Gimbutas, *Goddesses and Gods of Old Europe*, 238.
17. Mellaart, *Catal Huyuk*. See, e.g., 108–9.
18. Ibid., 113.
19. See, e.g., Neumann, *The Great Mother*.
20. Mellaart, *Catal Huyuk*, 77.
21. Gimbutas, *Goddesses and Gods of Old Europe*, 80.
22. See, e.g., Jane Harrison, *Prolegomena to the Study of Greek Religion* (London: Merlin Press, 1903, 1962), 260–63.

23. Mellaart, *Catal Huyuk*, 225.
24. Mellaart, *Neolithic of the Near East*, 100; Mellaart, *Catal Huyuk*, chap. 6.
25. Mellaart, *Catal Huyuk*, chap. 9.
26. Ibid., 201.
27. Harrison, *Prolegomena to the Study of Greek Religion*, 262.
28. Mellaart, *Catal Huyuk*, 60.
29. Ibid., 202, 208.
30. Gimbutas, *Goddess and Gods of Old Europe*, 232, fig. 248. See also figs. 84–91 in Mellaart, *Catal Huyuk*, for examples of male figurines.
31. Gimbutas, *Goddesses and Gods of Old Europe*, 217, where Gimbutas notes that seventh and sixth millennium B.C.E. Goddess figurines often had long, cylindrical necks reminiscent of a phallus, that there were also phallic representations in the form of simple clay cylinders that sometimes had female breasts, and that the combining of female and male characteristics in one figure did not completely die out after the sixth millennium B.C.E.
32. Edwin Oliver James, *The Cult of the Mother Goddess* (London: Thames & Hudson, 1959), 87.
33. Mellaart, *Catal Huyuk*, 184.
34. Gimbutas, *Goddesses and Gods of Old Europe*, 237.
35. See, e.g., "the caveat that such a social order need not imply the domination of one sex, which the term 'matriarchy' would by its semantic analogue to patriarchy infer," in Kate Millett, *Sexual Politics* (New York: Doubleday, 1970), 28, n. 9; or Adrienne Rich's comment that "the terms 'matriarchy,' 'mother-right,' or 'gynocracy' tend to be used imprecisely, often interchangeably," in *Of Woman Born* (New York: Bantam, 1976), 42–43. Rich also notes that "Robert Briffault goes to some pains to show that matriarchy in primitive societies was not simply patriarchy with a different sex in authority" (p. 43). For a discussion of how the term *gylany* avoids this semantic confusion, see chapter 8.
36. Abraham Maslow, *Toward a Psychology of Being*, 2d ed. (New York: Van Nostrand-Reinhold, 1968).
37. Mellaart, *Catal Huyuk*, 184.
38. This distinction will be discussed at length in Riane Eisler and David Loye, *Breaking Free* (forthcoming). It is a distinction that is central to the new feminist ethic now being developed by many thinkers. See, e.g., Jean Baker Miller, *Toward a New Psychology of Women* (Boston: Beacon, 1976); Carol Gilligan, *In a Different Voice* (Cambridge: Harvard University Press, 1982); Wilma Scott Heide, *Feminism for the Health of It* (Buffalo: Margaretdaughters Press, 1985). Of particular interest in this context is Anne Barstow, "The Uses of Archaeology for Women's History: James Mellaart's Work on the Neolithic Goddess at Catal Huyuk," *Feminist Studies* 4 (October 1978): 7–18, who independently arrived at a similar conclusion about the way power was probably conceptualized in the societies that worshiped the Goddess (see p. 9).

CHAPTER 3: The Essential Difference: Crete (pp. 29–41)

1. Walter Emery, quoted in Merlin Stone, *When God Was a Woman* (New York: Harcourt Brace Jovanovich, 1976), xxii.
2. Ibid. The androcentric bias Stone noted in archaeology has its counterpart in most other fields. But it is important to note that there are also male scholars who have made important contributions to knowledge about women and so-called women's issues. A notable contemporary example is Ashley Montagu, who in *The Natural Superiority of Women* (New York: Macmillan, 1968) and other works dispels many popular misogynist misconceptions about the female half of humanity and "the inevitability of patriarchy." Another is Fritjof Capra, who in *The Turning Point: Science, Society and the Rising Culture* (New York: Simon & Schuster, 1982) and other works recognizes the centrality of feminism to the movement for a more peaceful and humane future.

3. Nicolas Platon, *Crete* (Geneva: Nagel Publishers, 1966), 15.
4. Ibid., 16, 25.
5. Ibid., 26–47.
6. Jacquetta Hawkes, *Dawn of the Gods: Minoan and Mycenaean Origins of Greece* (New York: Random House, 1968), 153.
7. Ibid., 109.
8. Platon, *Crete*, 148, 143.
9. Hawkes, *Dawn of the Gods*, 45, 73; Platon, *Crete*, 148, 161.
10. Hans Gunther Buchholtz and Vassos Karageorghis, *Prehistoric Greece and Cyprus: An Archaeological Handbook* (London: Phaidon, 1973), 20; Platon, *Crete*, 148. See also Hawkes, *Dawn of the Gods*, 186.
11. Woolley, quoted in Hawkes, *Dawn of the Gods*, 73.
12. Ibid., 73–74.
13. Platon, *Crete*, 178.
14. Ibid., 147, 163.
15. Ibid., 148, 161–62.
16. Ibid., 161, 165.
17. Hawkes, *Dawn of the Gods*, 90.
18. Ibid., 58.
19. Ibid., 50; Platon, *Crete*, 181.
20. Platon, *Crete*, 179.
21. Ibid., 181–82.
22. Reynold Higgins, *An Archaeology of Minoan Crete* (London: The Bodley Head, 1973), 21.
23. Hawkes, *Dawn of the Gods*, 124, 125.
24. As is still the practice for most world religions, these Minoan rites were often in the form of ritual offerings, such as flowers, fruit, wine, or grains. By contrast with later Mesopotamian and Egyptian finds of massive and seemingly routine human sacrifices (e.g., the interment with a pharaoh of retinues of courtiers and slaves), the only find of a Cretan ritual sacrifice (excavated in a shrine at the foot of a mountain called the birthplace of Zeus) seems to have represented, in Joseph Alsop's words, "a desperate measure to stave off what must have looked like the end of the world." Indeed, for the protagonists of the drama recently unearthed by archaeologists, it was. The temblors of a massive earthquake brought down the roof (interrupting what seems to have been a priest stabbing a young man) and killing them both (Joseph Alsop, "A Historical Perspective," *National Geographic* 159 [February 1981]: 223–24). See also note 67, chap. 5.
25. Platon, *Crete*, 148.
26. Hawkes, *Dawn of the Gods*, 75–76.
27. Ibid., 75–76. Platon also stresses that the change from Minoan to Mycenaean times was a shift from a "love of life" to a mounting concern with death, and that the Mycenaeans were responsible for the "newly introduced worship of heroes" (Platon, *Crete*, 68).
28. Ruby Rohrlich-Leavitt, "Women in Transition: Crete and Sumer," in *Becoming Visible*, Renate Bridenthal and Claudia Koonz, eds. (Boston: Houghton Mifflin, 1977), 49, 46.
29. Platon, *Crete*, 167, 147, 178.
30. Rohrlich-Leavitt, "Women in Transition," 49.
31. In fact, Rohrlich-Leavitt argues that the status of women became even higher than it had been during the Neolithic (ibid., 42).
32. See, e.g., William Masters and Virginia Johnson, *The Pleasure Bond: A New Look at Sexuality and Commitment* (Boston: Little, Brown, 1975).
33. Hawkes, *Dawn of the Gods*, 156.
34. Arnold Hauser, quoted in ibid., 73. Or as Platon writes, "a fine artistic sense, a delight in beauty, grace and movement, enjoyment of life and closeness to nature, these were the qualities that distinguish the Minoans from all the other great civilizations of their time" (*Crete*, 143).

35. Charles Darwin, *The Descent of Man,* one-volume ed. (New York: Appleton, 1879), 168. The footnote is to J. C. Nott and George R. Gliddon, *Types of Mankind* (Philadelphia: Lippincott, Grambo, 1854).
36. This tendency persisted among Egyptologists until the U.S. civil rights movement of the 1960s forced a change of scholarly perception. See, e.g., John Hope Franklin, *From Slavery to Freedom* (New York: Knopf, 1967), or David Loye, *The Healing of a Nation* (New York: Norton, 1971), for information on the black leadership strain in ancient Egypt.
37. Arthur Evans, quoted in Higgins, *An Archaeology of Minoan Crete,* 40.
38. Buchholtz and Karageorghis, *Prehistoric Greece and Cyprus,* 22.
39. Platon, *Crete,* 161, 177.

CHAPTER 4: Dark Order Out of Chaos (pp. 42–58)

1. James Mellaart, *Catal Huyuk* (New York: McGraw-Hill, 1967), 67.
2. Ibid., 225: "The population of Catal Huyuk appears to have been of two different races."
3. Thus, in sharp contrast to the later priestly quarters around monumental temples, in Catal Huyuk the shrines (where the priestesses and priests also lived) were interspersed among the people's dwellings and, although sometimes larger, of the same plan as other living quarters (ibid., chap. 6). Similarly, in Crete there are no monumental temples to harsh and punitive gods of thunder and war administered by a male priesthood in the service of all-powerful male rulers.
4. A later book will explore this question, as well as various theories on the beginnings of male dominance.
5. James Mellaart, *The Neolithic of the Middle East,* 280.
6. Ibid., 275–76.
7. Marija Gimbutas, "The First Wave of Eurasian Steppe Pastoralists into Copper Age Europe," *Journal of Indo-European Studies* 5 (Winter 1977): 277. Dates for Kurgan Wave One revised in accordance with private communication with Gimbutas in 1986.
8. Modern scholarship no longer uses the term *Indo-European* as racial identity. Indo-European refers to a group of languages with common roots that are found from the British Isles to the Bay of Bengal. The more recent field research of physical anthropologists demonstrates that the so-called Indo-Europeans were of different racial stocks. The original use of the term by western European scholars in the late eighteenth and nineteenth centuries to refer to both race and language was part of a commonly held ideology that sought to classify the world by race, placing great value on racial purity, which they saw affirmed by the Hindu caste system. See Louis Fisher, *The Life of Mahatma Gandhi* (New York: Harper & Brothers, 1950), 138–41, for an interesting discussion of the earlier culture.
9. See, e.g., James Mellaart, *The Chalcolithic and Early Bronze Ages in the Near East and Anatolia* (Beirut: Khayats, 1966).
10. See, e.g., Cyrus Gordon, *Common Background of Greek and Hebrew Civilization* (New York: Norton, 1965); Merlin Stone, *When God was a Woman* (New York: Harcourt Brace Jovanovich, 1976).
11. Frederick Engels, *The Origins of the Family, Private Property, and the State* (New York: International Publishers, 1972).
12. The film *2001* and Robert Ardrey, *African Genesis* (New York: Atheneum, 1961), are examples of popular works that present the dawn of human consciousness as the discovery of how to use tools to kill. For a very different view, see, e.g., Richard Leakey and Roger Lewin, *People of the Lake* (New York: Doubleday Anchor, 1978), largely based on the Leakey family's famous discoveries and careful analysis of our earliest ancestor's fossil remains in the African Rift Valley.
13. See Marija Gimbutas, "The Beginning of the Bronze Age in Europe and the Indo-Europeans: 3500–2500 B.C.," *Journal of Indo-European Studies* 1 (1973): 166.
14. Ibid., 168.

15. Engels, *Origins of the Family.*
16. Gimbutas, "Beginning of the Bronze Age," 174–75.
17. Ibid. See also Gimbutas, "First Wave of Eurasian Steppe Pastoralists."
18. Gimbutas, "Beginning of the Bronze Age," 166.
19. Relative rapidity in evolutionary time may seem a long time when measured by our customary standards. However, the main point is that change is not necessarily gradual, nor is it necessarily a unidirectional movement from lower to higher stages.
20. See, e.g., Gimbutas, "First Wave of Eurasian Steppe Pastoralists," 281.
21. Ibid.
22. Gimbutas, "Beginning of the Bronze Age," 201.
23. Ibid., 202.
24. Ibid., 202–3.
25. Gimbutas, "First Wave of Eurasian Steppe Pastoralists," 297.
26. Ibid., 302.
27. Ibid., 294, 302.
28. Ibid., 302, 293, 285.
29. Ibid., 304–05.
30. Ibid., 284–85.
31. Ibid., 297.
32. Ibid., 281.
33. Ibid., 285. Gimbutas, "Beginning of the Bronze Age," 177.
34. V. Gordon Childe, *The Dawn of European Civilization,*" sixth edition (New York: Alfred Knopf, 1958), 109.
35. Ibid., 119.
36. Ibid., 119, 123.
37. Gimbutas, "First Wave of Eurasian Steppe Pastoralists," 289.
38. Ibid., 288, 290.
39. Ibid., 292.
40. Ibid., 294.
41. Jacquetta Hawkes, *Dawn of the Gods: Minoan and Mycenaean Origins of Greece* (New York: Random House, 1968), 186.
42. See, e.g., Nicolas Platon, *Crete* (Geneva: Nagel Publishers, 1966), 198–203, for a discussion of some of the scholarly controversy about how Minoan civilization came to an end, as well as about the general decline in cultural and artistic levels during the Mycenaean phase.
43. Hawkes, *Dawn of the Gods,* 233.
44. Ibid., 235.
45. Ibid., 236.
46. Ibid., 241.
47. Ibid.
48. Platon, *Crete,* 202.
49. Homer, *The Odyssey.*
50. Clearly, movement toward greater technological and social complexity is not the same as movement toward a technology and society that will enhance the human condition. A second book, Riane Eisler and David Loye, *Breaking Free,* will examine the relationship between social, technological, and cultural evolution in detail.
51. The Dartmouth Bible, annotated by Roy Chamberlain and Herman Feldman, with the counsel of an advisory board of biblical scholars (Boston: Houghton Mifflin, 1950), 78–79.
52. Judges 3:2; Joshua 23:13; Exodus 23:29. See also the commentary by biblical scholars in The Dartmouth Bible, 187–88.

CHAPTER 5: Memories of a Lost Age (pp. 59–77)

1. Hesiod, *Works and Days,* quoted in John Mansley Robinson, *An Introduction to Early Greek Philosophy* (Boston: Houghton Mifflin, 1968), 12–13.

2. Ibid., 13–14.
3. Ibid., 14.
4. Ibid., 15.
5. Ibid., 16.
6. Ibid., 15–16.
7. J. V. Luce, *The End of Atlantis* (London: Thames & Hudson, 1968), 137, 20.
8. Nicolas Platon, *Crete* (Geneva: Nagel Publishers, 1966), 69. Platon stresses that to explain the "Greek miracle" we must look to pre-Hellenic tradition. Another scholar who makes this point is Jacquetta Hawkes (*Dawn of the Gods: Minoan and Mycenaean Origins of Greece* [New York: Random House, 1968]).
9. See, e.g., Spyridon Marinatos, "The Volcanic Destruction of Minoan Crete," *Antiquity* 13 (1939): 425–39, one of the earliest scientific papers on this subject, as well as Luce, *End of Atlantis*, for a good, and more recent, overview.
10. Luce, *End of Atlantis*, 158. For some of the conflicting views about just how, when, and why Cretan civilization came to an end, see, e.g., Arthur Evans, *The Palace of Minos*, vols. 1–4 (London: Macmillan, 1921–35); Leonard Palmer, *Mycenaeans and Minoans* (London: Faber & Faber, 1961); Platon, *Crete*.
11. Marinatos, "Volcanic Destruction of Minoan Crete"; Luce, *End of Atlantis*; Platon, *Crete*, p. 69.
12. Merlin Stone, *When God was a Woman* (New York: Harcourt Brace Jovanovich, 1976), 82. In the introduction, Stone recounts that, in traveling from museum to museum and from library to library, gathering her material about early female deities, many of her sources were only to be found on the back shelves, and how exasperating it was that so much of the relevant "ancient writing and statuary must have been intentionally destroyed." On top of that she had to "confront the fact that even the material there is has been almost completely ignored in popular literature and general education" (pp. xvi–xvii).
13. Ibid., 219.
14. Ibid., 42–43.
15. H. W. F. Saggs, quoted in ibid., 39. See also Walter Hinz, quoted in ibid., 41.
16. Ruby Rohrlich-Leavitt, "Women in Transition: Crete and Sumer," in *Becoming Visible*, Renate Bridenthal and Claudia Koonz, eds. (Boston: Houghton Mifflin, 1977), 53.
17. See, e.g., Leonard Woolley, *The Sumerians* (New York: Norton, 1965), 66; George Thompson, *The Prehistoric Aegean* (New York: Citadel, 1965), 161.
18. Stone, *When God Was a Woman*, 41.
19. Ibid. See also Rohrlich-Leavitt, "Women in Transition," 55.
20. Stone, *When God Was a Woman*, 82.
21. Ibid.
22. Ibid., 3.
23. Ibid., 84.
24. See, e.g., Jacquetta Hawkes and Leonard Woolley, *Prehistory and the Beginning of Civilization* (New York: Harper & Row, 1963), 265, who write, "It is generally accepted that owing to her ancient role as the gatherer of vegetable foods, woman was responsible for the invention and development of agriculture." See also Ester Boserup, *Woman's Role in Economic Development* (London: Allen & Unwin, 1970); and Stone, *When God Was a Woman*, 36, citing Diodorus.
25. See, e.g., James Mellaart, *Catal Huyuk* (New York: McGraw-Hill, 1967), particularly chaps. 4 (architecture), 5 (the town plan), 6 (shrines and reliefs), 7 (wall paintings), 8 (sculpture), 10 (crafts and trade), 11 (the people and the economy). But as Mellaart writes in *The Neolithic of the Near East* (New York: Scribner, 1975), "Although archaeological research has made great progress in the last quarter of a century, interpretation has not kept up with discoveries and much of the theory of cultural development seems sadly out of date" (p. 276).
26. See, e.g., Mellaart, *Catal Huyuk*, chap. 10, where Mellaart notes, "Prospecting and trade formed a most important item of the city's economy and undoubtedly contributed appreciably to its wealth and prosperity" (p. 213).

27. See, e.g., Jane Harrison, *Prolegomena to the Study of Greek Religion* (London: Merlin Press, 1903, 1962), 261, quoting Aeschysus's prayer-poem to "before all other gods . . . the primaeval prophetess."

28. See, e.g., Stone, *When God Was a Woman*, esp. intro. and chaps. 2, 3.

29. For some earlier scholars who alluded to the major contribution of women to our principal physical and spiritual inventions, see Robert Briffault, *The Mothers* (New York: Johnson Reprint, 1969); and Erich Neumann, *The Great Mother* (Princeton, NJ: Princeton University Press, 1955).

30. Nancy Tanner, *On Becoming Human* (Boston: Cambridge University Press, 1981); Jane Lancaster, "Carrying and Sharing in Human Evolution," *Human Nature* 1 (February 1978): 82–89; Lila Leibowitz, *Females, Males, Families: A Biosocial Approach* (North Scituate, Mass.: Duxbury Press, 1978); Adrienne Zihlman, "Motherhood in Transition: From Ape to Human," in *The First Child and Family Formation*, Warren Miller and Lucille Newman, eds. (Chapel Hill, NC: Carolina Population Center, 1978). For a good summary of various theories of our hominid origins (as well as fascinating data about female primates), see Linda Marie Fedigan, *Primate Paradigms: Sex Roles and Social Bonds* (Montreal: Eden Press, 1982). See also Ashley Montagu, *The Nature of Human Aggression* (New York: Oxford University Press, 1976) for an excellent marshalling of evidence debunking the idea that, as Robert Ardrey wrote, "Man had emerged from the anthropoid background for one reason only: because he was a killer." Robert Ardrey, *African Genesis* (New York: Atheneum, 1961), 9.

31. See note 30. See also Richard Leakey and Roger Lewin, *People of the Lake* (New York: Doubleday Anchor, 1978).

32. Tanner, *On Becoming Human*, 190.

33. Ibid., chaps. 10 and 11. See particularly pp. 258–62 on tool use, expanded cranial capacity, and dental reduction.

34. Ibid., 268.

35. Ibid., 146, 268.

36. See note 25.

37. Ester Boserup, *Woman's Role in Economic Development* (London: Allen & Unwin, 1970); *The State of the World's Women 1985* (compiled for the United Nations by New Internationalist Publications, Oxford, U.K.); Barbara Rogers, *The Domestication of Women: Discrimination in Developing Societies* (New York: St. Martin's, 1979).

38. See, e.g., Stone, *When God Was a Woman*, 36, citing Diodorus about Isis; 3, on Ninlil.

39. See, e.g., Neumann, *The Great Mother*; Mara Keller, "The Mysteries of Demeter and Persephone, Ancient Greek Goddesses of Fertility, Sexuality, and Rebirth" *Journal of Feminist Studies in Religion*, Spring 1988, Vol.4, #1. Keller's in-depth study of the Eleusinian mysteries is a very important contribution to the understanding of the system of rituals involved in the ancient worship of the Goddess. It also traces the degeneration to practices involving both blood sacrifice and commercialization of these rites by classical Greek times.

40. Briffault, *The Mothers*, 1:473–74; Neumann, *The Great Mother*, 134–36, emphasis in original.

41. Stone, *When God Was a Woman*, 4.

42. Neumann, *The Great Mother*, 178.

43. Stone, *When God Was a Woman*, 200.

44. Ibid., p. 201–2. See also Barbara G. Walker, *The Woman's Encyclopedia of Myths and Secrets* (San Francisco: Harper & Row, 1983).

45. Harrison, *Prolegomena to the Study of Greek Religion*, 261.

46. Diodorus Siculus, quoted in Stone, *When God Was a Woman*, 36.

47. Harrison, *Prolegomena*, 343.

48. Stone, *When God Was a Woman*, 199, 3.

49. Marija Gimbutas, *The Early Civilization of Europe* (Monograph for Indo-European Studies 131, University of California at Los Angeles, 1980), chap. 2, 17.

50. Marija Gimbutas, *The Goddesses and Gods of Old Europe, 7000–3500 B.C.* (Berkeley and Los Angeles: University of California Press, 1982), 22–23, citing Professor Vasic.

51. Ibid., 22–25.
52. Ibid.
53. Ibid.
54. Gimbutas, *Early Civilization of Europe*, chap. 2, 72.
55. Ibid., chap. 2, 78.
56. Ibid., chap. 2, 75–77.
57. Ibid., chap. 2, 78.
58. See also Hawkes, *Dawn of the Gods*, 68.
59. See note 24.
60. There is much controversy about whether ritual sacrifice was practiced in connection with the worship of the Goddess. The mass human sacrifices found in tombs of Egyptian and Babylonian times only appear later, and seem to be elaborations on the theme of sacrificing a man's wives, concubines, and/or servants introduced into Europe and India by the Indo-Europeans. But there are also some archaeological data that seem to indicate instances of ritual sacrifice in the Neolithic. See, e.g., Gimbutas, *Goddesses and Gods of Old Europe*, 74. Most of the data, however, are mythical: see, e.g., Sir James Frazer, *The Golden Bough* (New York: Macmillan, 1922). Frazer was a leading nineteenth-century exponent of the theory that kings were regularly sacrificed in what he called matriarchal societies. It may be that ritual sacrifice was a regular practice, as Frazer believed. Or it may have been an emergency measure designed to avert impending disaster. As previously noted, in the one find of Minoan ritual sacrifice, it was most probably the latter. Here a priest was interrupted in the sacrifice of a young man by an earthquake that killed both (Yannis Sakellarakis and Sapouna Sakellarakis, "Drama of Death in a Minoan Temple," *National Geographic* 159 (February 1981): 205–22). This, as well as the fact that no other evidence of Minoan ritual sacrifice has ever been found, leads to the inference, as Joseph Alsop writes, that human sacrifice was not a regular Minoan practice. Rather, like similar instances in later classical Greek times, it appears that "this was a desperate measure to stave off what must have looked like the end of the world" (Joseph Alsop, "A Historical Perspective," *National Geographic* 159 (February 1981): 223–24). We do know that as late as the fifth century B.C.E. the ancient Greeks occasionally sacrificed a *pharmakos*, or "scapegoat" (usually a condemned criminal), as an act of ritual purification (see e.g., Harrison, *Prolegomena*, 102–5). However, on the question of whether such sacrifices were regularly practiced opinion is very divided. Some scholars, such as Elinor Gadon, though not asserting that this was a universal, or even common, practice, point to evidence that in the Indian Harappan culture that flourished from ca. 3000 to 1800 B.C.E., ritual human sacrifice was practiced (private communications with Gadon, 1986). Other scholars, such as Nancy Jay and Mara Keller, argue that even blood sacrifices of animals were not practiced by the agrarian peoples who worshiped the Goddess. For example, in the familiar biblical story of Cain and Abel, Cain (representing the farming people of Canaan) offers Jehovah fruits and grains. This offering is, however, rejected by Jehovah, who does accept the blood sacrifice of Abel (representing the pastoral invaders). (For an early reexamination of this myth, see E. Cecil Curwen, *Plough and Pasture* [London: Cobbett Press, 1946].) There are also indications that in Catal Huyuk there were no blood sacrifices of any kind. The worship of Demeter, which dates from before the Indo-European invasions, also originally involved only offerings of fruits and grains (Mara Keller, "The Mysteries of Demeter and Persephone, Ancient Greek Goddesses of Fertility, Sexuality, and Rebirth").
61. In the formulation of this definition of rational and irrational, I am indebted to the philospher Herbert Marcuse's discussion of reason in *One-Dimensional Man* (Boston: Beacon Press, 1964), 236–37.
62. Julian Jaynes, *The Origin of Consciousness in the Breakdown of the Bicameral Mind* (Boston: Houghton Mifflin, 1977).
63. See, e.g., C. A. Newham, *The Astronomical Significance of Stonehenge* (Leeds: John Blackburn, 1972). Similarly, Mellaart describes Catal Huyuk as possessing "advanced

technology in the crafts of weaving, woodwork, and metallurgy" and "advanced practices in agriculture and stock breeding" (*Catal Huyuk,* ii).

64. J. E. Lovelock, *Gaia* (New York: Oxford University Press, 1979).
65. James Mellaart, *Excavations at Hacilar* (Edinburgh: Edinburgh University Press, 1970), 2:iv.
66. Ibid., vi.
67. Ibid., 249.

CHAPTER 6: Reality Stood on Its Head, Part I (pp. 78–89)

1. Aeschylus, *Oresteia* (Chicago: University of Chicago Press, 1953), 158.
2. Ibid.
3. Ibid., 161.
4. Ibid., 163.
5. See, e.g., Hugh Lloyd-Jones, Introduction to *Agamemnon, The Libation Bearers, The Eumenides* (Englewood Cliffs, NJ: Prentice-Hall, 1970).
6. Joan Rockwell, *Fact in Fiction: The Use of Literature in the Systematic Study of Society* (London: Routledge & Kegan Paul, 1974), chap. 5.
7. George Thompson, *The Prehistoric Aegean* (New York: Citadel, 1975); H. D. F. Kitto, *The Greeks* (Baltimore: Penguin Books, 1951), 19.
8. Rockwell, *Fact in Fiction,* 163.
9. Ibid., 162.
10. Ibid.
11. Aeschylus, *Oresteia,* 167.
12. Rockwell, *Fact in Fiction,* 150.
13. Aeschylus, *Oresteia,* 164.
14. For an excellent analysis of Spencer and other androcentric nineteenth-century theorists, see Martha Vicinus, ed., *Suffer and Be Still: Women in the Victorian Age* (Bloomington, IN: Indiana University Press, 1972), esp. 126–45.
15. See, e.g., Numbers 32, 1 Chronicles 5.
16. See David Loye and Riane Eisler, "Chaos and Transformation: Implications of Nonequilibrium Theory for Social Science and Society," in *Behavioral Science,* 32 (1987), 53–65.
17. See, e.g., Humberto Maturana, "The Organization of the Living: A Theory of the Living Organization," in *Journal of Man-Machine Studies* 7 (1975): 313–32; and Vilmos Csanyi, *General Theory of Evolution* (Budapest: Akademiai Kiado, 1982).
18. See, e.g., Vilmos Csanyi and Georgy Kampis, "Autogenesis: The Evolution of Replicative Systems," in *Journal of Theoretical Biology* 114 (1985): 303–21.
19. See, e.g., 2 Kings 18:4; Numbers 31; 2 Chronicles 33.
20. George Orwell, *1984* (New York: New American Library, 1971); originally published under the title *Nineteen Eighty Four* (London: Gollancz, 1949).
21. See Mary Daly, *Gyn/Ecology: The Metaethics of Radical Feminism* (Boston: Beacon Press, 1978), for this important insight.
22. See *The Dartmouth Bible* (Boston: Houghton Mifflin, 1950) for an account of how scholars have now been able to reconstruct how the Bible was put together over several hundred years by various "schools" of rabbis and priests. See esp. 5–11.
23. Ibid., 9.
24. Ibid., 10.
25. Ibid., 10.
26. Ibid.
27. Ibid.
28. Marija Gimbutas, *The Goddesses and Gods of Old Europe, 7000–3500 B.C.* (Berkeley and Los Angeles: University of California Press, 1982), 93.
29. Ibid., 149. See, e.g., plate 59, Erich Neumann, *The Great Mother* (Princeton, NJ: Princeton University Press, 1955).
30. For an overview of the unbiquity of serpent images associated with the Goddess, in

Near Eastern, European, Asiatic, and even American cultures, see plates in Neumann, *The Great Mother.*

31. See, e.g., Joseph Campbell, *The Mythic Image* (Princeton, NJ: Princeton University Press, 1974), 295.

32. See, e.g., ibid., 296. See also Jane Harrison, *Prolegomena to the Study of Greek Religion* (London: Merlin Press, 1903, 1962), for an overview of the origins of the serpent in Greek mythology.

33. Gimbutas, *The Goddesses and Gods of Old Europe,* 149.

34. Merlin Stone, *When God Was a Woman* (New York: Harcourt Brace Jovanovich, 1976), 67.

35. *The Dartmouth Bible,* 146; 2 Kings 18:4.

36. Campbell, *The Mythic Image,* 294.

37. 2 Kings 18:4.

38. For a discussion of Eve's origins, see, e.g., Robert Graves and Raphael Patai, *Hebrew Myths* (New York: McGraw-Hill, 1963), 69.

39. Genesis 3:16. The passage "unto the woman he said, I will greatly multiply thy sorrow and thy conception; in sorrow thou shalt bring forth child, and thy desire shall be to thy husband, and he shall rule over thee" makes eminent sense when the fall from paradise story is seen as an androcratic fable about how the equalitarian farming (or gardening) people who worshiped the Goddess were conquered by male-dominated, warlike pastoralists and how this marked the end of both sexual and reproductive freedom for women. The passage "I will greatly multiply thy sorrow and thy conception" strongly suggests that at that time women not only lost the right to choose who they would have sex with but also the right to use birth control technologies. That the use of contraceptives goes back to antiquity is verified by ancient Egyptian papyri describing the use of spermicides. See Norman Himes, *Medical History of Contraception* (New York: Schocken, 1970), 64.

40. For an extraordinary nineteenth-century work challenging not only the conventional scholarship of its time, but the Bible itself, see Elizabeth Cady Stanton, *The Woman's Bible* (reprinted in *The Original Feminist Attack on the Bible,* intro. by Barbara Welter [New York: Arno Press, 1974]). First published in 1895 over the objections of many other feminists, who saw it as either horribly sacrilegious or no longer relevant in a secular or enlightened age, *The Woman's Bible* is the work of a number of feminist scholars. Though some of them sought to reconcile the Bible with feminist aspirations, Elizabeth Cady Stanton, who is probably the most remarkable of the nineteenth-century feminists, went directly to the heart of the matter, identifying and objecting to the many passages in which women are supposed to be divinely decreed as lesser creatures. Since then, particularly during the 1970s and 1980s, many women have reexamined the Bible, making important contributions to religious scholarship. For some overviews on this new research, see Gail Graham Yates, "Spirituality and the American Feminist Experience," *Signs* 9 (Autumn 1983): 59–72; Anne Barstow Driver, "Review Essay: Religion," *Signs* 2 (Winter 1976): 434–42; Rosemary Ruether, "Feminist Theology in the Academy," *Christianity and Crisis* 45 (1985): 55–62; Also see Carol P. Christ and Judith Plaskow, eds. *Womanspirit Rising* (New York: Harper & Row, 1979); Nancy Auer Falk and Rita Gross, eds., *Unspoken Worlds* (New York: Harper & Row, 1980): Charlene Spretnak, ed., *The Politics of Women's Spirituality* (New York: Doubleday Anchor, 1982); Elisabeth Schussler Fiorenza, *In Memory of Her* (New York: Crossroad, 1983); Rosemary Radford Ruether, ed., *Religion and Sexism: Images of Women in Jewish and Christian Traditions* (New York: Simon & Schuster, 1974); Mary Daly, *Beyond God the Father* (Boston: Beacon, 1973); Susannah Herschel, ed., *On Being a Jewish Feminist* (New York: Schocken Books, 1982). A recent and excellent short paper is Carol P. Christ, "Toward a Paradigm Shift in the Academy and in Religious Studies," in *Transforming the Consciousness of the Academy,* Christy Farham, ed. (Bloomington, IN: Indiana University Press, 1987). For a fascinating reinterpretation of the biblical story of Sarah, see Savina J. Teubal, *Sarah the Priestess: The First Matriarch of Genesis* (Chicago: Swallow Press, 1984).

CHAPTER 7: Reality Stood on Its Head, Part II (pp. 90–103)

1. Marija Gimbutas, "The First Wave of Eurasian Steppe Pastoralists into Copper Age Europe," *Journal of Indo-European Studies*, 5 (Winter 1977): 297.
2. Numbers 31, Joshua 6, 7, 8, 10, 11.
3. In modern times greater technological and social complexity is also creating new roles, and one of the major contemporary issues is whether the more lucrative and prestigious ones should again go mainly to men. *Breaking Free*, the sequel to this book, examines this issue. For an interesting discussion dealing with this question of technology and social organization in prehistory from a male-centered perspective, see Lewis Mumford, *The Myth of the Machine: Technics and Human Development* (New York: Harcourt, Brace & World, 1966).
4. See chapter 3 for a discussion of how greater social and technological complexity does not necessarily lead to male dominance, and how in Crete women retained their positions of power and status as long as a partnership model of social organization prevailed.
5. Edwin Oliver James, *The Cult of the Mother Goddess* (London: Thames & Hudson, 1959), 89. In *When God Was a Woman*, (New York: Harcourt Brace Jovanovich, 1976), Merlin Stone specifically notes in this connection how important it is to distinguish between the forms Goddess worship took *before* and *after* the imposition of male dominance. But unfortunately in much of this otherwise excellent work, Stone does not clearly separate the two. As a result, we often find female deities worshiped in male-dominant times discussed in the same context as those representing the earlier Goddess, with no distinction between Athene, Ishtar, or Cybele (all deities associated with war) and the Goddess of prehistory, such as the pregnant "Venus" figures of the Paleolithic and the Great Mother Goddess of Catal Huyuk, who are primarily identified with the regeneration of life.
6. Rohrlich-Leavitt, "Woman in Transition: Crete and Sumer," in *Becoming Visible*, Renate Bridenthal and Claudia Koonz, eds. (Boston: Houghton Mifflin, 1977), 55. For an excellent collection of scholarly essays relating to the broader question of how later religions have reflected and perpetuated the degradation and subjugation of women, see Rosemary Radford Ruether, *Religion and Sexism: Images of Women in Jewish and Christian Traditions* (New York: Simon & Schuster, 1974). Some more recent works are Carol Christ and Judith Plaskow, *Womanspirit Rising: A Feminist Reader in Religion* (San Francisco: Harper & Row, 1979); Charlene Spretnack, ed., *The Politics of Women's Spirituality* (New York: Doubleday Anchor, 1982); and Mary Daly, *Gyn/Ecology: The Metaethics of Radical Feminism* (Boston: Beacon Press, 1978). See also Riane Eisler, "Our Lost Heritage: New Facts on How God Became A Man," *The Humanist* 45 (May/June 1985): 26–28.
7. Raphael Patai, *The Hebrew Goddess*, (New York: Avon, 1978), 12–13. Even in the Bible we read that Solomon's temple was also used to worship gods, and goddesses, other than Jehovah.
8. Ibid., 48–50. Despite all the data this work reports of our gynocentric religious heritage, Patai's interpretation is generally within the dominator paradigm. For a different approach from a feminist perspective, see Carol P. Christ, "Heretics and Outsiders: The Struggle over Female Power in Western Religion," *Soundings* 61 (Fall 1978): 260–80.
9. See, e.g., Jeremiah 44:17. Stone, *When God Was a Woman*, contains an excellent discussion of this point. See also Elizabeth Gould Davis, *The First Sex* (New York: Penguin Books, 1971), which contains interesting documentation of the enormous strength of Goddess worship, not only among women, but also men, well into medieval times. For example, Davis cites Cyril's letters, where we read that in the fifth century C.E., when they were informed that henceforth the Church was willing to allow them to "worship the Virgin Mary as the Mother of God," the people of Ephesus danced in the streets (p. 246).
10. For an interesting analysis of the etymology of the Hebrew word for deity, *Elohim*,

see S. L. MacGregor Mathers, *The Kabbalah Unveiled* (London: Routledge & Kegan Paul, 1957), discussed in June Singer, *Androgyny* (New York: Anchor Books, 1977), 84. Mathers not only points out that *Elohim* is the feminine noun for deity with a masculine ending, but that the Hebrew word *ruach* (Holy Spirit) is feminine, as is, of course, the word *hochma* (Wisdom), all ancient appellations of the Goddess.

11. For a very powerful analysis of how earlier myths and symbols have "been stolen and reversed, contorted and distorted" (p. 75), see Daly, *Gyn/Ecology*, esp. chap. 2. A fascinating aspect of this and other analyses of this subject is how through independent routes many scholars are today arriving at the same basic insight: so successful was the job of dominator remything that Orwell's "prophecies" in *1984* "are descriptions of what already happened." For it is not only that our true prehistory—and with it the Goddess—has been erased; the crippling of thinking wrought by the expurgation of sexually equalitarian words from our language has made it impossible "to follow heretical thought further than the perception that it *was* heretical." As in *1984*, the necessary words no longer exist (Daly, *Gyn/Ecology*, 330–31; Orwell, *1984*, 252). For some earlier, nonfeminist attempts to untangle religious and classical myths that, in distorted form, date back to pre-dominator times, see, e.g., Robert Briffault, *The Mothers* (New York: Johnson Reprint, 1969); Jane Harrison, *Prolegomena to the Study of Greek Religion* (London: Merlin Press, 1903, 1962); M. Esther Harding, *Woman's Mysteries* (New York: Putnam, 1971); Erich Neumann, *The Great Mother* (Princeton, NJ: Princeton University Press, 1955); Robert Graves, *The White Goddess* (New York: Vintage Books, 1958); Helen Diner, *Mothers and Amazons* (New York: Julian Press, 1971); Frazer, *The Golden Bough* (New York: Macmillan, 1922); J. J. Bachofen, *Myth, Religion and Mother Right*, trans. Ralph Manheim (Princeton, NJ: Princeton University Press, 1861, 1967). The term *mother-right*, although sometimes used in a different way, means simply a system of matrilineal rather than patrilineal succession, in other words, descent traced through the mother rather than, as in our time, through the father.

12. See, e.g., Joshua 6:21; Deuteronomy 12:2–3. Because Jews have in Christian tradition often been blamed for the killing of the Son of God and for other "abominations" that for much of European history served to rationalize persecuting and killing them, it is imperative to stress that such practices were not Hebrew inventions but characteristic of dominator societies. For two important articles frontally dealing with mistaken allegations (or implications) that the Jews are to blame for patriarchy, see Judith Plaskow, "Blaming Jews for Inventing Patriarchy," and Annette Daum, "Blaming Jews for the Death of the Goddess," both in *Lilith*, 1980, no. 7:11–13.

13. *The Dartmouth Bible* (Boston: Houghton Mifflin, 1950), 146. Like most conventional sources, *The Dartmouth Bible* calls the first part of the Judeo-Christian Bible the Old Testament, even though Jewish scholars point out that for Jews there is only one holy book and therefore the terms *Hebrew Scriptures* or *Hebrew Bible* would be more appropriate than *Old Testament*. In this book I would have preferred using the term *Hebrew Bible*. But it soon became evident that this would cause a good deal of confusion, as most people I queried assumed that it meant the Apocryphal Writings or even newly found Hebrew scrolls (like the Dead Sea Scrolls), rather than the first part of the Bible.

14. See, e.g., Numbers 31:18.

15. Exodus 12:7.

16. Numbers 31:9, 17, 18.

17. Judges 19:24. That readers, including biblical scholars, have for so long been able to placidly ignore what such passages say about man's inhumanity to woman is a horrifying testimony to the power of the prevailing paradigm. That today a new wave of biblical analysts are independently reassessing such passages and independently coming to the same conclusions (see, e.g., Mary Daly, *Beyond God the Father* [Boston: Beacon, 1973]), is a heartening testimony of the power of the contemporary resurgence of a partnership worldview—a subject we will return to.

18. Judges 19:25–28.

19. Genesis 19.
20. Leviticus 12:6–7.
21. Neuman, *The Great Mother*, 313.
22. Ibid., 312.
23. *New Catholic Encyclopedia*, vols. 2, 5: *Hastings Encyclopedia of Religion and Ethics*, vol. 1.
24. See, e.g., Joseph Campbell, *The Mythic Image* (Princeton: Princeton University Press, 1974), 59–64.
25. Daly, *Gyn/Ecology*, 17–18, 39. Daly, a theologian, angrily writes, not only has the tree of life been replaced by "the necrophilic symbol of a dead body hanging on dead wood," but also "partriarchy" is "itself the prevailing religion of the entire planet, and its essential message is necrophilia."

CHAPTER 8: The Other Half of History, Part I (pp. 104–119)

1. The preferred pronunciation for gylany is *gi-lan-ee*. The *g* is hard, as in *gift*. The accent is on the first syllable. The word *gylany* as a whole has the same syllabic emphasis and rhythm as the word *progeny*.
2. Jane Harrison, *Prolegomena to the Study of Greek Religion* (London: Merlin Press, 1903, 1962), 646.
3. Jacquetta Hawkes, *Dawn of the Gods: Minoan and Mycenaean Origins of Greece* (New York: Random House, 1968), 261.
4. Later Greek plays such as Aeschylus's *Oresteia* confirm this, as here queens like Clytemnestra are clearly in charge and their husbands are referred to as consorts.
5. Hesiod, *Works and Days*, quoted in John Mansley Robinson, *An Introduction to Early Greek Philosophy* (Boston: Houghton Mifflin, 1968), 4.
6. Heraclitus, quoted in Edward Hussey, *The Pre-Socratics* (New York: Scribner, 1972), 49.
7. Hesiod, quoted in Robinson, *Early Greek Philosophy*, 5.
8. J. V. Luce, *The End of Atlantis* (London: Thames & Hudson, 1968), 158.
9. Ibid., 159.
10. Ibid.
11. For example, Anaximander (born ca. 612 B.C.E.) in some rudimentary respects fore-shadowed Darwin's theory of evolution. He said of the origins of human life that the prototypes of human beings were originally produced as fishlike creatures that upon reaching maturity left the water for land and shed their fishlike exterior, emerging in human form. These ideas suggest Anaximander may have known something of the development of the human embryo (Hussey, *The Pre-Socratics*, 26; Robinson *Early Greek Philosophy*, 33–34).
12. Robinson, *Early Greek Philosophy*, 46.
13. Hussey, *The Pre-Socratics*, 14.
14. Ibid., 13.
15. Ibid.
16. As already noted, scholars such as Nicolas Platon and Jacquetta Hawkes have written of the Cretan roots of Greek civilization. As Platon wrote, "A brilliant civilization produced by such dynamic people could not vanish without leaving any traces" (Nicolas Platon, *Crete* [Geneva: Nagel Publishers, 1966], 69). It is also significant that leading pre-Socratic philosopher-scientists like Xenophanes of Calophon, Pythagoras of Samos, and Thales, Anaximander, and Anaximenes of Miletus lived in islands in the eastern Mediterranean and cities on the southern Anatolian coast, sites of mil-lennia of Goddess-worshipping cultures, which were not destroyed until the Dorian onslaught that ushered in the Greek Dark Age.
17. The idea of a unified, interrelated universe (earlier symbolized by the Goddess as the Mother and Giver of All) in which everything is interconnected or linked rather than, as in androcratic theological and scientific theories, ranked, is expressed in some of Anaxagoras's statements. "In everything," he wrote, "the things in the one

world-order are not separated from one another, or cut off with an axe—neither the hot from the cold nor the cold from the hot" (quoted in Robinson, *Early Greek Philosophy*, 177–81).

18. Hussey, *The Pre-Socratics*, 17.
19. Ibid., 19.
20. See, e.g., Robinson, *Early Greek Philosophy*, 34, 35, 89, 94, 137, 168.
21. Marija Gimbutas, *The Goddesses and Gods of Old Europe, 7000–3500 B.C.* (Berkeley and Los Angeles: University of California Press, 1982), 102, 196.
22. Ibid., 198.
23. Erich Neumann, *The Great Mother* (Princeton, NJ: Princeton University Press, 1955), 275.
24. Hussey, *The Pre-Socratics*, 14.
25. Robinson, *Early Greek Philosophy*, 70.
26. Ibid., 80.
27. Harrison cites Aristoxenus as the source of the information that Pythagoras was taught ethics by Themistocleia (*Prolegomena*, 646). Hawkes writes that as a reformer of Orphism, Pythagoras adopted "a strong feminism." (*Dawn of the Gods*, 283.)
28. Harrison, *Prolegomena*, 646.
29. Ibid.; Hawkes, *Dawn of the Gods*, 284.
30. Harrison, *Prolegomena*, 647.
31. Plato, *Republic*, book 4.
32. See also illustrations on a cinerary urn showing initiation ceremonies in which Demeter is enthroned and her great snake, coiled about her, is caressed by the initiate. To Demeter's left stands another female figure, her daughter and twin Goddess, Persephone. (Harrison, *Prolegomena*, 546). For a new, and fascinating, study of the Eleusinian Mysteries, see Keller, "The Mysteries of Demeter and Persephone, Ancient Greek Goddesses of Fertility, Sexuality, and Rebirth" (unpublished manuscript). As Keller points out, the Eleusinian Mysteries preserved many of the elements of the ancient worship of the Goddess. She writes: "The rites of Demeter and Persephone speak to the experiences of life remaining through all times the most mysterious—birth, sexuality, death; and the greatest mystery of all, enduring love. In this Mystery religion, people of the ancient Mediterranean world expressed their joy in the beauty and abundance of nature, including the provident harvest of their crops; in personal love, sexuality and procreation; and in the rebirth of the human spirit, even through suffering and death. Cicero wrote of these rites: 'We have been given a reason not only to live in joy, but also to die with better hope.'"
33. Augustine, quoted in Harrison, *Prolegomena*, 261.
34. Hawkes, *Dawn of the Gods*, 286.
35. Elise Boulding, *The Underside of History* (Boulder, CO: Westview Press, 1976), 260–62. As the feminist philosopher Mara Keller notes, it is significant that Aspasia appears to have come from Anatolia, where the Goddess was still primary and women were still to a large degree independent (private communication with Mara Keller, 1986). Aspasia, who arrived in Athens ca. 450 B.C.E., opened a school for women and also lectured widely. Her lectures were attended by Socrates, Pericles, and other famous men (Will Durant, *The Life of Greece* (New York: Simon & Schuster, 1939), 253.
36. Harrison, *Prolegomena*, 646.
37. Mary Beard, *Woman as a Force in History* (New York: McMillan, 1946), 326.
38. *Sappho: Lyrics in the Original Greek*, trans. by Willis Barnstone (New York: Anchor, 1965). Most of Sappho's works were burned by Christian zealots, along with other "pagan" writings. But as Keller asks, why was Homer (who extolled war) spared and the works of women like Sappho (who extolled love) destroyed? For discussions of Sappho, whom Plato spoke of as the tenth muse, see, e.g., Hawkes, *Dawn of the Gods*, 286; Boulding, *Underside of History*, 260–62.
39. Boulding, *Underside of History*, 262–63.
40. Examples are Aristophanes' *The Women at Demeter's Festivals* and *The Women in Politics*.

41. Robinson, *Early Greek Philosophy*, 269–70.
42. Ibid., 286, 285.
43. Thucydides, *History of the Peloponnesian War*, 267.
44. Robinson, *Early Greek Philosophy*, 287.
45. Aristotle, *Politics*.
46. Genesis 1–3.
47. Fritjof Capra, *The Turning Point: Science, Society, and the Rising Culture* (New York: Simon & Schuster, 1982), 282.

CHAPTER 9: The Other Half of History, Part II (pp. 120–134)

1. Leonard Swidler, "Jesus was a Feminist," *The Catholic World*, January 1971, 177–83.
2. See, e.g., John 20:1–18.
3. Interview with Professor S. Scott Bartchy, in "Tracing the Roots of Christianity," *The UCLA Monthly* 11 (November-December 1980): 5.
4. See, e.g., Elisabeth Schussler Fiorenza, "Women in the Early Christian Movement," in Carol Christ and Judith Plaskow, eds. *Womanspirit Rising: A Feminist Reader in Religion* (San Francisco: Harper & Row, 1979), 91–92; Elise Boulding, *The Underside of History* (Boulder, CO: Westview Press, 1976), 359–60. Fiorenza's *In Memory of Her* (New York: Crossroad, 1983) is a major work of New Testament scholarship from a feminist perspective.
5. James Robinson, ed., *The Nag Hammadi Library* (New York: Harper & Row, 1977). This is by no means to say that these ancient Christian gospels are not androcratic documents. It is difficult to judge to what extent this is the function of the various translations they underwent. For instance, the last translation, from Coptic to English, was the work of the Coptic Gnostic Library Project of the Institute for Antiquity and Christianity. But the prevailing imagery of the language clearly shows that these are documents written in a time when men and masculine conceptualizations of deity were already dominant. However, there is also no question that one of the major heresies of these gospels is that a number of them contain a return to the preandrocratic conception of the powers that rule the universe in feminine form, with references to the creative powers and wisdom of the Mother. (See, e.g., *Gospel of Thomas*, 129; *Gospel of Philip*, 136–42; *The Hypostasis of the Archons*, *The Sophia of Jesus Christ*, 206; *The Thunder, Perfect Mind*, 271; *The Second Treatise of the Great Seth*, 330). Perhaps the salient heresy that runs through all these rather diverse gospels (which draw from a variety of philosophical and religious traditions) is that they challenge the tenet that ranking is divinely ordained. Even beyond such gylanic motifs as the symbolization of divine power as female and references to Mary Magdalene as Jesus' most beloved and trusted companion is the fact that we here find the outright rejection of the notion that *gnosis*, or knowledge, can only be obtained through the church hierarchy—through the popes, bishops, and priests—which became, and still is, the hallmark of orthodox Christianity.
6. Elaine Pagels, *The Gnostic Gospels* (New York: Random House, 1979), xix.
7. Ibid., xix. Note that Constantine's Edict of Milan was in 313 C.E. marking the beginning of the alliance of the Christian Church and the Roman ruling classes.
8. Helmut Koester, "Introduction to the Gospel of Thomas," *The Nag Hammadi Library*, 117.
9. Mark 16:9–20; Robinson, ed., *Nag Hammadi Library*, 471–74; Pagels, *The Gnostic Gospels*, 11.
10. Robinson, ed., *Nag Hammadi Library*, 43, 138. For an excellent analysis of these passages, see Pagels, *The Gnostic Gospels*, chap. 1.
11. See Pagels, *The Gnostic Gospels*, 11–14.
12. Ibid., 14. Some of the official Christian scriptures still contain traces of this gylanic message. See, e.g., John 8:32: "and ye shall know the truth, and the truth shall make you free."
13. Ibid., chap. 3.

14. Ibid., xvii, 41.
15. Ibid., 41–42, emphasis in original.
16. Ibid., 42–43.
17. Ibid., 42.
18. Ibid., 54.
19. Robinson, ed., *Nag Hammadi Library*, 461–62.
20. Pagels, *The Gnostic Gospels*, 52.
21. Ibid., 56–57.
22. Ibid., 52–53.
23. Ibid., 49.
24. Ibid., chap. 3; see esp. p. 50 and what follows.
25. Ibid., 52–53.
26. Interview with Prof. S. Scott Bartchy, in "Tracing the Roots of Christianity," 5.
27. Ilya Prigogine and Isabel Stengers, *Order Out of Chaos* (New York: Bantam, 1984), esp. chaps. 5, 6.
28. Constance Parvey, "The Theology and Leadership of Women in the New Testament," in Rosemary Radford Ruether, ed., *Religion and Sexism: Images of Women in Jewish and Christian Traditions* (New York: Simon & Schuster, 1974), 118.
29. Pagels, *The Gnostic Gospels*, 62–63.
30. Abba Eban, *My People: The Story of the Jews* (New York: Random House, 1968).
31. Pagels, *The Gnostic Gospels*, 63.
32. Ibid., p. 49.
33. Ibid., xviii.
34. See, e.g., *New Columbia Encyclopedia* (New York: Columbia University Press, 1975), 634; H. G. Wells, *The Outline of History* (New York: Garden City Publishing, 1920), 520; Elizabeth Gould Davis, *The First Sex* (New York: Penguin Books, 1971), 234, 237; Hendrik Van Loon, *The Story of Mankind* (New York: Boni & Liveright, 1921), 135.
35. See, e.g., Wells, *Outline of History*, 522–26; Davis, *The First Sex*, chap. 14; G. Rattray Taylor, *Sex in History* (New York: Ballantine, 1954).
36. Pagels, *The Gnostic Gospels*, 69.
37. Ibid., 57, emphasis added.
38. See, e.g., *New Columbia Encyclopedia*, 61; Davis, *The First Sex*, 420.
39. *New Columbia Encylopedia*, 705, 1302; Davis, *The First Sex*, 420.
40. Pagels, *The Gnostic Gospels*, 68.
41. Will Durant and Ariel Durant, *The History of Civilization* (New York: Simon & Schuster), vol. 4, *The Age of Faith*, 843.

CHAPTER 10: The Patterns of the Past (pp. 135–155)

1. Ilya Prigogine and Isabel Stengers, *Order out of Chaos* (New York: Bantam, 1984); Edward Lorenz, "Irregularity: A Fundamental Property of the Atmosphere," *Tellus*, 1984, no. 36A: 98–110; Ralph Abraham and Christopher Shaw, *Dynamics: The Geometry of Behavior* (Santa Cruz, CA: Aerial Press, 1984).
2. Prigogine and Stengers, *Order out of Chaos*, 169–70.
3. Abraham and Shaw, *Dynamics: The Geometry of Behavior*.
4. Ibid.
5. Prigogine and Stengers, *Order out of Chaos*, 189–90.
6. Ibid., Quotations (in order) from 187, 176–177.
7. For cyclic theories of history and economics, see, e.g., Walter Kaufman, *Hegel: A Reinterpretation* (Garden City, NY: Doubleday, 1965); Oswald Spengler, *The Decline of the West* (New York: Knopf, 1926–1928); Pitirim Sorokin, *The Crisis of Our Time* (New York: Dutton, 1941); R. Hamil, "Is the Wave of the Future a Kondratieff?" *The Futurist*, October 1979; Arthur Schlesinger, Sr., *The Tides of Politics* (Boston: Houghton Mifflin, 1964); David Loye, *The Leadership Passion* (San Francisco: Jossey-Bass, 1977).
8. Henry Adams, *The Education of Henry Adams* (New York: Houghton Mifflin, 1918), 441–42.

9. Ibid., 388. For an interesting interpretation stressing Adams's high valuing of the "feminine," see Lewis Mumford, "Apology to Henry Adams," in *Interpretation and Forecasts: 1922–1972* (New York: Harcourt Brace Jovanovich, 1973), 363–65.

10. G. Rattray Taylor, *Sex in History* (New York: Ballantine, 1954).

11. See, e.g., Wilhelm Reich, *The Mass Psychology of Fascism* (New York: Farrar, Straus, Giroux, 1980).

12. Taylor, *Sex in History*, chap. 5.

13. Ibid. See particularly the Patrist/Matrist Comparison table on p. 81.

14. For an excellent biography (and history of her time), see Marion Meade, *Eleanor of Aquitaine* (New York: Hawthorn Books, 1977). See also Robert Briffault, *The Troubadors* (Bloomington, IN: Indiana University Press, 1965).

15. Taylor, *Sex in History*, 84.

16. Ibid., 91.

17. Ibid., 85.

18. Heinrich Kramer and James Sprenger, *Malleus Maleficarum*, trans. Montague Summers (London: Pushkin Press, 1928), originally published in 1490 with the pope's blessings as the handbook for Inquisitors in hunting witches.

19. Gregory Zilboorg, quoted in Barbara Ehrenreich and Deirdre English, *Witches, Midwives, and Nurses: A History of Women Healers* (Old Westbury, NY: Feminist Press, 1973), 7.

20. Ibid.

21. Ibid., 10. For an excellent treatment of this subject, see also Wendy Faulkner, "Medical Technology and the Right to Heal," in Wendy Faulkner and Erik Arnold, eds., *Smothered by Invention: Technology in Women's Lives* (London: Pluto Press, 1985). This well-documented piece reports research showing that as the Church went into the business of training doctors in universities sanctioned by the Church (which excluded women) the traditional healers (wisewomen or "witches" now accused of having "magical powers") had to be first discredited and then eliminated. It was also decreed that at these "witch trials" doctors should be brought in to adjudicate whether a person's state of health (good or bad) was the result of natural causes or sorcery. Not only was the Church successful in squeezing out women (both the literate ones and the peasant healers), it also succeeded in discrediting many of these women's age-old remedies—fresh air and baths, for example, which the new Church-trained physicians labeled harmful. They substituted instead such "heroic remedies" as incisions for bleeding, applications of leeches, and prescription of poisonous purges. These "cures" were still commonly prescribed by medical men as late as the nineteenth century.

22. A central theme in *The Malleus Maleficarum* is that the devil acts through the female, just as he did in the Garden of Eden. "All witchcraft comes from carnal lust, which in women is insatiable," it declared, continuing that it is therefore "no matter for wonder that there are more women than men found infected with the heresy of witchcraft. . . . And blessed be the Highest Who has so far preserved the male sex from so great a crime" (quoted in Ehrenreich and English, *Witches, Midwives, and Nurses*, 10). The first work to present the view that "witchcraft" represents in part the survival of pre-Christian religion was Margaret Alice Murray, *The Witch-Cult in Western Europe* (London: Oxford University Press, 1921). This analysis, which is now more widely accepted, also in part underlies Jules Michelet, *Satanism and Witchcraft* (New York: Citadel Press, 1970). For other, more contemporary feminist writings, on the persecutions of witches as measures to suppress women, see, e.g., Elizabeth Gould Davis, *The First Sex* (New York: Penguin Books, 1971), chap. 18; Mary Daly, *Gyn/Ecology: The Metaethics of Radical Feminism* (Boston: Beacon Press, 1978). For some works reinterpreting the nature religion of witches (Wicca) and their craft in healing and midwifery, see Starhawk, *Dreaming the Dark: Magic, Sex, and Politics* (Boston: Beacon, 1982); Margot Adler, *Drawing Down the Moon: Witches, Druids, Goddess Worshippers and Other Pagans in America Today* (Boston: Beacon, 1981); Starhawk, *The Spiral Dance* (New York: Harper & Row, 1979).

23. Taylor, *Sex in History*, 77.
24. Ibid., 126.
25. Ibid., 99–103. Since they viewed women as equal human beings, friendship or non-sexual bonding between the sexes was a Cathar principle. One ironic result was that "chaste love" or "agape" was fiercely denounced by the official Church. They accused these "heretics," who, following Christ's teachings called their church the Church of Love, not only of wishing to exterminate the human race by refraining from procreation, but of all forms of sexual perversion.
26. Ibid., 125.
27. Ibid., 151.
28. There is continuing debate among feminist scholars on the question that Joan Kelly-Gadol's article asks, whether women even had a Renaissance (Kelly-Gadol, "Did Women Have a Renaissance?" in *Becoming Visible*, Renate Bridenthal and Claudia Koonz, Editors [Boston: Houghton Mifflin, 1977]). The earlier Burckhardt-Beard school of thought saw improvements for women during the Italian Renaissance (Mary Beard, *Woman as a Force in History*, (New York: McMillan, 1946), 272). Ruth Kelso and Kelly-Gadol now argue that women actually lost ground, and were better off during the feudal period. Certainly some women of the feudal ruling classes, notably Eleanor of Aquitaine and her daughter Marie of Champagne, had some small measure of independence (although Eleanor was imprisoned by her husband for many years) and exerted great influence in developing and popularizing the troubadour ideal of the veneration rather than derogation of women. But as E. William Monter and others have pointed out, there is also a great deal of controversy about whether women actually made any real social and legal gains during the Middle Ages (see, e.g., E. William Monter, "The Pedestal and the Stake," in Bridenthal and Koonz, *Becoming Visible*, 125). Similarly, during the Italian Renaissance, though normative writers like Castiglione advocated equal education for women, opposed the bourgeois notion of women's exclusively domestic role, and at least debated the sexual double standard, as Kelly-Gadol points out, with a few notable exceptions like Caterine Sforza, the Renaissance lady was hardly a politically and economically independent agent. In other words, in *neither* period do we find any fundamental alteration of women's subservience to men. What we see instead are more "feminine" humanistic values struggling to the fore during *both* the feudal troubadour and the Italian Renaissance periods. We also see some expanding rights and options for women—or at least some direct challenge of their subservience to men (such as the challenge to women's sexual slavery and vilification). The troubadours' idealization of women and the celebration of their sexual independence and the Renaissance's ideal of equal education for women are examples. But in the end, what we see is the failure of the gylanic thrust to overthrow the entrenched androcratic order, be it feudal or statist, thirteenth-century or fifteenth-century. What we also see is that this ongoing and periodically heightened gylanic-androcratic conflict is still going on in our time.
29. Taylor, *Sex in History*, 126. The violent reimposition of androcratic controls has historically been particularly important in relation to any fundamental alteration in the male-dominator/female-dominated human relations model that is the linchpin of androcracy. In other words, all the historical attempts to elevate the status of women (and with them, "feminine" values) could only be permitted to go so far and no further if the androcratic character of the system was to be maintained. Thus, any fundamental alteration in the subdominant position of women had to be prevented at all costs. This is not to say that the androcratic resistance was not there from the beginning of any period of gylanic upsurge. It obviously was. But what we see again and again in the alternation between more gylanic and more androcratic periods is how, as the gylanic resurgence mounts, so also does the androcratic resistance, with the end result a period of, at least for a time, even more repressive androcratic controls. For example, the Protestant Reformation, with its rebellion against the absolute authority of the church fathers and against the derogation of sexual relations

between women and men through the ideal of priestly chastity seemed for a time to promise some improvement in the situation of women. Indeed, some of the progressive Catholic humanists who were forerunners of the Reformation, such as Erasmus and Thomas More, advocated education for women and taught that the "doctrine of Christ casts aside no age, no sex, no fortune or position in life" (Erasmus in the *Paraclesis*). Moreover, the technological changes of the advancing industrial revolution made this an era of social and economic upheaval, when fundamental changes in institutions and roles would have been possible. But in the end there was no real change in either the subordination of women or in the basically hierarchical character of this new institutionalization of Christianity, with Puritanism in fact ushering in a period of punitive androcratic controls. (For an interesting overview of the Reformation, with the focus on women, see Sherrin Marshall Wyntjes's "Women in the Reformation Era," in Bridenthal and Koonz, *Becoming Visible*).

30. David Winter, *The Power Motive* (New York: Free Press, 1973).
31. Ibid., 172.
32. Ibid.
33. Ibid., chaps. 6, 7.
34. Kate Millett, *Sexual Politics* (New York: Doubleday, 1970); Roszak, "The Hard and the Soft," in *Masculine/Feminine*, Betty Roszak and Theodore Roszak, eds. (New York: Harper Colophon, 1969).
35. Millett, *Sexual Politics*.
36. Roszak, "The Hard and the Soft."
37. Ibid., 90.
38. Ibid., see esp. p. 102.
39. Ibid. The first two quotations are from page 92, and the third from page 91.
40. David McClelland, *Power: The Inner Experience* (New York: Irvington, 1975).
41. Ibid., 340.
42. Ibid., 324.
43. Ibid., 320–21.
44. Ibid.
45. Ibid., 319.
46. Jessie Bernard, *The Female World* (New York: Free Press, 1981); Carol Gilligan, *In a Different Voice* (Cambridge: Harvard University Press, 1982); Jean Baker Miller, *Toward a New Psychology of Women* (Boston: Beacon Press, 1976).
47. Miller, *Toward a New Psychology of Women; Women and Power*.
48. Bernard, *The Female World*.
49. Gilligan, *In a Different Voice*.
50. Lynn White, Jr., *Medieval Technology and Social Change* (New York: Oxford University Press, 1962), p. V.
51. Beard, *Woman as a Force in History*.
52. Ibid., 255, 323–29.
53. Ibid., 312.
54. Davis, *The First Sex*.
55. See, e.g., Bridenthal and Koonz, eds., *Becoming Visible*; Elise Boulding, *The Underside of History* (Boulder, CO: Westview Press, 1976); Nancy Cott and Elizabeth Pleck, eds., *A Heritage of Her Own* (New York: Simon & Schuster, 1979); Nawal El Sadawii, *The Hidden Face of Eve: Women in the Arab World* (London: ZED Press, 1980); Gerda Lerner, *The Majority Finds Its Past: Placing Women in History* (New York: Oxford University Press, 1979); La Frances Rodgers-Rose, ed., *The Black Woman* (Beverly Hills, CA: Sage, 1980); Martha Vicinus, ed., *Suffer and Be Still: Women in the Victorian Age* (Bloomington, IN: Indiana University Press, 1972); Susan Mosher Stuard, ed., *Women in Medieval Society* (Philadelphia: University of Pennsylvania Press, 1976); Tsultrim Alione, *Women of Wisdom* (London: Routledge & Kegan Paul, 1984); Marilyn French, *Beyond Power: On Women, Men, and Morals* (New York: Ballantine, 1985); Carl Degler, *At Odds: Women and the Family in America from the Revolution to the Present* (New York: Oxford University Press, 1980); Lester A. Kirkendall and Arthur E. Gravatt, eds., *Marriage*

and the Family in the Year 2020 (Buffalo: Prometheus Books, 1984), to name but a few examining the fluctuating status of women in different times and places.

56. Charles Fourier, quoted in Sheila Rowbotham, *Women, Resistance and Revolution* (New York: Vintage, 1974), 51.

57. See, e.g., Eleanor Flexner, *A Century of Struggle* (Cambridge: Belknap Press of Harvard University Press, 1959).

58. Ibid. See also Boulding, *The Underside of History;* Carol Hymowitz and Michele Weissman, eds., *A History of Women in America* (New York: Bantam, 1978); Ruth Brin, *Contributions of Women: Social Reform* (Minneapolis: Dillon, 1977).

59. See, e.g., Riane Eisler, "Women and Peace," *Women Speaking* 5 (October–December 1982): 16–18; Boulding, *The Underside of History.* The historian Gerda Lerner points out that "historical interpretation of the community-building of women is urgently needed" (*The Majority Finds Its Past,* 165–67).

60. For an excellent discussion of Christine de Pisan's *Book of the City of Ladies* in this context, see Joan Kelly, "Early Feminist Theory and the *Querelles des Femmes,* 1400–1789," *Signs* 8 (Autumn 1982): 4–28.

61. See, e.g., *Take Back the Night,* Laura Lederer, ed. (New York: William Morrow, 1980).

62. Roszak, "The Hard and the Soft."

63. See, e.g., Caryl Jacobs, "Patterns of Violence: A Feminist Perspective on the Regulation of Pornography," *Harvard Women's Law Journal* 7 (1984): 5–55, also citing FBI figures reporting that the number of rapes committed in the United States increased by over 95 percent during the 1960s. Even making allowance for increased reporting of rapes by women, this indicates an enormous increase. The increase of pornography equating sexual pleasure with violence against women (reflecing the androcratic resistance to the women's liberation movement) has coincided with this rise.

64. See, e.g., Riane Eisler "Violence and Male Dominance: The Ticking Time Bomb," *Humanities in Society* 7 (Winter–Spring, 1984): 3–18; Eisler and Loye, "Peace and Feminist Theory: New Directions," *Bulletin of Peace Proposals,* 1986, no. 1.

65. Although there are many unprecedented aspects to the modern women's movement, it is a mistake to think that women have never before vigorously challenged male dominance. Ancient stories about Medusa and the Amazons indicate their rebellion has very deep roots. But as Dale Spender writes, the androcratic system has systematically erased these attempts at self-assertion and rebellion, so that every women is left with the feeling there is something abnormal (and unheard of) about such acts—and even such thoughts (*Feminist Theorists: Three Centuries of Key Women Thinkers* [New York: Pantheon, 1983]).

CHAPTER 11: Breaking Free (pp. 156–171)

1. Henry Aiken, *The Age of Ideology* (New York: Mentor, 1956).

2. Alvin Toffler, *The Third Wave* (New York: Bantam, 1980).

3. Riane Eisler and David Loye, *Breaking Free* (forthcoming).

4. Abbé de Saint-Pierre, quoted in Mary Beard, *Woman as a Force in History* (New York: Macmillan, 1946), 330.

5. Ibid., 150. The Levellers, a sect that supported the Cromwellian revolution that overthrew the British monarchy in 1649, had also held that "by naturall birth all men are equally and alike born to like propriety [property], liberty, and freedom . . . every man by nature being a King, Priest, and Prophet in his own naturall circuite and compasse."

6. Jean Jacques Rousseau, *The Social Contract* (New York: Hafner Press, 1954).

7. Mary Wollstonecraft, "A Vindication of the Rights of Woman," in *Feminism: The Essential Historical Writings,* Miriam Schneir, ed. (New York: Vintage Books, 1972), 6–16.

8. For Comte, see Aiken, *The Age of Ideology,* 128. For Mill and Marx, see Alburey Castell, *An Introduction to Modern Philosophy* (New York: Macmillan, 1946), 455, 535.

9. Ronald Fletcher, "The Making of the Modern Family," in *The Family and Its Future,* Katherine Elliott, ed. (London: J & A Churchill, 1970), 183.

10. Randolph Trumbach, *The Rise of the Egalitarian Family: Androcratic Kinship and Domestic Relations* (New York: Academic Press, 1978).
11. See, e.g., Max Weber, *The Protestant Ethic and the Spirit of Capitalism* (London: Allen & Unwin, 1930); and R. H. Tawney, *Religion and the Rise of Capitalism* (New York: Harcourt Brace, 1926).
12. See, e.g., Robert Heilbroner, *The Worldly Philosophers* (New York: Simon & Schuster, 1961).
13. George Gilder, *Wealth and Poverty* (New York: Basic Books, 1981).
14. See chapter on Saint-Simon in Timothy Raison, ed., *The Founding Fathers of Sociology* (Baltimore: Peguin Books, 1969); discussion on Charles Fourier in Heilbroner, *The Worldly Philosophers*; Karl Marx, *Das Kapital.*
15. Frederick Engels, *The Origin of the Family, Private Property, and the State* (New York: International Publishers, 1972), 58, 50.
16. Sheila Rowbotham, *Women, Resistance and Revolution* (New York: Vintage, 1974); Kate Millett, *Sexual Politics* (New York: Doubleday, 1970); Riane Eisler and David Loye, "The 'Failure' of Liberalism: A Reassessment of Idology from a New Feminine-Masculine Perspective," *Political Psychology* 4 (1983): 375–91; Eisler and Loye, *Breaking Free.*
17. Leon Trotsky, *The Revolution Betrayed*, trans. Max Eastman (New York: Merit, 1965), Trotsky points out, "You cannot 'abolish' the family, you have to replace it." (145).
18. See, e.g., Dale Spender, ed., *Feminist Theorists: Three Centuries of Key Women Thinkers* (New York: Pantheon, 1983); Schneir, ed., *Feminism.*
19. Ellen Carol Du Bois, ed., *Elizabeth Cady Stanton, Susan B. Anthony: Correspondence, Writings, Speeches* (New York: Schocken, 1981), 29.
20. See Castell, 421–52, 123–41, 321–36.
21. Ibid., 340.
22. Ibid. Quotations from Nietzsche (in order) from pp. 358–59, 352, 353; Adolf Hitler, *Mein Kampf* (Boston: Houghton Mifflin, 1962).
23. See, e.g., Bertram Gross, *Friendly Fascism* (Boston: South End Press, 1980); *Liberty* 79 (July–Aug. 1984) and 80 (Nov.–Dec. 1985); Eugen Weber, *The Nationalist Revival in France: 1905–1914* (Berkeley and Los Angeles: University of California Press, 1959); Riane Eisler, "Human Rights: The Unfinished Struggle," *International Journal of Women's Studies* 6 (September/October 1983): 326–35; Riane Eisler, "The Human Life Amendment and the Future of Human Life," *The Humanist* 41 (September/Octorber 1981): 13–19; Alan Crawford, *Thunder on the Right* (New York: Pantheon Books, 1980).
24. See, e.g., Riane Eisler, "Women's Rights and Human Rights," *The Humanist* 40 (November/December 1980): 4–9; Eisler and Loye, "The 'Failure' of Liberalism"; Edward L. Ericson, *American Freedom and the Radical Right* (New York: Frederick Ungar, 1982). See also *Liberty* 79 (July/August 1984).
25. Fred Brenner, "Khomeini's Dream of an Islamic Republic," *Liberty* 74 (July–Aug. 1979): 11–13.
26. Ibid., 12.
27. *Atlas World Press Review*, September 1979.
28. Brenner, "Khomeini's Dream of an Islamic Republic."
29. *Women's International Network News* 9 (Autumn 1983): 42. These women are not the first Baha'i to die for their faith, which espouses the equality of men and women. Tahiri, one of the original disciples of the Bab (who founded the Baha'i faith) went to her death proclaiming, "You may kill me as soon as you like, but you cannot stop the emancipation of women" (quoted in John Huddleston, *The Earth Is But One Country* [London: Baha'i Publishing Trust, 1976], 154).
30. This will be examined in depth in Eisler and Loye, *Breaking Free.* See also notes 23 and 24 above.
31. This includes women as well as men, so that women will not only accept their own domination, but will support men's acts of violence against others. This is examined in Eisler and Loye, *Breaking Free.*
32. See e.g., Wilma Scott Heide, *Feminism for the Health of It* (Buffalo: Margaretdaughters

Press, 1985); Mary Daly, *Gyn/Ecology: The Metaethics of Radical Feminism* (Boston: Beacon Press, 1978); Adrienne Rich, *Of Woman Born* (New York: Bantam, 1976); Sonia Johnson, *From Housewife to Heretic* (Garden City, NY: Anchor Doubleday, 1983). *Breaking Free*, by Riane Eisler and David Loye, analyzes the dynamics that lie behind the relation between male dominance and warfare in depth, focusing on contemporary history. Here a distinction between warlike societies and times of war should be noted. That the status of women tends to be generally low in warlike societies does not necessarily mean that the position of women always declines during periods of warfare. In fact, there are some situations in which the absence of men in wars produces a temporary improvement in the status of women, who then get the opportunity to take over some of the more highly valued "men's work." Examples are parts of feudal Europe when the men left on the Crusades and parts of the United States during World War II. But the crux is that the greater independence and status of women is gained only for a temporary period. Since there is no rise in the valuation of women and "feminine" traits such as compassion, caring, and nonviolence, the women are again relegated to "women's work" and subservience when the men return—and the system continues to be male-dominated and warlike.

33. New Paradigm Symposium, Esalen Institute, Big Sur, California, Nov. 29–Dec. 4, 1985.

34. See, e.g., John Platt, "Women's Roles and the Great World Transformation," *Futures* 7 (October 1975); David Loye, "Men at the U.N. Women's Conference," *The Humanist* 45 (November/December 1985). Robert Jungk, one of the "fathers" of the European peace movement, has also actively supported the greater participation of women in politics, recognizing this as a prerequisite for peace.

35. *The Promise of World Peace* (Haifa: Baha'i World Center, 1985), 11–12.

36. See e.g., Heide, *Feminism for the Health of It*; Fran Hosken, *The Hosken Report: Genital and Sexual Mutilation of Females* (Lexington, MA: Women's International Network News, 1979); Helen Caldicott, *Nuclear Madness* (New York: Bantam Books, 1980); Pam McAllister, ed., *Reweaving the Web of Life: Feminism and Nonviolence* (Philadelphia: New Society Publishers, 1982); Charlene Spretnak, ed., *The Politics of Women's Spirituality* (New York: Doubleday Anchor, 1982); Elizabeth Dodson-Gray, *Green Paradise Lost* (Wellesley, MA: Roundtable Press, 1979); Hilkka Pietila, "Tomorrow Begins Today," ICDA/ISIS Workshop in Forum, Nairobi, 1985.

37. See, e.g., Abida Khanum, *The Black-Eyed Houri: Women in the Moslem World* (work in progress); Susan Griffin, *Women in Nature* (New York: Harper Colophon Books, 1978); Paula Gunn Allen, *The Woman Who Owned the Shadows* (San Francisco: Spinster's Ink, 1983); Jean O'Barr, *Third World Women: Factors in Their Changing Status* (Durham, NC: Duke University Center for International Studies, 1976); Judy Chicago, *The Dinner Party* (Garden City, NY: Doubleday, 1979); Alice Walker, *The Color Purple* (New York: Harcourt Brace Jovanovich, 1982); Rosemary Radford Ruether, ed., *Religion and Sexism: Images of Women in Jewish and Christian Traditions* (New York: Simon & Schuster, 1974); Evelyn Fox Keller, *A Feeling for the Organism: The Life and Work of Barbara McClintock* (San Francisco: W. H. Freeman, 1983).

38. An excellent work on this subject is Fritjof Capra and Charlene Spretnak, *Green Politics* (New York: Dutton, 1984).

39. As the futurist Stuart Conger points out, in the same way that paper and pen, buggies and airplanes, or abacuses and computers are technological inventions, the institutions we take for granted, like courts of law, schools, and churches are social inventions. All are products of the human mind (*Social Inventions* [Prince Albert, Saskatchewan: Saskatchewan Newstart Incorporated, 1970]).

CHAPTER 12: The Breakdown of Evolution (pp. 172–184)

1. Norbert Wiener, *The Human Use of Human Beings* (New York: Avon, 1950, 1967), see esp. chaps. 2–3.

2. As Wiener writes from his systems perspective, "Cybernetics takes the view that the

structure of the machine or of the organism is an index of the performance that may be expected from it. . . . It is as completely natural for a human society to be based on learning as for an ant society to be based on an inherited pattern" (Ibid., 79, 81). Or, as Ashley Montagu has extensively documented, the traits that characterize our species—and make it unique—are our great flexibility and thus our capacity for inventiveness. See particularly Ashley Montagu, *The Direction of Human Development* (New York: Harper, 1955); *On Being Human*, 2d ed. (New York: Dutton/Hawthorn Books, 1966); *Growing Young* (New York: McGraw-Hill, 1981); *Touching*, 3d ed. (New York: Harper & Row, 1986).

3. Thus Wiener writes that "the orderly state of permanently allotted functions" is *not* congruent with the structure of the human organism or with "the irreversible movement toward a contingent future which is the true condition of human life"—much less with a democratic form of social organization (*Human Use of Human Beings*, 70–71).

4. Ibid., 71, chap. 3.

5. See, e.g., Edward Cornish, *The Study of the Future* (Washington, D.C.: The World Future Society, 1977).

6. See, e.g., Mihajlo Mesarovic and Eduard Pestel, *Mankind at the Turning Point* (New York: Dutton, 1974); *The Global 2000 Report to the President* (Washington, D.C.: U.S. Council on Environmental Quality, U.S. Department of State, 1980); Ervin Laszlo, "The Crucial Epoch," *Futures* 17 (Feb. 1985): 2–23; William Neufeld, "Five Potential Crises," *The Futurist* 18 (April 1984).

7. *The Global 2000 Report to the President*, 3.

8. Ibid., 2–3.

9. Ruth Sivard, *World Military and Social Expenditures 1983* (Washington, D.C.: World Priorities, 1983), 26.

10. Ibid., 26.

11. *The Global 2000 Report to the President*, 1, 26. There have been projections that population growth will level off. But as Jonas Salk points out in *World Population and Human Values: A New Reality* (New York: Harper & Row, 1981), for this to be achieved in a humane way will require effective human intervention.

12. During the decade of 1974 to 1984 alone, the number of people on earth increased by 770 million, to 4.75 billion. The World Bank estimates that in 2025, global population could nearly double, to about 8.3 billion, and that out of that total, about 7 billion will be residents of the undercapitalized, undernourished Third World (*Time*, 6 August, 1984, 24). The most alarming projections are for the African continent, where population is now *doubling* every twenty-three years, making the continent's future, in the words of the Economic Commission for Africa, "a nightmare" (*ZPG Reporter*, 16 [March/April 1984]: 3).

13. Mesarovic and Pestel, *Mankind at the Turning Point*, 72.

14. See, e.g., Lester Brown, "A Harvest of Neglect: The World's Declining Croplands," *The Futurist* 13 (April 1979): 141–52; Lester Brown, *State of the World Nineteen Eighty Five* (New York: Norton, 1985); "World Population Growth and Global Security," *Population*, Sept. 1983; Stephen D. Mumford, *American Democracy and the Vatican: Population Growth and National Security* (Amherst, NY: Humanist Press, 1985).

15. The U.S. position paper dated May 30, 1984, prepared for the Mexico City population conference, stated, "Population growth is, of itself, a neutral phenomenon. It is not necessarily good or ill." To the astonishment of economists, it further asserted, "The relation between population growth and economic development is not a negative one" (Draft of U.S. position paper prepared by White House Office of Policy Development and the National Security Council, reprinted in *ZPG Reporter* 16 [May/ June 1984]: 3). The credibility of these statements was frontally challenged by the World Bank's *World Development Report*, released in July of 1984. This 286-page document pointed out that "in some countries development may not be possible at all unless slower population growth can be achieved soon." It also declared that the economic advancement of the world's poorer nations will be drastically held back

as a result of population growth, and that increased family planning and funding are essential (*ZPG Reporter* 16 (July/August 1984): 2). The consensus of most population experts is that the U.S. position and its criticism of family planning and population control efforts was dictated by ideological motives. The ICP World Plan of Action, adopted at the Mexico City conference, also stressed that population is "a fundamental element in development planning," and that "priority should be given to action programmes integrating all essential population and development factors" (*ZPG Reporter* 16 (July/August 1984): 4).

16. See, e.g., Riane Eisler, "Thrusting Women Back to Their 1900 Roles," *The Humanist* 42 (March/April 1982); "The Human Rights Amendment and the Future of Human Life," *The Humanist* 41 (Sept./Oct. 1981).

17. *National Now Times*, Jan./Feb. 1985, 5.

18. See, e.g., Riane Eisler, "Population: Women's Realities, Women's Choices," *Congressional Record*, 98th Cong., 2d sess., 1984.

19. Rafael M. Salas, *The State of World Population 1985: Population and Women*, available from Information Division, UNFPA, 220 E. 42nd St. New York, NY 10017.

20. As Dr. Esther Boohene, Coordinator of Zimbabwe's National Child Spacing and Fertility Association, stressed, reproductive freedom is not a reality for most African women, who still "must have the permission of their husbands" to practice birth control. (*Popline* 7 [August 1985]: 2). Through interviews with Third World women, Perdita Huston's *Third World Women Speak Out* (New York: Praeger, 1979), provides dramatic insight into this problem.

21. See, e.g., *Draper Fund Report No. 9: Improving the Status of Women* (Washington, D.C. Oct. 1980); Kathleen Newland, *Women and Population Growth* (Washington, D.C.: Worldwatch Paper 16, Dec. 1977); Robert McNamara, *Accelerating Population Stabilization Through Social and Economic Progress* Development Paper 24 (Washington, D.C.: Overseas Development Council, 1977).

22. See, e.g., Julian L. Simon and Herman Kahn, eds., *The Resourceful Earth: A Response to Global 2000* (New York: Basil Blackwell, 1984). Simon's argument is that the earth can comfortably support twice the present global population, and more: in fact, since human ingenuity is essential to creating the kind of future we want, more people are an asset rather than a problem. Simon also argues that population will stabilize naturally as the benefits of material progress are more widely shared throughout the world. But as for how this is to happen, he argues that no fundamental changes are necessary. Presumably this too will happen naturally through continued economic growth—a welcome message for the Heritage Foundation's wealthy business supporters.

23. Ibid. See also Herman Kahn: "The Unthinkable Optimist," *The Futurist* 9 (Dec. 1975): 286, in which Kahn concedes that, despite his great optimism about the future, there will be tragedy, the most likely being widespread starvation.

24. See, e.g., Julian Simon, "Life on Earth Is Getting Better, Not Worse," *The Futurist* 17 (August 1983): 7–15. See Lindsey Grant, "The Cornucopian Fallacies: The Myth of Perpetual Growth," *The Futurist* 17 (August 1983): 16–23; and Herman Daly, "Ultimate Confusion: The Economics of Julian Simon," *Futures* 17 (Oct. 1985): 446–50 for some searing critiques of this view.

25. Sivard, *World Military and Social Expenditures 1983*, 5.

26. See notes 22, 23, and 24. For another critique of the position that economic growth is the answer, see Gita Sen, with Caren Grown, *Development, Crisis, and Alternative Visions: Third World Women's Perspectives* (New Delhi: Dawn, 1985). Addressing some of the structural roots of hunger and poverty, this approach looks at the problem of poverty from the perspective of those most directly affected: Third World women.

27. See, e.g., *State of the World's Women 1985* (compiled for the United Nations by New Internationalist Publications, Oxford, U.K.); Riane Eisler, "The Global Impact of Sexual Equality," *The Humanist* 41 (May/June 1981); Barbara Rogers, *The Domestication of Women* (New York: St. Martin's, 1979).

28. See, e.g., *Disadvantaged Women and Their Children*, U.S. Commission on Civil Rights,

May 1983; Karin Stallard, Barbara Ehrenreich, and Holly Sklar, *Poverty in the American Dream: Women and Children First* (Boston: South End Press, 1983); *Women in Poverty*, National Advisory Council on Economic Opportunity, Final Report, September 1981; *A Women's Rights Agenda for the States*, Conference on Alternative State and Local Politics, Washington, D.C., 1984.

29. The result of over a decade of unprecedented governmental and nongovernmental studies coordinated by the United Nations are summarized in *The State of the World's Women 1985*. It reports that even though "most women work a double day" and "grow around half the world's food," they "own hardly any land, find it difficult to get loans," "are concentrated in the lowest-paid occupations," and "still earn less than three quarters of the wages of men doing similar work" (p. 1).

30. That women are not only the mass of the world's poor, but also the majority of the world's hungry is now being extensively documented. This has in fact long been implicitly recognized, as for example in Hugh Downs's UNICEF Appeal Letter of January 1981, in which he wrote that "in Ethiopia most of the five million victims of drought and civil war are mothers and children."

31. See, e.g., June Turner, ed., *Latin American Women: The Meek Speak Out* (Silver Springs, MD: International Educational Development, 1981); and Huston, *Third World Women Speak Out*.

32. For example, in 1982 the U.S. Agency for International Development (AID) only allocated 4 percent of its development aid to programs for women (Ruth Sivard, *Women . . . a world survey, 1985* [Washington, D.C.: World Priorities], 17).

33. See, e.g., Barbara Bergmann, "The Share of Women and Men in the Economic Support of Children," *Human Rights Quarterly* 3 (Spring 1981), on the poverty caused by the failure of American men to pay child support.

34. See, e.g., *Law and the Status of Women: An International Symposium* (New York: U.N. Centre for Social Development & Humanitarian Affairs, 1977), for specific data on how, according to traditional as well as modern legal codes, in many African societies a man has no obligation, legal or otherwise, to take care of his wife and children. See also interview with Fran Hosken, editor of *Women's International News*, discussing this problem in Riane Eisler and David Loye, "Fran Hosken: Global Humanitarian," *The Humanist*, September/October 1982.

35. See, e.g., *State of the World's Women 1985; Review and Appraisal: Health and Nutrition*, World Conference to Review and Appraise the Achievements of the U.N. Decade for Women, A/Conf. 116/5/Add. 3; Rogers, *The Domestication of Women*; Sivard, *Women . . . a world survey*.

36. Sivard, *Women . . . a world survey*, 25.

37. Jacques Ellul, *The Technological Society* (New York: Knopf, 1964).

38. See, e.g., Herman Kahn and Anthony Weiner, *The Year 2000* (New York: Macmillan, 1967), 189.

39. See, e.g., Hannah Arendt, *The Origins of Totalitarianism* (New York: Meridian Books, 1958); Robert A. Brady, *The Spirit and Structure of German Fascism* (New York: Viking, 1937); Ernst Nolte, *The Faces of Fascism* (London: Trinity Press, 1965); George Mosse, *Nazi Culture* (New York: Grosset & Dunlap, 1966).

40. Lewis Mumford, *The Myth of the Machine: Technics and Human Development* (New York: Harcourt, Brace & World, 1966).

41. The analysis of the androcratic character of Hitler's Germany and Stalin's Russia will be developed in Riane Eisler and David Loye, *Breaking Free*.

42. For a vivid picture of these medieval events, see Marion Meade, *Eleanor of Aquitaine* (New York: Hawthorn Books, 1977). A fascinating commonality between Nazi and medieval church pageants is the way both lasted for many hours and used repetitive chanting as a means of exhausting people, thus making them more suggestible.

43. Alburey Castell, *An Introduction to Modern Philosophy* (New York: Macmillan, 1946), 357.

44. Claudia Koonz, "Mothers in the Fatherland: Women in Nazi Germany," in Renate

Bridenthal and Claudia Koonz, eds., *Becoming Visible: Women in European History* (Boston: Houghton Mifflin, 1977), 469.

45. Scholars like Carl Jung and Lewis Mumford, as well as Robert Graves and Mircea Eliade, have brought out the need for balancing our "intuitive" and "rational" perceptions. More recently, in *The Psychology of Consciousness*, Robert Ornstein attempts to understand, and reconcile, these two kinds of perceptions. He notes that the intuitive is characteristically devalued as being of a more "feminine" and thus lower order (*The Psychology of Consciousness* [San Francisco: Freeman, 1972], 51). One of the most powerful cases for the necessity of what he calls the "recovery of participating consciousness" is made by Morris Berman in *The Reenchantment of the World* (Ithaca, NY: Cornell University Press, 1981), who notes that feminism, ecology, and spiritual renewal, which ostensibly have nothing in common politically, appear to be converging toward a common goal. See also Gregory Bateson, *Steps to an Ecology of Mind* (New York: Ballantine, 1972) for another important work on the need for a more holistic view which does not devalue our dreamier, more intuitive, "feminine" side.

CHAPTER 13: Breakthrough in Evolution (pp. 185–203)

1. Frank Herbert, *Dune* (Philadelphia: Chilton, 1965).
2. Charlotte Gilman, *Herland* (New York: Pantheon Books, 1979 reprint).
3. For example, E. O. Wilson illustrates "aggressive behavior" as a "form of competitive technique" in evolution by citing ant colonies, which he describes as "notoriously aggressive toward one another." See E. O. Wilson, *Sociobiology: The New Synthesis* (Cambridge: Harvard University Press, 1975), 244. He also uses insect societies to back up the theory of "intrasexual selection," which he writes "is based on aggressive exclusion among the courting sex," stating there is "rampant machismo" among some species of beetles (p. 320). He then goes on to some examples of violent male dominance among insects, for instance the yellow dung fly, where the male forcefully immobilizes the female for long periods of time to prevent rival males from mounting her (pp. 321–24). In some of his writings Wilson makes a point of distinguishing insect from human behavior. For example, he writes how "the mosquito is an automaton" in which "a sequence of rigid behaviors programmed by the genes" must "unfold swiftly and unerringly from birth," whereas "rather than specifying a single trait, human genes prescribe a *capacity* to develop a certain array of traits" (*On Human Nature* [Cambridge: Harvard University Press, 1978], 56, emphasis in original). But the overall import of what Wilson says is such that it is not hard to see why he is so often cited to prove notions of inevitable male aggression and male dominance. For instance, in explaining his evolutionary theory of "paternal investment," Wilson writes that since "males invest relatively little with each mating effort . . . it is to their advantage to tie up as many of the female investments as they can"—which presumably only the most aggressive males can do, thus eliminating the genes of "inferior" males (*Sociobiology*, 324–25). Again, he illustrates the sociobiological theory that evolution favors male aggression with an insect experiment that is a favorite of sociobiologists: the 1948 Bateman experiment involving the mating of ten *Drosophila melanogaster*, a species of fly (p. 325). This is followed by a discussion of how animals are fundamentally polygamous because the mating of the "fittest" males with more than one female gives an evolutionary advantage to the entire species (p. 327). Elsewhere Wilson contends that the "reproductive advantages confered by dominance" extend to our species as well. To substantiate this, he cites one sole example: the Yanomama Indians of Brazil, a highly warlike, rigidly male-dominant tribe where female infanticide is practiced. Here, "the politically dominant males father a disproportionate number of children." And here, Wilson reports, the impression of the anthropologists describing what they termed a type of "natural selection" was that "the polygynous Indians, especially the headmen, tend to be more intelligent than the nonpolygynous." On this basis, Wilson implies that his hypothesis of "domi-

nance advantage in reproductive competition" is founded on "persuasive" evidence (p. 288).

4. See, e.g., Vilmos Csanyi, *General Theory of Evolution* (Budapest: Akademiai Kiado, 1982); Ervin Laszlo, *Evolution: The Grand Synthesis* (Boston: New Science Library, 1987); Niles Eldredge, *Time Frames* (New York: Simon & Schuster, 1985). As Margaret Mead summed it up, "There were options and turning points throughout cosmic and biological evolution. If you look seriously at the process of evolution, it did not have to take the present course. It could have taken many others" ("Our Open Ended Future," *The Next Billion Years,* Lecture Series, UCLA, 1973).

5. Sherwood Washburn, "Tools and Human Evolution," *Scientific American* 203 (Sept. 1960): 62.

6. Ilya Prigogine and Isabel Stengers, *Order out of Chaos* (New York: Bantam, 1984), esp. 160–76; Eldredge, *Time Frames,* 189.

7. Ervin Laszlo, "The Crucial Epoch," *Futures* 17 (Feb. 1985): 16.

8. Jonas Salk, *Anatomy of Reality* (New York: Columbia University Press, 1983), 12–15.

9. See, e.g., Marija Gimbutas, *The Goddesses and Gods of Old Europe, 7000–3500 B.C.* (Berkeley and Los Angeles: University of California Press, 1982), 91.

10. During the Crusades and the Inquisition, the cross again became associated with killing and torturing. A grisly modern use of the cross as a symbol of death and oppression is its use by the Ku Klux Klan in the United States.

11. See, e.g., *Liberty* 80 (Nov.–Dec. 1985): 4, quoting President Ronald Reagan, who on at least eleven occasions has suggested that the end of the world is coming—a sobering statement from a man who could bring this end on.

12. This re-mything is also being countered by the global regression to "fundamentalism"—a code word for androcratic religious mythology. This regression is so strong precisely because of the enormous movement worldwide to both create new myths and reinterpret old ones in more gylanic ways.

13. There is also a new genre of modern Goddess art. See, e.g., Gloria Orenstein, "Female Creation: The Quest for the Great Mythic Mother," slide lecture; and Gloria Orenstein, "Artist as Shaman," art exhibit at Women's Building Gallery, Los Angeles, California, Nov. 4–28, 1985.

14. It is also significant that the birth of the ecology movement is often said to have been the publication of a book by a woman: Rachel Carson's *The Silent Spring* (Boston: Houghton Mifflin, 1962). As former Secretary of the Interior James Udall wrote, "A great woman has awakened the nation by her forceful account of the danger around us."

15. See, e.g., Francoise D'Eaubonne, *Le Feminism ou La Mort (Feminism or Death)* (Paris: Pierre Horay, 1974); Elizabeth Dodson-Gray, "Psycho-Sexual Roots of Our Ecological Crises" (paper distributed by Roundtable Press, 1974); and Susan Griffin, *Woman and Nature* (New York: Harper Colophon, 1978), for analyses linking our ecological crises and our male and masculine values–dominated system.

16. Shirley McConahay and John McConahay, "Sexual Permissiveness, Sex Role Rigidity, and Violence Across Cultures," *Journal of Social Issues,* 33, (1977), 134–43.

17. This is detailed in Riane Eisler and David Loye, *Breaking Free.* See also Eisler, "Violence and Male Dominance: The Ticking Time Bomb," *Humanities in Society* 7 (Winter/ Spring 1984): 3–18.

18. The term *consciousness raising* was a contribution of the women's liberation movement during the late 1960s when women came together in groups to share a growing understanding of how many of their supposedly personal problems are the common social problems of half of humanity in androcratic society.

19. This will be examined in depth in Eisler and Loye, *Breaking Free,* forthcoming.

20. See also Eisler and Loye, "Peace and Feminist Theory: New Directions," *Bulletin of Peace Proposals,* No. 1 (1986); Eisler, "Women and Peace," *Women Speaking* 5 (Oct.– Dec. 1982): 16–18; Eisler, "Our Lost Heritage: New Facts on How God Became a Man," *The Humanist* 45 (May/June 1985): 26–28.

21. For example, veterans of the Vietnam War were in December 1985 leafletting in front

of toystores to raise consciousness about how destructive war toys are. As one veteran put it in a TV interview, if they sell Rambo and GI Joe dolls glamorizing war, they ought to at least make some of them amputees to show what war really is like.

22. *The Futurist*, Feb. 1981, 2.

23. The growth of the international women's movement has been enormously accelerated during the First United Nations Decade for Women (1975–1985), with more and more men also beginning to recognize that there can be no real social or economic development without major changes in the status of women. For instance, at the opening of the End of United Nations for Women Conference held in Nairobi, Kenya, in July 1985, Kenyan president Daniel Arap Moi said that "a twenty-first century of peace, development, and the universal observance of human rights will remain elusive without the full partnership of women." Kenya's vice-president Mwai Kibaki recently spoke of how African women, who now often give birth every thirteen months "are helpless, weak, and miserable in the difficult task of having to cook for and suckle three or four children . . . with yet another waiting . . . and must be liberated" (Moi and Kibaki quoted in David Loye, "Men at the U.N. Women's Conference," *The Humanist* 45 [Nov./Dec. 1985]: 28, 32).

24. See, e.g., Mary Daly, *Gyn/Ecology: The Metaethics of Radical Feminism* (Boston: Beacon, 1978); and Wilma Scott Heide, *Feminism for the Health of It* (Buffalo: Margaretdaughters Press, 1985).

25. See Louise Bruyn, *Feminism: The Hope for a Future* (Cambridge, MA: American Friends Service Committee, May 1981) for a forceful articulation of what Daly terms the "misogynistic roots of androcratic aggression" (*Gyn/Ecology*, 357). See also Eisler and Loye, "Peace and Feminist Theory: New Directions"; and "Peace and Feminist Thought: New Directions," *World Encyclopedia of Peace*, Laszlo and Yoo, eds. (London: Pergamon Press, 1986).

26. Jean Baker Miller, *Toward a New Psychology of Women* (Boston: Beacon, 1976), 86.

27. Ibid., 69.

28. Ibid. Quotations (in order) from 83, 87, and 69.

29. Ibid. Quotations (in order) from 95 and 83 (emphasis in original).

30. Abraham Maslow, *Toward a Psychology of Being* (New York: Van Nostrand-Reinhold, 1968).

31. Alfred Adler, *Understanding Human Nature* (Greenwich, CT: Fawcett, 1954).

32. Research bearing on the different characteristics of androcratic and gylanic personality types is reported in Eisler and Loye, *Breaking Free* (forthcoming). See also Riane Eisler, "Gylany: The Balanced Future," *Futures* 13 (Dec. 1981): 499–507.

33. Maslow, *Toward a Psychology of Being*.

34. Fritjof Capra, *The Turning Point: Science, Society, and the Rising Culture* (New York: Simon & Schuster, 1982).

35. It is ironic that only now, as male scientists are discovering how limited the traditional "masculine" linear approach is, there is more openness to the idea that both sexes probably have similar innate thinking capabilities. Although there are some biological differences, women's ability to process information more holistically is probably mainly due to sexually stereotyped socialization and roles. For instance, unlike men, women have been socialized to see their lives primarily in terms of relationships and to be more attuned to the needs of others.

36. Salk, *Anatomy of Reality*, 11–19.

37. The definitive work on McClintock is Evelyn Fox Keller, *A Feeling for the Organism: The Life and Work of Barbara McClintock* (San Francisco: W. H. Freeman, 1983).

38. Ashley Montagu, quoted in *Woodstock Times*, August 7, 1986.

39. Hillary Rose, "Hand, Brain, and Heart: A Feminist Epistemology for the Natural Sciences," *Signs* 9 (Autumn 1983): 81.

40. See, e.g., Evelyn Fox Keller, *Reflections on Gender and Science* (New Haven: Yale University Press, 1985); Carol Christ, "Toward a Paradigm Shift in the Academy and in Religious Studies," in Christie Farnham, ed., *Transforming the Consciousness of the Academy* (Bloomington, IN: Indiana University Press, 1987); Rita Arditti, "Feminism

and Science," in *Science and Liberation*, Rita Arditti, Pat Brennan, and Steve Cavrak, eds. (Boston: South End Press, 1979).

41. Salk, *Anatomy of Reality*, 22.
42. Miller, *Toward a New Psychology of Women*, chap. 11.
43. Ibid., 130.
44. For an overview of the nineteenth-century feminist struggle for the vote, see Eleanor Flexner, *A Century of Struggle* (Cambridge: Belknap Press of Harvard University Press, 1959). For an overview of the nineteenth-century struggle for access to higher education, see Mabel Newcomer, *A Century of Higher Education for Women* (New York: Harper & Brothers, 1959). Some sources on the twentieth-century women's liberation movement are Vivian Gornick and Barbara Moran, *Woman in Sexist Society* (New York: Basic Books, 1971); Robin Morgan, ed., *Sisterhood Is Powerful* (New York: Random House, 1970); Johnson, *From Housewife to Heretic* (Garden City, NY: Doubleday Anchor, 1983); Riane Eisler, *The Equal Rights Handbook* (New York: Avon Books, 1978).
45. For a discussion of Gandhi's approach, see Marilyn Ferguson, *The Aquarian Conspiracy: Personal and Social Transformation in the 1980s* (Los Angeles: Tarcher, 1980), 119–200. See also Louis Fisher, *The Life of Mahatma Gandhi* (New York: Harper & Brothers, 1950).
46. Miller, *Toward a New Psychology of Women*, 116. The distinction between power *for* and power *over* is the distinction symbolized by the Chalice and the Blade.
47. See, e.g., Morgan, ed., *Sisterhood Is Powerful*; Marilyn French, *Beyond Power: On Women, Men, and Morals* (New York: Ballantine, 1985); Adrienne Rich, *Of Woman Born* (New York: Bantam, 1976); Devaki Jain, *Woman's Quest for Power: Five Indian Case Studies* (Ghanziabad: Vikas Publishing House, 1980); Marielouise Janssen-Jurreit, trans. Verne Moberg, *Sexism: The Male Monopoly on History and Thought* (New York: Farrar, Straus & Giroux, 1982).
48. Erich Neumann, *The Great Mother* (Princeton, NJ: Princeton University Press, 1955), 333–34.
49. Alvin Toffler, *The Third Wave* (New York: Bantam, 1980).
50. Ruth Sivard, *World Military and Social Expenditures 1983* (Washington, D.C.: World Priorities, 1983), 5, 26.
51. Willis Harman, "The Coming Transformation," *The Futurist*, Feb. 1977, 5–11.
52. Mihajlo Mesarovic and Eduard Pestel, *Mankind at the Turning Point* (New York: Dutton, 1974), 157.
53. Ibid., 146–47.
54. John McHale, *The Future of the Future* (New York: Ballantine, 1969), 11.
55. See, e.g., T. W. Adorno, Else Frenkel-Brunswik, Daniel Levinson, R. Nevitt Sanford, *The Authoritarian Personality* (New York: Harper & Row, 1950), particularly the work of Frenkel-Brunswik on how individuals brought up in rigidly hierarchic families are particularly prone to substitute material acquisition for the emotionally satisfactory relations they are incapable of having. These social and personality dynamics are examined in depth in Eisler and Loye, *Breaking Free*.
56. John Stuart Mill, *Principles of Political Economy,* W. J. Ashley, ed., new edition of 1909 based on the 7th ed. of 1871 (New York: Longman, Green, 1929). See also Heilbroner, *The Worldly Philosophers* (New York: Simon & Schuster, 1961).
57. *State of the World's Women 1985* (compiled for the United Nations by New Internationalist Publications, Oxford, U.K.), 1.
58. Ibid.
59. Hazel Henderson, *The Politics of the Solar Age* (New York: Anchor Books, 1981), 171.
60. Ibid. Quotations (in order) are from 337, 364, and 373.
61. James Robertson, *The Sane Alternative* (St. Paul, MN: River Basin Publishing, 1979).
62. Joseph Huber, "Social Ecology and Dual Economy," an English excerpt from *Anders Arbeiten–Anders Wirtshaften* (Frankfurt: Fischer-Verlag, 1979).
63. I am indebted to Hillary Rose's "Hand, Brain, and Heart: A Feminist Epistemology for the Natural Sciences" for her forceful articulation of this central point. (See note 39.)

64. This economic transformation is discussed in more depth in Eisler and Loye, *Breaking Free* and Riane Eisler, *Emergence* (work in progress).

65. See Riane Eisler, "Pragmatopia: Women's Utopias and Scenarios for a Possible Future," paper presented at Society for Utopian Studies Eleventh Conference, Asilomar, California, October 2–5, 1986, for the first introduction of the concept of *pragmatopia* (which in Greek means a real place, and a realizable future, as contrasted to the conventional term *utopia*, which literally means "no place.")

66. Since present population growth rates cannot be sustained by the earth's ecological system, the issue is not whether population growth will stabilize, but how. See, e.g., Jonas Salk, *World Population and Human Values: A New Reality* (New York: Harper & Row, 1981). See also Riane Eisler, "Peace, Population and Women's Roles," in *World Encyclopedia of Peace*, Laszlo and Yoo, eds.

67. This issue will be discussed in more depth in Eisler, *Emergence*. See also D'Eaubonne, *Le Feminism ou La Mort; Elizabeth Dodson-Gray, Green Paradise Lost* (Wellesley, MA: Roundtable Press, 1979); and other eco-feminist works.

68. See, e.g., *The State of the World's Women 1985;* Barbara Rogers, *The Domestication of Women: Discrimination in Developing Societies* (New York: St. Martin's, 1979); Mayra Buvinic, Nadia Joussef, and Barbara Von Elm, *Women-Headed Households: The Ignored Factor in Development Planning* (Washington, D.C.: International Center for Research on Women, 1978); May Rihani, *Development as if Women Mattered* (Washington, D.C.: Overseas Development Council, 1978); Riane Eisler, "The Global Impact of Sexual Equality," *The Humanist* 41 (May/June 1981).

69. See, e.g., Sivard, *World Military and Social Expenditures 1983;* Riane Eisler and David Loye, "The 'Failure' of Liberalism: A Reassessment of Ideology from a New Feminine-Masculine Perspective," *Political Psychology* 4 (1983): 375–91.

70. See, e.g., Luther Gerlach and Virginia Hine, *People, Power, Change: Movements of Social Transformation* (Indianapolis: Bobbs-Merrill, 1970).

71. See, e.g., E. F. Schumacher, *Small Is Beautiful* (New York: Harper & Row, 1973); Henderson, *The Politics of the Solar Age.*

72. For the androcratic scenario on new birth control technologies see, e.g., Wendy Faulkner and Erik Arnold, eds., *Smothered by Invention: Technology in Women's Lives* (London: Pluto Press, 1985); and Rita Arditti, Renate Duelli Klein, and Shelley Minden, eds., *Test Tube Women: What Future for Motherhood?* (London: Routledge & Kegan Paul, 1984).

73. For a work exploring some of these possibilities, see Martin Carnoy and Derek Sherer, *Economic Democracy* (New York: Sharpe, 1980).

74. Henderson, *The Politics of the Solar Age,* both quotations from 365.

75. Riane Eisler, "Human Rights: The Unfinished Struggle," *International Journal of Women's Studies* 6 (Sept./Oct. 1983): 326–35.

76. Riane Eisler, *Dissolution: No-Fault Divorce, Marriage, and the Future of Women* (New York: McGraw-Hill, 1977).

77. Mead, "Our Open-Ended Future"; Riane Eisler and David Loye, "Childhood and the Chosen Future," *Journal of Clinical Child Psychology* 9 (Summer 1980).

78. David Loye, *The Sphinx and the Rainbow: Brain, Mind, and Future Vision* (Boston: New Science Library, 1983).

Figures

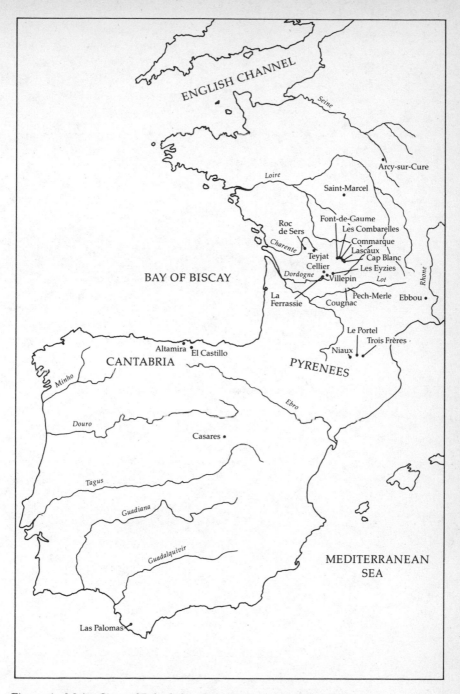

Figure 1. Major Sites of Paleolithic Cave Art in Western Europe
Paleolithic art also has been found at sites in Eastern Europe.

Source: Adapted from André Leroi-Gourhan, "The Evolution of Paleolithic Art," *Scientific American* 218, no. 2 (February 1968): 62.

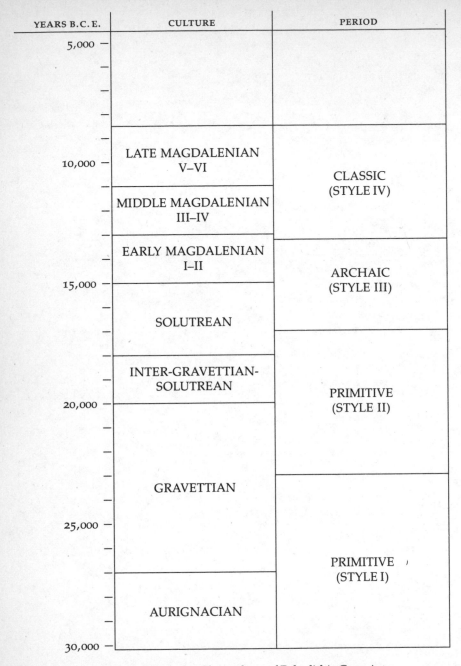

YEARS B.C.E.	CULTURE	PERIOD
5,000 —		
10,000 —	LATE MAGDALENIAN V–VI	CLASSIC (STYLE IV)
	MIDDLE MAGDALENIAN III–IV	
	EARLY MAGDALENIAN I–II	ARCHAIC (STYLE III)
15,000 —	SOLUTREAN	
	INTER-GRAVETTIAN-SOLUTREAN	PRIMITIVE (STYLE II)
20,000 —		
	GRAVETTIAN	PRIMITIVE (STYLE I)
25,000 —		
	AURIGNACIAN	
30,000 —		

Figure 2. André Leroi-Gourhan's Chronology of Paleolithic Cave Art
(ca. 30,000 B.C.E. to ca. 10,000 B.C.E.)

Source: André Leroi-Gourhan, "The Evolution of Paleolithic Art," *Scientific American* 218, no. 2 (February 1968): 63.

HACILAR

c. 5000 BCE · · · · · · · · · · · · · · ·

    Id

   −Ic

c. 5250 ———— Ia   *5247 ± 119*

    IIb

c. 5435 ———— IIa   *5434 ± 131*

    III

    IV

c. 5500 ————

    V

c. 5600 ————

    VI   *5620 ± 79*

    VII

    VIII

    IX   *5614 ± 92*

          →5706

c. 5700 ————

Radiocarbon dates in italic type.
→extreme tolerance.
All dates calculated with half-life of
   5730.
Doubtful dates in brackets

ÇATAL HÜYÜK

	O		
	I		
c. 5720			
c. 5750	II	*5797 ± 79*	
	III		
c. 5790		*5807 ± 94*	
c. 5830	IV	*(6329 ± 99)*	
	V	*5920 ± 94*	
c. 5880			
	VI A	*5781 ± 96*	destruction
		5800 ± 93	
		5815 ± 92	beginning
c. 5950		*5850 ± 94*	
	VI B	*5908 ± 93*	
c. 6050/6070		*5986 ± 94*	beginning
c. 6200	VII	*6200 ± 97* (?)	
c. 6280	VIII		
c. 6380?	IX	*6486 ± 102*	
c. 6500	X	*6385 ± 101*	

Pre-X floor levels (not yet dated)

Figure 3. James Mellaart's Chronology for Hacilar and Çatal Hüyük
          (ca. 6500 B.C.E. to ca. 5000 B.C.E.)

          Chart reads from bottom to top. Larger numerals indicate older levels. Roman numerals indicate levels of excavation corresponding to levels of development.

          Source: James Mellaart, *Çatal Hüyük* (New York: McGraw-Hill, 1967): 52.

245

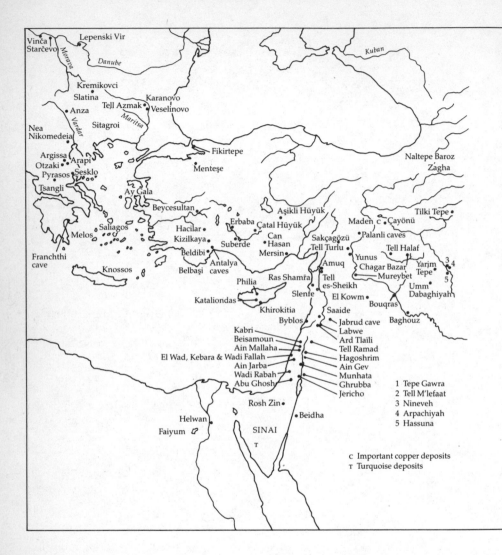

Vinča
Starčevo
Lepenski Vir
Morava
Danube
Kuban
Kremikovci
Slatina
Anza
Tell Azmak
Karanovo
Veselinovo
Maritsa
Sitagroi
Vardar
Nea
Nikomedeia
Fikirtepe
Naltepe Baroz
Zagha
Argissa
Otzaki Arapi
Pyrasos Sesklo
Tsangli
Ay Gala
Mentese
Beycesultan
Tilki Tepe
Saliagos
Melos
Franchthi
cave
Knossos
Hacilar
Kizilkaya
Beldibi
Antalya caves
Belbaşi
Erbaba
Aşikli Hüyük
Çatal Hüyük
Can
Hasan
Mersin
Suberde
Maden c Çayönü
Palanli caves
Sakçagözü
Tell Turlu
Tell Halaf
Yunus
Chagar Bazar
Mureybet
Yarim
Tepe
Umm
Dabaghiyah
Amuq
Philia
Ras Shamra
Tell
es-Sheikh
El Kowm
Slenfe
Bouqras
Baghouz
Kataliondas
Khirokitia
Byblos
Saaide
Jabrud cave
Labwe
Ard Tlaïli
Tell Ramad
Hagoshrim
Ain Gev
Munhata
Ghrubba
Jericho
Kabri
Beisamoun
Ain Mallaha
El Wad, Kebara & Wadi Fallah
Ain Jarba
Wadi Rabah
Abu Ghosh
Rosh Zin
Beidha
Helwan
Faiyum
SINAI
T

1 Tepe Gawra
2 Tell M'lefaat
3 Nineveh
4 Arpachiyah
5 Hassuna

c Important copper deposits
T Turquoise deposits

246

Figure 4. The Near East Showing Epipaleolithic and Neolithic Excavation Sites

The term *Epipaleolithic* is used to designate the transitional period between the Paleolithic and the Neolithic (or beginning of agriculture). Proliferation of sites shows extent of early cultural development.

Source: Adapted from James Mellaart, *The Neolithic of the Near East* (New York: Charles Scribner's Sons, 1975): 20, 21 (copyright Thames and Hudson, London).

247

Figure 5. Approximate Area for Early Civilization of Old Europe
(ca. 7000 B.C.E. to 3500 B.C.E.)

The term Old Europe was introduced to designate the civilization that lasted
from ca. 7000 to 3500 B.C.E. in southeastern Europe, but the term may also be
used for all of Europe before the Indo-European invasions, including the megalithic cultures of western Europe (Ireland, Malta, Sardinia, and parts of Great
Britain, Scandinavia, France, Spain, and Italy) from the 5th to the 3rd millennium B.C.E.

Source: Adapted from Marija Gimbutas, *Goddesses and Gods of Old Europe* (Berkeley and Los Angeles: University of California Press, 1982): 16.

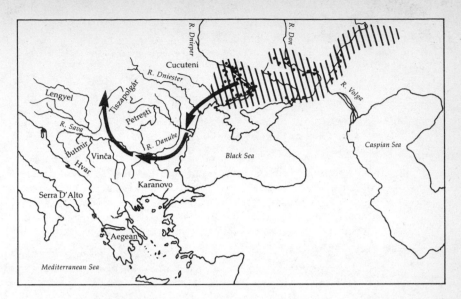

Figure 6. Kurgan Wave One (ca. 4300 B.C.E. to 4200 B.C.E.)

Arrows show main invasion routes for earliest Kurgan incursion primarily into Old European cultures of Karanova, Vinča, Lengyel, and Tiszapolgar.

Source: 1986 revision for this book by Marija Gimbutas of map originally appearing in *The Journal of Indo-European Studies* 5, no. 4 (Winter 1977): 283.

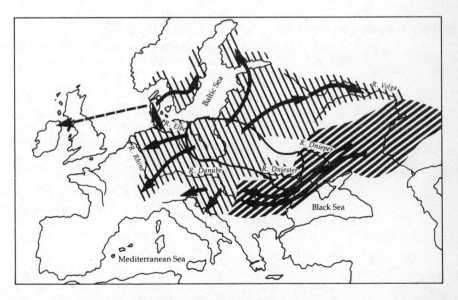

Figure 7. Kurgan Wave Three (ca. 3000 B.C.E. to 2800 B.C.E.)

Arrows and shaded areas show later incursions by Kurgans from steppes (eastern area of dark bars) and from hybridized cultures (e.g., oblong area in center of map). Dotted line shows possible route to Ireland.

Source: 1986 revision for this book by Marija Gimbutas of map originally appearing in *The Indo-Europeans in the Fourth and Third Millennia* (Karoma Publishers, 1982).

Figure 8. Marija Gimbutas's Chronology of the Flowering and Destruction of Old European Culture (ca. 7000 B.C.E. to 2500 B.C.E.)

Source: 1986 revision for this book by Marija Gimbutas of chronology originally appearing in syllabus for Indo-European Studies 131, UCLA, 1980, pp. 5–7.

B.C.E.	Major Events
7000–6500:	Beginning stage of food production and settled village life in the valleys of the coastal zones of the Aegean Sea.
6500–6000:	Full-fledged Neolithic, with pottery, in the Aegean, central Balkan, and Adriatic regions. Cultivation of wheat, barley, vetch, and peas. All domesticated animals except the horse. Large agglomerated villages appear. Closely grouped rectangular houses of mudbrick and timber with courtyards. First temples. Coastal and deep sea navigation. Trade in obsidian, marble, and spondylus shells.
6000–5500:	Spread of the agricultural economy to the lower and middle Danube basin (Yugoslavia, Hungary, Romania), to the Marica plain in central Bulgaria, and emergence in the Dniester-Bug region.
5500–5000:	Spread of the food-producing economy from east central to central Europe: Moravia, Bohemia, southern Poland, Germany, and Holland (the Linear Pottery culture). Beginning of copper metallurgy in Yugoslavia, Romania, and Bulgaria. Increase in size of villages. Sacred script emerged for use in the religious cult. Rise of the Vinča, Tisza, Lengyel, Butmir, Danilo, and Karanovo cultures.
5000–4500:	Climax of Old European culture. Efflorescence of ceramic art and architecture (including two-story temple buildings). Emergence in Moldavia and the western Ukraine of the Cucuteni (Tripolye) culture; the Petreşti in Transylvania.
4500–4000:	Continuous florescence of Old Europe. Proliferating use of copper and gold, and increase of trade. Vehicles (models of miniature wheels in clay) and domesticated horse appear. The latter brought by the Steppe pastoralist Wave One which started the disintegration of the Karanovo, Vinča, Petreşti, and Lengyel cultures.
4000–3500:	Initial Kurganization: marked changes in habitation pattern, social structure, economy, and religion. Dwindling of Old European art; cessation of figurines, polychrome ceramics, and temple building. Emergence in the lower Danube basin and Dobruja of a Kurganized Cernavoda culture.
3500–3000:	Wave Two of the Kurgan people from north of the Black Sea. Beginning of the Bronze Age. Formation of the Circum-Pontic metallurgical province. Disintegration of the Cucuteni civilization, and the emergence of the Usatovo-Gorodsk-Forteşti complex, an amalgam of Cucuteni with Kurgan. The Ezero complex in Bulgaria and the Baden culture in the mid-Danube region are formed from the crossing of the Old European substratum with eastern (Kurgan) elements. Emergence in northern central Europe of the Globular Amphora culture.

3000–2500: A new upheaval throughout east-central Europe caused by Kurgan Wave Three (or "Jamna") from the lower Dnieper–lower Volga steppe. Ethnic shifts: late Baden and Vučedol into Bohemia and central Germany, Bosnia, and the Adriatic coast. Long range wanderings of the Bell Beaker people (probably Kurganized Central Europeans) into western Europe. Formation between Rhine and Dnieper of the Corded Ware complex from the fusion of the Globular Amphora, Funnel-necked Beaker cultures, and new eastern ("Jamna") elements, followed by the wide dispersal of the Corded Pottery carriers to southern Scandinavia, the East Baltic, and areas of the upper Dnieper and upper Volga.

Figure 9. Comparison of Old European and Kurgan Cultures

Source: 1986 revision for this book by Marija Gimbutas of chart originally appearing in *The Journal of Indo-European Studies* 5, no. 4 (Winter 1977). 283.

	Old European Culture	Kurgan Culture
Economy	Agricultural (without the horse), sedentary	Pastoral (with the horse)
Habitat	Large aggregates villages and townships no hillforts	Small villages with semi-subterranean houses chieftains ruling from the hillfort
Social Structure	Egalitarian matrilinear	Patriarchal, patrilocal
Ideology	Peaceful, art-loving woman creatress	Warlike man creator

Figure 10. Chronological Comparison of Crete with Other Ancient Civilizations

Development of Cretan civilization, based on chronologies of
Sir Arthur Evans and Nicolas Platon, compared with highlights from
other ancient civilizations (dates are only approximations).

Dates B.C.E.	Crete Platon's Chronology	Crete Evans' Chronology	Other Ancient Civilizations Selected Chronological Highlights
6000	Early Neolithic I	Early Neolithic	Çatal Hüyük flourishes in Anatolia. Rice cultivated in Thailand. Agrarian cultures develop in Europe and Near East.
5000	Early Neolithic II	Middle Neolithic	Colonization of Mesopotamian alluvial plain. Agrarian settlements develop in Egypt. Corn cultivated in Mexico.
4000	Middle Neolithic		Neolithic economy imported into Britain. Early Megalithic monuments in Brittany. Silk moth domesticated in China.
3000	Late Neolithic	Late Neolithic	Cycladic cultures develop in Mediterranean. Arable farming techniques spread to central Africa. First pottery in Americas. First Egyptian dynasty.
2600	Pre-Palace Phase I	Early Minoan I	Growth of civilization in Indus Valley. First dynasty of Ur. Cheops pyramid erected in Egypt.
2400	Pre-Palace Phase II	Early Minoan II	Akkad period of Sumer. Fifth Egyptian dynasty.
2200	Pre-Palace Phase III	Early Minoan III	Seventh Egyptian dynasty. Neo-Sumerian period.

2000	Old Palace Phase I	Middle Minoan I	Elephant domesticated in Indus valley. Third dynasty of Ur. Middle kingdom of Egypt.
1900	Old Palace Phase II	Middle Minoan II	First dynasty of Babylon.
1800	Old Palace Phase III		Hammurabi rules in Babylon.
1700	New Palace Phase I	Middle Minoan III	Hyksos takeover in Egypt.
1600	New Palace Phase II	Late Minoan I	Shang civilization develops in China.
1450	New Palace Phase III	Late Minoan II	Aryan-language-speaking people conquer India.
1400	Post-Palace Phase I	Late Minoan III	Hittite Empire rises.
1320	Post-Palace Phase II		Assyria rises as military power. Hebrew tribes conquer Canaan.
1260	Post-Palace Phase III		Hittite empire collapses.
1150	Subminoan	Subminoan	Shang dynasty overthrown in China. Mycenaean civilization collapses in Mediterranean. Assyrian conquests of Near East intensify under Tiglath-pileser I.

Sources: Sir Arthur Evans, *The Palace of Minos at Knossos*, Vols. I–IV. (London: Macmillan & Company Ltd., 1921–1935); Nicolas Platon, *Crete* (Geneva: Nagel Publishers, 1966); James Mellaart, *The Neolithic of the Near East* (New York: Charles Scribners Sons, 1975); and encyclopedias and atlases of world history.

Figure 11. Principal Sites of Minoan Crete

Source: Adapted from Jacquetta Hawks, *Dawn of the Gods: Minoan and Mycenaean Origins of Greece* (New York: Random House, 1968): 59.

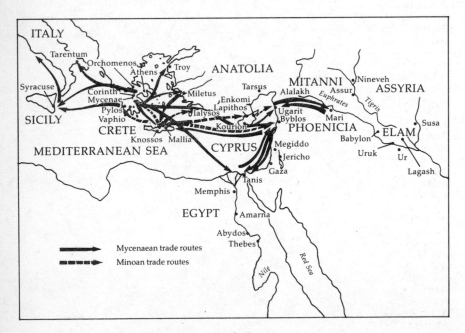

Figure 12. Minoan and Mycenaean Trade Routes

Source: Adapted from Jacquetta Hawks, *Dawn of the Gods: Minoan and Mycenaean Origins of Greece* (New York: Random House, 1968): 21.

Index